Alexandre Kojève

Alexandre Kojève

A Man of Influence

Edited by Luis J. Pedrazuela

LEXINGTON BOOKS
Lanham • Boulder • New York • London

Published by Lexington Books
An imprint of The Rowman & Littlefield Publishing Group, Inc.
4501 Forbes Boulevard, Suite 200, Lanham, Maryland 20706
www.rowman.com

86-90 Paul Street, London EC2A 4NE

British Library Cataloguing in Publication Information Available

Library of Congress Cataloging-in-Publication Data

Names: Pedrazuela, Luis J., 1968- editor.
Title: Alexandre Kojève : a man of influence / edited by Luis J. Pedrazuela.
Description: Lanham, Maryland : Lexington Books, 2022. | Includes bibliographical
    references and index. | Summary: "Alexandre Kojève: A Man of Influence offers a
    multifaceted approach to the work of Alexandre Kojève, in which eleven international
    scholars combine their perspectives on key aspects of the Russo-French thinker's
    work. The result: an original reappraisal of its significance that prompts a better
    understanding of the contemporary world"— Provided by publisher.
Identifiers: LCCN 2022031486 (print) | LCCN 2022031487 (ebook) | ISBN
    9781793654465 (cloth) | ISBN 9781793654472 (epub) | ISBN 9781793654489
    (paperback)
Subjects: LCSH: Kojève, Alexandre, 1902-1968.
Classification: LCC B2430.K654 A44 2022 (print) | LCC B2430.K654 (ebook) | DDC
    194—dc23/eng/20220815
LC record available at https://lccn.loc.gov/2022031486
LC ebook record available at https://lccn.loc.gov/2022031487

Contents

Acknowledgments   vii

Introduction   1
Luis J. Pedrazuela

**PART I: THREE SOURCES OF INFLUENCE: ART,
RELIGION, AND PHILOSOPHY**   25

Chapter One: From the Inexistent to the Concrete: Kojève after
Kandinsky   27
Isabel Jacobs

Chapter Two: Between Kant and Hegel: Alexandre Kojève and the
Absolute State   53
Jeff Love

Chapter Three: Kojève and Christianity   75
José María Carabante

Chapter Four: History and Nothingness: Kojève's Re-Leveraging of
Hegel's Dialectic of Freedom   93
Waller R. Newell

Chapter Five: Kojève and Marx: Elusive Affinities and Divergences   103
Igor Shoikhedbrod

Chapter Six: Alexandre Kojève and Carl Schmitt: Mythologies of
Enmity   121
Massimo Palma

**PART II: ACTION/REVOLUTION—END OF HISTORY/
WISDOM: THE CONCEPT TOWARD CONCRETION**   139

Chapter Seven: Wisdom, Self-Consciousness, and Empire   141
  Alexei Rutkevich

Chapter Eight: Tyranny or Wisdom?: A Reading of the Strauss–
  Kojève Debate   161
  José Daniel Parra

**PART III: THREE CONCRETE KOJÈVEAN OUTCOMES
AND THEIR LIKELIHOOD: AUTHORITY, THE
MIRROR STAGE, AND GLOBAL TRADE**   181

Chapter Nine: Authority and Legitimacy in Alexandre Kojève's *The
  Notion of Authority*   183
  Bryan-Paul Frost

Chapter Ten: The Specular Philosopher: Alexandre Kojève and
  Jacques Lacan   209
  Trevor Wilson

Chapter Eleven: Alexandre Kojève's Economic Undertakings   225
  Luis J. Pedrazuela

Index   241

About the Contributors   249

Acknowledgments

I would like to thank the following people without whom this book would not have been possible:

Each and every one of its contributors for their confidence and knowledge, with special thanks to Igor Shoikhedbrod for having suggested the idea to me in October 2020.

Chris O'Malley for his help with the English.

My wife and daughter for their support and patience.

Leeds, May 31, 2022

Introduction

Luis J. Pedrazuela

In the *Diary of a Philosopher* which he kept at the time, a nineteen-year-old Alexandre Kojève wonders in an entry dated August 1920 if the whole truth of humanity cannot be contained in Kosma Prutkov's aphorism "Swat a mare in the nose and it will wag its tail."[1] Meaningless as it sounds, it is precisely its lack of a determinate signification, Kojève reflects further in his diary, which lies at the root of whatever possible meaning. Forty-three years later, Kojève, aged sixty-one, chooses another of Prutkov's aphorisms—as well as two other quotes evoking the obligation of remaining silent before the ineffable, from the emperor Julian the Apostate and Ludwig Wittgenstein, respectively—as the introductory words to his substantious "The Emperor Julian and His Art of Writing." As in the quotation from his youth, the main characters of this quote are also animals: "If you see a 'buffalo' sign on an elephant's cage, do not trust your eyes."[2]

Kosma Petrovich Prutkov was a fictional author invented by the Russian author Aleksey Konstantinovich Tolstoy (1817–1875) and his cousins, the brothers Zhemchuzhnikov. The four used this pseudonym as a collective pen-name to publish parody aphorisms, fables, and epigrams, as well as satiric, humorous, and nonsensical verses. According to the fictional biographical data on Kosma Prutkov, the latter worked his entire adult life as a clerk in the Ministry of Finance for the government of the Russian Empire, and in 1820 entered military service as a hussar only for the uniform.

Alexandre Kojève spent from 1945 until his death with his boots on, half of his adult life working as a high civil servant for the Ministry of Economy of France, a country, which, not being exactly an empire back then, certainly became the head of Europe's integration during the 1950s and 1960s in parallel to Kojève's career inside its administration. In 1964 the Russo-French philosopher was even awarded the highest state distinction—"La

1

Légion d'honneur"—by the then finance minister of France, Valery Giscard d'Estaing, for his official career. As for Kojève's military service, it was also evoked by a writer fond of "satire, humor, and nonsense," only this time by not a Russian but a French writer. The title of Raymond Queneau's book *Loin de Rueil* refers to the small town ten kilometers outside of Paris where Kojève was barracked as a *fascicule blue*, a reserve soldier who could be called only in case of necessity. When this necessity eventually arose, France's swift defeat before the Nazi troops in June 1940 spared Kojève from soiling his military uniform. He made up for such *a tragic leave* by joining the French "Resistance" in 1942. However, this didn't prevent him from playing a double game as *a resistant*, on the one hand, and on the other, as someone who not only held "a correct attitude to the government of Vichy,"[3] according to the police files of the time, but who had a close relation to Vichy's Minister of State, Henri Moysset, who in those days was engaged in drafting the regime's constitution as well as its workers' rights act.[4] Besides their exchange of letters regarding such matters, Kojève kept Moysset posted on his progress on "The notion of the Authority" and the "Outline of a Phenomenology of Right" he was then writing. Moreover, if the evidence of his cooperation with the secret services of the government of Soviet Russia since 1940 is taken into account[5] one cannot discard a triple nature of the aforementioned double game.

Be that as it may, my purpose by linking Prutkov—a fictional character of Russian literature—to Kojève—a Russian in flesh and blood who was naturalized as a French citizen in 1939 and who seemingly loved Tolstoy's and his cousins' literary creation throughout his life, is to underline the *mise-en-abyme* perspective from which the work and influence of the Russo-French thinker is addressed in the edited volume that we are now introducing. The multifaceted nature of said work and influence acquires, from such a perspective, the form of a set of matryoshka dolls whose wholeness is not comprehensible if a figurine is left out.

Kojève's prewar Hegel lectures at the Sorbonne in Paris in the 1930s, which shaped a generation of top-notch French intellectuals, unquestionably make up one of the most colorful figurines of said matryoshka set. Still, one can't help having the impression that these lectures, cut from the continuum that flows from the initial quotation of Prutkov by a young Kojève to the last by a much older one, have usually been granted the "belle of the ball" status at the expense of the other figurines. The overall purpose of this edited volume is not to deny such a status but rather to claim that the impact of the lectures roots in influences that Kojève received earlier in his life and that, notwithstanding their brilliance, they can also be rated as a landmark within Kojève's broader concern of making something real and concrete in the world out of the concept that is thought. To probe to what extent such influences—even if reworked and enriched by Kojève's reception of Hegel, itself conditioned by previous ones of other authors and subjects—may have steered both his thought and action toward exercising a practical and effective influence on the only world his atheism deemed worthy of the name, to wit, this earthly one, this volume gathers an international group of leading scholars. By pooling their expertise on Kojève's work, its aim is to reassess the Russo-French thinker's influence in the light of contrasting approaches so as to open that work up to further scrutiny. As if the build-up of matryoshka dolls were inexhaustible or, alternatively, as if the Prutkov mirror in which Kojève seemed fond of viewing himself was made up, in turn, of the reflection of other, still to be discovered, looking-glasses, the scope of this book is to contribute to a broadening of the range of perspectives on Kojève's work rather than to become "the Bible" that puts an end to discussion, as Kojève himself wanted the book of the end of history to be.[6]

The scope of *Alexandre Kojève: A Man of Influence* seeks thus to survey Alexandre Kojève's influence by exploring both the philosophical and nonphilosophical influences he received. This survey brings with it an assessment of the increasingly practical nature of the influence he himself might have sought to exercise.

Kojève's name is commonly associated with Hegel and with Marx. As to the former, Kojève himself said that his was nothing but an *update* of Hegel's work. As to the latter, suffice it to say that Allan Bloom described Kojève as "the most intelligent Marxist of the twentieth century."[7] Rather than building on these statements, this book takes up the challenge of tracing Kojève's thought back to the time when the Russo-French thinker, still a young man, assimilated the nonphilosophical influences of religion and of his uncle, Wassily Kandinsky's, *concrete* paintings. Starting here, the book moves on to explore not only Kojève's reception of Hegel and Marx from a new perspective but also his probable early assimilation of Carl Schmitt's theories. Adding to this innovative approach to the roots of his thought, the book offers cutting-edge research on a still-unpublished and barely deciphered 900-page Russian manuscript written in 1941, in which Kojève makes the link that binds his notion of wisdom to the realization of a final State at the end of history more explicit than he did in his lectures on Hegel. By drawing next upon the debate that he held with Leo Strauss on the phenomenon of tyranny in the 1950s, the book tackles Kojève's theory of action. Kojève's claim in his exchange with Strauss that "the conflict of the philosopher confronted with the tyrant is nothing else than the conflict of the intellectual faced with action"[8] lingers over the three final chapters of the book. These chapters examine how Kojève's keenness for *true successful action (réussite)* might have led him to expand his influence in three increasingly practical fields, namely: that of authority embodied in a particular conception of willing obedience, that of psychology through his influence on the French psychiatrist Jacques Lacan, and that of global trade by his becoming a Statesman who tirelessly strove for globalization in his post at the French Ministry of Economic Affairs.

The book is structured, in three parts:

Part I: Chapters 1 to 6 "Three Sources of Influence: Art, Religion, and Philosophy"

Part II: Chapters 7 to 8 "Action/Revolution—End of History/Wisdom: The Concept toward Concretion"

Part III: Chapters 9 to 11 "Three Concrete Kojèvean Outcomes and Their Likelihood: Authority, the Mirror Stage, and Global Trade"

CHAPTER 1: "FROM THE INEXISTENT TO THE CONCRETE: KOJÈVE AFTER KANDINSKY"

The book's first essay, "From the Inexistent to the Concrete: Kojève after Kandisnky," is written by Isabel Jacobs, who starts her survey of Kojève's relationship with art and specifically both with visual art and the aesthetic conceptions of his uncle, Vassily Kandinsky, by depicting the small water-color that the latter gave him in 1912 when he was only ten years old. Uncle and nephew would remain close for thirty-two years, until the death of the former in 1944. Only this may already give us an idea of how relevant this relationship was for both. They would even draft a four-handed essay in 1936 entitled "Kandinsky's Concrete paintings," the main body of the text written by Kojève and the notes by the painter and art theoretician. Such a collaborative format was not altogether alien to the Russo-French thinker. That same year he planned, in fact, to share the authorship of two more essays—one with Jacques Lacan on Hegel and Freud and the other with Leo Strauss on Hegel and Hobbes. Only the four-handed attempt with his relative came finally to fruition, which may attest to the importance that Kojève attached to the exchange on art with his uncle. In her chapter, Isabel Jacobs takes us from Kojève's early reflections on aesthetics and photography to the plastic nature of some of his late political reflections. The author explains as well both the significance within Kojève's work of his own practice as a photographer and the early influence that Buddhist notions such as "sunyata"—*boundlessness* rather than *emptiness*—exercised on his understanding of the artwork. Kandinsky's abstract paintings were, in Kojève's eyes, the first to exhaust the possibilities of painting. By giving birth to an *objectless art—objectless* to the extent that it disposes of *the real* which no longer seeks to represent—Kandinsky would have taken art to its utmost limit, bringing about not only the death of the author but also the death of originality as such.

Kojève's idea of the work of art implies, thus, that of its radical unoriginality in a post-historical age, Jacobs argues. What the wise man is in relation to knowledge—namely, the harbinger of an endless repetition in language—Kandinsky would be in relation to visual art. Jacobs's chapter addresses furthermore the Russo-French thinker's harsh criticism of surrealism and the sort of tension that Kojève sees running through the work of art between its *representational* and *concrete* aspects. This tension would only be overcome when, having reached its utmost limit, the work of art becomes independent from its object, that is, becomes a subject-object itself. By achieving through his paintings "a uni-totality that exists in the same way as do trees, animals, rocks, men, States, clouds," Kandinsky encountered the limit beyond which art would do nothing but repeat itself. A similar fate is that which our technical or cultural world eventually meets, according to Kojève in his lectures on Hegel and in some of his other nonaesthetical writings. If nature is completely conquered and replaced at the end of history by the concept taken as a concrete "self-contained whole," henceforward there's no point in wasting a word that somebody else has, for certain, uttered before us. It is perhaps worth adding, in this introduction to Jacobs's chapter, Kojève's judgment of the bourgeois domination after 1848 and its aesthetical implications in his book *The Notion of Authority*, because what he states here may well feature the aforementioned world in more than one way. The social hegemony of the bourgeoisie is one, according to Kojève, that leads to the hegemony of the present and the animal instincts. The possibilities of real action exhausted, past, and future take shelter in that society within the aesthetic domain. Here they are reproduced virtually in the respective shapes of Romanticism and the Futurist revolution. Classicism has no place in the bourgeois social milieu because the active element on which it is based is absent. The bourgeois negation of classicism gives way to the preference of writing as a mode of expression, because, unlike tradition, which rest on oral or spectacular sources, writing allows for a separation of the work from its author, "as if it were conceived outside of time."[9]

CHAPTER 2: "BETWEEN KANT AND HEGEL: ALEXANDRE KOJÈVE AND THE ABSOLUTE STATE"

Jeff Love's essay, "Between Kant and Hegel: Alexandre Kojève and the Absolute State," contains two strains of thought. One is summarized in his introductory quote from Kojève's lectures on Hegel's words "Human existence is a mediated suicide" and refers us to Kojève's notion of "atheism." The other focuses on Kant and Hegel as making up the philosophical orbit around which the radical implications of Kojève's notion of atheism revolve—the abandonment of individuality by surrendering one's own biological life. Love relates these radical implications to the Russo-French thinker's assimilation of certain Buddhist principles that equate annihilation and the definitive interruption of the cycle of life with the achievement of emancipation. In the same vein we also find Kojève's own suggestion that, had he been born in Asia, Kant's own anthropology would have been Buddhist.[10] Love's chapter, thus, can be considered as one that deals substantially with religion or, more exactly, with its reverse, to wit, with Kojève's notion of atheism and its necessary counterpart, suicide as the human death *par excellence,* or alternatively, suicide as the real actualization of a Kojèvean *Nirvana.* According to Love, Kojève as an interpreter of Hegel, bets everything—at first glance no matter the cost—on the realization of the end of history in the form of a Universal and Homogeneous State. The mutual recognition among equal human beings that reigns in such a State renders right redundant. On the other hand, the satisfaction that ensues leads to an absence of desire that resembles the Buddhist conception of death as a total extinction of biological urges. But Kojève as a reader of Kant holds back. He realizes the unfeasible and *"limit case" character* of such a State. Correspondingly, he makes certain concessions to a less ambitious and more realistic goal, namely, to the establishment of "a sort of surrogate instinct and new or second nature." This second nature takes the shape of a system of right that is meant to "adjudicate" the conflicts that arise from an individuality that hangs onto life driven by its fear of death and to keep its inclinations at bay. Whereas Kojève's radicalism as an interpreter of Hegel is based for Love both on the "Buddhist subtext that is explicit in 'Atheism' (1931) and in Kojève's book on Kant (1951)," as well as, if we may add, on the early notes on Buddhism in his *Diary of a Philosopher* (1920s), Kant as the inspiration of the system of right that Kojève sets up in his *Outline of a Phenomenology of Right* (1943) provides the necessary tools to scale down the radicality intrinsic to the Buddhist conceptual apparatus. Still, as Love explains further, both the Kantian system of right and the Hegelian final State and even Kojève's own reticence to be *uncompromisingly* consequent with his own premises in *Atheism* fall short of delivering on their emancipatory promises since all three end up shirking the effective "actualization of the possibility of suicide." Such an actualization would freely oppose the *maintenance in being* that the will of self-preservation imposes. Interestingly, the political aspect of the State is portrayed by Kojève in *Outline of a Phenomenology of Right* as exclusively concerned with issues that have to do with the State's maintenance whereas its perfect justice at the end of time implies the abandonment of any concern relative to the State's own self-preservation.[11]

CHAPTER 3: "KOJÈVE AND CHRISTIANITY"

"Atheism," "death," and "radicality" may be the terms that best express the common thread that links Love's essay to the third chapter of the book written by José María Carabante. Kojève's relationship with religion continues to be at the center of the debate but this time Christianity, or rather, its dismantling by Kojève, gains the upper hand with respect to Buddhism. If Jeff Love already noted the "Christian salvation" undertones that resound in Kojève's interpretation of history, José María Carabante comes to confirm Kojève's resolve to fulfill the revelation that human history contains no matter the consequences and the strange void in which such a fulfillment results. As Carabanate notes, the groundworks had already been laid to a certain extent by Hegel when the German philosopher declared that philosophy was a science and, in doing so, rescued it from the hold of its Christian interpreters. Hegel also sensed the existential problem that this meant for any theological understanding. It is not by chance then that Kojève took over the courses on Hegel's philosophy of religion from his friend Alexandre Koyré, which the latter was giving at the Sorbonne in the 1930s, nor that he saw in the fight for recognition between master and slave of Hegel's *Phenomenology of Spirit* a philosophical atheism whose potential had been overlooked by others. Something in Hegel's philosophy must have struck Kojève as particularly promising for his purpose. However, Hegel never ceased to consider Christian religion as legitimate a path as philosophy to access science or absolute knowledge, even if that meant downrating them to mere transient landmarks along that path. And this difference, according to Professor Carabante, is not a negligible one, because it leads to two disparate readings of Hegel, namely: one that implies the immanentization of the Absolute and the other, the Kojèvean one, that brings with it a "radical inversion of theology" and leads to the formulation of "a philosophy of death." Kojève's intent is to suppress every trace of theology from the surface of human knowledge and to establish, instead, man's deathly fate as the absolute. This means two things. First, to turn Vladimir Soloviev's metaphysics, to which Kojève had consecrated his doctoral thesis at Heidelberg, on its head and secondly, to denounce Hegel's monism and philosophy of nature in the *Encyclopedia* after his bold attempt at overcoming transcendence in his *Phenomenology*. But the "philosophy of death" put forward by Kojève, Carabante further explains, does not imply the claim that God should be replaced by man or by any other petty deity at hand, nor for that matter, by any "attainable end in the world." Very much like Prutkov's quotation in his early *Diary of a Philosopher*, Kojève claims rather that the gap of God's absence should be left wide open, for it is precisely in the lack of meaning entailed by such a gap where human meaning begins. For Carabante this turns Kojève into a "philosophical Kirillov," that is, into someone for whom the liberation from God puts an end to the fear of death. A Kirillov of a particular kind, if we may add, since Kojève himself admits that one may dispose of God and overcome the fear of death and yet remain attached to a religious distrust toward worldly satisfaction that leads to the belief that everything is permitted provided one's own conduct accelerates one's salvation through death.[12] All in all, the emancipation from the Christian God is equivalent to the emancipation from the last remnant of nature, understood as a master that overpowers human self-consciousness from within. Ridding oneself of God requires, Carabante concludes, an ultimate effort that strongly calls to mind Love's featuring suicide and self-annihilation as the most incontestable Kojèvean evidence of a true assumption of mortal finitude, with the caveat that where Love sees the traces of a Buddhist type of extinction, Carabante sees a "defeat of God" intrinsic to the logic of Christianity itself.

CHAPTER 4: "HISTORY AND NOTHINGNESS. KOJÈVE'S RE-LEVERAGING OF HEGEL'S DIALECTIC OF FREEDOM"

If the volume's first three chapters show how Kojèvean concerns that, strictly speaking, lie outside the theoretical realm, converge, or are led to do so by Kojève into Hegel's thought, Waller Newell's chapter, "History and Nothingness: Kojève's Re-Leveraging of Hegel's Dialectic," explicitly aims at "emphasizing some important differences between Kojève's transformation of Hegel and Hegel's own teaching" within an overall "attempt to assess the general significance of Kojève's theoretical enterprise." Such an attempt starts by calling the attention of the reader to a fact that is also pointed out in the essays by Love, Carabante, Shoikhedbrod, and Rutkevich in this volume, namely, the marginal role that Hegel assigns to the master-slave dialectic within the *Phenomenology of Spirit* as a whole. In contrast to the modern and individualistic perspective, Newell explains in his chapter, from which Hegel gives a first account of the sequence of shapes (master, slave, stoic, skeptic, unhappy consciousness) in the *Phenomenology of Spirit*, the historical perspective from which he gives the second enhances the role that the *unhappy consciousness* plays in the formation of self-consciousness in detriment to all the other shapes, including that of the master and the slave. As a religious internalization of said sequence, the shape *unhappy consciousness* proves essential for such formation to be fully accomplished. This accomplishment is not for Hegel, according to Newell, a mere result of an individualistic striving for recognition, but rather a synthesis between said efforts and the communal or historical setting, including tradition, ethics (*Sittlichkeit*), and family life. In line with what Rutkevich holds in his chapter, Newell sees no reason to blame Kojève for this misunderstanding because his purpose would have lain elsewhere. Where? In the adaptation of Hegel's ideas to the historical circumstances of Kojève's own time. And how? By means of both a Marxist-inspired reduction of the Hegelian spirit to historical action and by referring human action to a sort of Heideggerian *nothingness,* determined by "sheer finitude," but fully detached at the same time from being. As Newell states, Kojève privileges a notion of man that results in a modern subject at the same time dispossessed of inner content and made up of nothing but compulsive outward action, a subject fully focused on submitting the "inert fodder of nature" to his will—a Fichtean, rather than a Hegelian subject, Newell adds. Hegel and Kojève's different understandings of revelation may in the final analysis relate to this. For Hegel, the author further explains, understands *Spirit* as comprising two poles: the pole *subject* and the pole *substance.* While the former corresponds with modern values like "morality typified by Rousseau's general will and by Kant's categorical imperative" or "political liberalism," the pole *substance* reflects "the divine law of the old hearth," that is, life not merely understood as a biological reality but raised to a sort of "Spinoza's life-world" that enables the passage from nature to civilization. Let us add in this regard that in *Outline of a Phenomenology of Right* Kojève elaborates further on his conception of *family-life.* He portrays the hearth as a first instance of human individuation whose goal is the human education of its new members with a view to maintaining the family patrimony. Family would be the realm of human love, of a love capable of attributing an absolute value to the being of its members. Said being would be human and not a mere biological reality insofar as the family conceives it as making up the spiritual essence of its members as opposed to the here and now of their actions. Still, this love for the essence of being gives rise to "the family veneration of the dead, which is the *religion* of the family, the manifestation of the religious phenomenon."[13] Kojeve's *active* way of treating this religious *specter* entrenched within the family realm can be best summarized by these words from *Outline of a Phenomenology of Right*: "The most general definition that can be given of 'the divine being' is maybe the following: A is divine with respect to B and for B (that is, for the conscience that B has of A) if A is supposed to be able to act upon B without B being able to react upon A."[14] As to the pole *substance*, alluded to by Newell, suffice it to say here that for Kojève, substance is society as such or that God is nothing but the social milieu turned into substance.[15]

CHAPTER 5: "KOJÈVE AND MARX: ELUSIVE AFFINITIES AND DIVERGENCES"

Kojève's approach to Hegel is routinely held as being strongly influenced by Marx. According to this interpretation, Kojève would be the poster child of an existentialist Marxism that exercised a deep influence on a whole generation of French Marxist philosophers. In his chapter, Igor Shoikhedbrod analyzes the extent to which such an interpretation is plausible. He does so, to start with, by taking with a pinch of salt, as Kojève would say, Kojève's self-professed Marxism and by not dismissing altogether Kojève's own statement that his lectures on Hegel served a propagandistic purpose. Going into more detail, the author expands on something highlighted as well in other chapters, namely, the disproportionate importance attached by Kojève to Hegel's passages on the master-slave dialectic in *The Phenomenology of Spirit*. Shoikhedbrod evokes the idea that Kojève might have wanted his audience to believe that Marx drew upon said passages when developing his ideas of estranged labor and class struggle. Kojève's placing a quote from Marx's *Economic and Philosophical Manuscripts* of 1844 at the beginning of his *Interpretation of the Reading of Hegel* would seek to support that belief. Yet what Marx really does in that quote, Shoikhedbrod explains, is to reproach Hegel for disregarding the material process of human work and instead focusing exclusively on mental or abstract labor. Interestingly, Kojève himself raises heavy objections to Hegel on a similar account. As a philosopher talking exclusively to other philosophers, Hegel, according to Kojève, neglects the other side of the coin that is necessary for history to progress, namely, the man of action. This leads Kojève to make this often-overlooked statement on Hegel: "I doubt that he (Hegel) is the Wiseman that accomplishes History."[16] We can certainly ask ourselves in this context whether what Kojève understands under "action" coincides with what Marx understands under "the material process of human work." The answer, as might be inferred from what is stated below, is yes and no. By resorting to Marx's *Grundrisse*, Shoikhedbrod's chapter provides further evidence of the forceful character of Kojève's interpretation of Marx's thought as principally based on the Hegelian master-slave dialectic. The importance of becoming aware of the alienating consequences that arise from accepting the separation between the "product as its own" and "the conditions of its realization" is an issue that *Grundrisse* brings to light. Now, if we take Kojève at his word in his *Outline of a Phenomenology of Right*, it is precisely such a separation that lies at the core of his notion of bourgeois property and the emancipatory consequences that its exchange has for the slave-bourgeois. In effect, the separation of the product from the worker's own body sets in motion a dynamic of trade which is potentially conducive to the final State at the end of history. Thereupon a turning point ensues, and exchange contracts can be reduced to a minimum, being no longer necessary since equality, or rather equity among human beings, has been achieved. This is, very succinctly exposed, one of Kojève's claims in his book on right. The contrast between Kojève and Marx, the former rating the separation between product and material work conditions as emancipatory and the latter as alienating, could not be greater. In his chapter, Shoikhedbrod also points out that the—concomitant with the master-slave dialectic—notion of *recognition for pure prestige* does not play a significant role in Marx's system of thought. Insofar as the latter is a system based on "the contradictions of material life," Kojève himself would have realized the salient divergences that exist between his *spiritual* stance on recognition and the *nothingness* it entails and Marx's own pattern of thinking. Shoikhedbrod expands further in his chapter on an analysis of the shape that the final State takes in the work of each author by coming back to the distinction between the "realm of necessity" and the "realm of freedom" that he exposes at the beginning of his essay. While for Kojève the realm of freedom puts an end to the struggle for recognition, so that fight and work are no longer necessary and the citizens of such a State enjoy the reciprocal recognition of their individualities, Marx's final State raises labor to "life's prime want" and does not bring about any *transcendence of necessity*. What type of freedom Kojève's final State features and what sort of labor Marx thinks of when he devises his, are legitimate questions that one can ask at this juncture. The answer to the first is ambivalent: on the one hand, a full conquest of nature allows the slave to free himself completely from the constraints of the given, on the other, the exhaustion of action and creative will means that freedom in Kojève's end state is something more apparent than real. The answer to the status of work in Marx's final State may, paradoxically, refer us to Kojève's starting point, when to the violent victory of the master he opposes the humanizing nature of work as something that increasingly permits the objectification of the slave's self-consciousness in the world. As Shoikhedbrod notes, in refuting Adam Smith's conception of labor, Marx portrays work as an "overcoming of obstacles" that, gradually liberating he who works from merely responding to "external natural urgencies," enables him more and more to become a free individual author of his work. Kojève might well have subscribed to this provided history was still there, which, by all accounts, is not the case.

CHAPTER 6: "ALEXANDRE KOJÈVE AND CARL
SCHMITT: MYTHOLOGIES OF ENMITY"

Massimo Palma explores in his chapter the relationship between Alexandre Kojève and Carl Schmitt. Both authors corresponded from 1955 to 1960, and finally met up personally when Schmitt invited Kojève to give a conference in January 1957 at the Rhein-Ruhr club in Düsseldorf. As the philosopher Jacob Taubes states, after a conference in Berlin to which, for his part, he had invited him in 1967 Kojève told him that he planned to visit the only man who was worth discussing with in Germany, meaning Schmitt. This suggests that the proponent of the friend-enemy relationship and the proponent of the master-slave dialectic may have met in person more frequently than just once in 1957. That their relationship was a close one is also evidenced by the fact that in 1955 Schmitt writes to Kojève thanking him for having entertained his only child, the then twenty-four-year-old Anima, during her stay in Paris. In his approach to their mutual influences, Palma distinguishes three different periods: the first coincides with Kojève's lectures on Hegel during the '30s, the second covers the war period during which Kojève writes both his *The Notion of Authority* and *Outline of a Phenomenology of Right*, and the third, the period in which Kojève gives his conference in Düsseldorf. The first period is marked by Kojève's reception of Schmitt's work, presumably through Leo Strauss. The most salient feature of this reception is the use that Kojève makes of the Schmittian notion of *"the real possibility" to kill the enemy,* since it is this notion that he uses to describe the emergence both of self-consciousness and the lack of it in the anthropogenic fight. Palma further connects the existentialist trait of said fight with the Schmittian "seriousness of the case" or *Ernstfall,* the "friend-enemy" decision owing its seriousness to nothing other than its being the source of political autonomy and freedom. As evoked above, in the middle of WWII, Kojève writes a short essay on authority and a much longer and "unwieldly" one on right. The fact that in the latter Kojève explicitly mentions Schmitt provides further evidence, according to Palma, of an influence that in the 1930s remained only latent. In effect, in Kojève's study of right the friendship that unites the victors of the fight within an equal society of masters is the prerequisite for the birth of the juridical; in other words, Kojève posits the political, as Schmitt understands it, as the condition for the existence of right. Palma furthermore calls attention to the fact that in Kojève's *Outline of a Phenomenology of Right,* Hegel's influence is not directly traceable, as one may initially expect, to the German thinker's *Philosophy of Right.* What we encounter instead is a Hegel read through Schmittian lenses. As Palma explains, through his assumption of the Schmittian characterization of *political hate* as something "undifferentiated"—opposed by definition to the differentiated and private nature that hate acquires inside the family realm—Kojève accepts Schmitt's reading of the "young Hegel's *Scientific Ways to Treat Natural Law.*" Worth noting is also, according to the author of the chapter, the use of the Schmittian distinction that Kojève makes during this war period between *legitimacy* and *legality.*

The influence between the two authors would balance in the 1950s and turn into a more reciprocal one. The seriousness of the political decision seems to give way in Schmitt to the *playfulness* and *joie de vivre* that Kojève at times so conspicuously attributes to the *victory of the slave* at the end of history. If Schmitt was fully committed in the prewar and war years to the preservation of his idea of the State whatever the cost, from the 1950s on he shows himself ready to declare—very much in line with Kojève's claims in their correspondence relative to Truman's point IV and the mere managerial and not political future that awaits humanity—that the statal form is definitively over,[17] as well as to acknowledge that the notion of "play" proves more apt to account for what was going on in the world back then. Through playfulness as opposed to seriousness enmity is conventionalized and, thanks to contrivances common to a global mass consumer society such as entertainment, sport or free time management, channeled away from the killing of the enemy.[18] Addressing, finally, Kojève's inversion of the Schmittian notion of "taking," Palma's chapter links the "giving" that results from such an inversion to Kojève's undertakings—"the philosopher in action"—as a high civil servant specialized in commercial policy in the French Ministry of Economic Affairs.

CHAPTER 7: "WISDOM, SELF-CONSCIOUSNESS, AND EMPIRE"

Three things should be said beforehand about Alexei Rutkevich's chapter, "Wisdom, Self-Consciousness and Empire": first, that it outlines with sharp precision matters that have come up in other chapters; second, that, by drawing upon a manuscript so far only partially deciphered and transcribed into Russian, it deals with the relevant issue of the status of historical experience in Kojève's work; and thirdly, that it acquaints the reader with valuable firsthand testimonies. Concerning the first question, Rutkevich's chapter categorically differentiates Hegel's own work from its Kojèvean interpretation. According to him, Kojève, in his lectures on Hegel of the 1930s, disguised his own thought in a Hegelian robe before his gullible French audience. Rutkevich's statement that Kojève "was not trying to find out things as accurately as possible 'as they really are'" may even be referred to Kojeve's own statement in his *Kant* that the wise and uncontradictory language of recognition and success does not stem from "an *intention* to speak the truth."[19] From this perspective, the question arises as to what extent a literal reading of Kojève's words to the Vietnamese philosopher Tran-Duc-Thao in 1948, claiming that his own interpretation of Hegel was nothing but a work of propaganda, is the most appropriate one. This leads us to ask two more questions, namely: one which regards the eventual goal of such philosophical propaganda and the other, the "different motivation" from which "Kojève's own doctrine" arises. Rutkevich's survey of the undeciphered manuscript by Kojève on *Sophia* or wisdom may help elucidate these questions. As Rutkevich explains, the manuscript is a first attempt by Kojève to present his system of thought without covering it entirely in the costumes of another thinker—maybe, we speculate, his *Outline of a Phenomenology of Right* was the work in which he exposed such a doctrine in the nude by dressing it up in the gowns of a socialist empire, this being, in turn, the reason why he felt so satisfied with that book. At any rate, as Rutkevich further reveals, from his system of thought Kojève awaits a concrete account of the whole since from the truth of said whole stems that of its individual parts. And the system of thought that Kojève designs runs counter not only to the abstract truths of Descartes's system, since the latter relies on a separation of the speaker cognizer (subject) from the thing cognized (object) that hinders the attainment of the truth of totality from the very outset, but also to the Spinozist axioms since the system of thought they build is one that excludes human experience. The whole, thus, whose account Kojève's has in mind is a whole made up of both experienced nature and experienced history, of their concrete and actual totality, and to become true this totality must encompass all its constituent parts, allowing them thereby to become true themselves. Hegel's dialectic and its circularity, Rutkevich continues, are the philosophical tools that best suit such a system because together they sanction the truth of the system's particular provisions by referring them to a true totality. The *salvific* limit of the system ensues the moment that its first provision, whichever this may be, contains all the rest and vice versa, that is, when the answer to no matter what question proves to contain all the logical answers and questions previously stated. Be it the beginning containing the end or vice versa, by reaching its limit the system of thought exhausts its logical possibilities, thereupon demonstrating its truth. Such exhaustion indeed affects human speech—the ideal—but existence—the real—is dragged into its circular motion not to a lesser degree, or maybe even far more. "All that can exist must actually exist," quotes Rutkevich. If that which must actually exist does not yet exist, the system proves not to have reached its truth and the speech to which it gives rise is false. True speech demands, therefore, the previous end of "the real development," or, in other words, the actual "stoppage of history." This stoppage in turn presupposes the emergence of a new form of state—if this term makes any sense in a context in which history has ended—and a new, concrete, knowledge of man—if the word "man" should likewise not be questioned based on the same historical exhaustion. Rutkevich further notes that, according to Kojève's *Sophia* manuscript, such state and knowledge are only attainable in a postrevolutionary communist society that has completed history. He also asserts that, for Kojève, bourgeois and communist revolutions are both "part of a single movement" toward the final state. The cursory nature of an introduction forbids us to expand on other intriguing considerations made by the author of the chapter. Still, if we briefly return to the questions we raised above, the precedence that Kojève grants in his system to "experienced" history over unexperienced speech to articulate a wise speech worthy of its name—"historiosophical scheme"—seems to justify a literal reading of Kojeve's reference to "propaganda" in the letter he wrote to Tran-Duc-Thao. In the light of this reading, propaganda appears as a useful means to achieve what is really serious, namely, that "Man does not miss definitively his human destiny and that History reaches its goal."[20]

CHAPTER 8: "TYRANNY OR WISDOM? A READING OF THE STRAUSS–KOJÈVE DEBATE"

José Daniel Parra's chapter "Tyranny or Wisdom? A Reading of the Strauss–Kojève Debate" gives a detailed account of Kojève's response to Strauss in their famous debate. Among the numerous questions that Professor Parra's essay raises, this introduction will focus on the question of "action" and the time constraint that is associated with it. As Parra notes in his essay, this question appears in Kojève's response almost from the very outset. An "exercise in political reflection" makes it advisable to the ancient tyrant not to waste time listening to the utopian advice of the philosopher. One would even say in this same line that the tyrant's attention to the latter holds just enough to avoid being blamed for impoliteness. Without uttering a word and not a single minute later, the ancient tyrant resumes the current business he was engaged in to bring it to conclusion. Kojève's concern with the shortage of time arises also in his *Outline of a Phenomenology of Right* and similarly in some of the official notes that he writes for the French Ministry of Economic Affairs, which reveal a Kojève urged by the need to find an all-knowledge solution for the problems of the world. In *Tyranny and Wisdom*, at any rate, Kojève draws upon Pascal and asserts that the business that the tyrant deals with—his undertaking political activity as opposed to the idle chatter of the philosopher—cannot be sorted out at an individual level, but only within the broader framework of that great individual that is History. According to this historical scheme, would-be tyrants build on the legacy of their predecessors until one of them sees the collective tyrannical task finally accomplished, namely, a perfect political regime in which the free will of its citizens coincides with the will of the tyrant and vice versa. The point seems to be, for Kojève, to let the flow of *current affairs* reach historical completion so that wisdom and its political counterpart, the universal and homogeneous State, can happen effectively at the end of History. Philosophy is there, at its best, to smoothen the flow that leads to the *exhaustion* of such *affairs*, at its worst, to clog it by housing prejudices that take the form of theistic and moral—and ultimately platonic—qualms. In his chapter, Parra suggests that the nonhistorical, non-Hegelian philosopher may be in Kojève's eyes "the intellectual." The intellectual philosopher as opposed to the dialectical one is he who yields, as the Christian atheist he is, to moral or theistic conceptions of virtue that make him shirk his *revolutionary* duty if, by chance, he reaches power.[21] This theistic penchant also affects those who hang on to the belief that they are revolutionaries even if the success of a revolution proves its own cancellation as such. Both moral prejudices, on the one hand, and the unwillingness to accept that the revolution has been successful, lead their proponents to overlook the post-revolutionary present as it is. Kojève distinguishes in this sense between actions that arise from a mere reformist will and "revolutionary" actions that seek a *radical reform*. It is worth expanding on this to avoid certain misunderstandings. For Kojève, by merely sticking to a reformist program, the tyrant to-be simply acknowledges the world that the master has previously established. This meek acceptance of the world as it is, underlies the slave condition of every reformist. The inescapable fact is that either one draws upon the terror that the world of the master inspires in him, summoning up therefrom the necessary courage to negate it through a matching terror, or one is forever unable to shake off his slave condition.[22] But the revolution in which such a negation issues is everything but a nihilistic or sceptic one. As Kojève understands it, the revolution does not lead to the disappearance of the social world or to an anarchic chaos, but rather to a new and concrete order. Only when true revolutionaries acknowledge first and incorporate after the tradition of the past to their idea of revolution, are they in a position to build something concrete and permanent that does not vanish in "the perfectly pure but unbreathable air of abstract theory or of dreams."[23] Yet, if, as above stated, once transformed into something concrete, the revolution cancels itself out, revolutionaries who are no longer needed should get ready for their own "suicide." As agents of the revolution in a postrevolutionary state the communist parties find themselves at a similar dead end, namely, that, as their goals have been achieved, their existence is superfluous. The former USSR is no exception to this. The years 1917–1957 make up the forty-year period that it took Russia, according to Kojève, to achieve the goals set by its communist party, namely, the "nationalization of the means of production and distribution."[24] Thereupon, the existence of such a party is rendered redundant. A communist individual in a post-Stalinist Russia proves therefore to be as untimely and incongruous as a communist individual in the United States or, for that matter, in a social-democratic Europe. Or, even, *mutatis mutandis*, as the philosopher was in the eyes of the ancient tyrant, with the caveat that whereas the latter had a long way to go before he brought his business to conclusion, the modern tyrant is just about to finish it up. If, as Parra states in his chapter, "For Kojève historical wisdom is an actual possibility," one cannot help but wonder whether, very much as seems to happen to Napoleon in relation to Hegel, it is not the modern tyrant—as a history maker—rather than any philosopher—as an abstract thinker—he who in matters of wisdom has the last say.

CHAPTER 9: "AUTHORITY AND LEGITIMACY IN ALEXANDRE KOJÈVE'S *THE NOTION OF AUTHORITY*"

Bryan-Paul Frost begins his chapter by making the point that the war period, paradoxically as it may sound, was particularly fruitful for Kojève's work as a philosopher. Between 1942 and 1945 the Russo-French thinker wrote three books, one of them of a considerable size and density. If we add to these the 1,000 or so pages of the 1941 still-undeciphered manuscript on *Sophia*, we may get an idea of how productive Kojève was during this time. It is noteworthy that neither of the two works on which Frost concentrates in his chapter, namely *The Notion of Authority* and *Outline of a Phenomenology of Right*, to say nothing of the aforementioned manuscript, were published during Kojève's lifetime. The French edition of the first appeared in 2004 and that of the second only in 1981. Kojève's disregard for the publication of his own writings, merits attention by itself: was writing for him a mode of expression particularly apt to record his prolific thoughts but useless if it turned into a mere intellectual means for one to get published and recognized, as he might suggest in *Tyranny and Wisdom* in 1954?[25] Or was he rather keener on the oral or spectacular nature of classical tradition that prevailed before the written artwork typical of the bourgeoisie and its universal pretensions became hegemonic, as he might allude to in his *The Notion of Authority*?[26] It is hard to know. Be that as it may, in his essay Frost makes a thorough survey of Kojève's war period writings, with a special focus on the latter. As Frost explains, *The Notion of Authority* not only exercised a deep influence on Kojève's positioning in the debate with Leo Strauss of the 1950s, but, in fact, "one might argue that 'Notion' is even more foundational than" Kojève's *Introduction to the Reading of Hegel* "given that the authority of the master is one of only four archetypes and it does not seem privileged over the other three in any strict sense." Frost signals in this respect something to which Carabante refers also in his chapter and that Kojève himself highlights in his lectures on Hegel, namely, that the desire for recognition and its counterpart, the fight to the death, make it difficult, if not altogether impossible, for the unsatisfied masters to build a stable political community based on their desire for recognition, since recognition presupposes the slavery of the one that recognizes. What is at stake here is, as Frost puts it, none other than the "origin of political life." Kojève's way of overcoming this "impasse" in his work of the 1930s is twofold. On the one hand, in his *Outline of a Phenomenology of Right* he devises a collective fight for recognition in which the contenders witness both their equal conditions at the outset and the unequal outcome of the fight. In the case of the victors, the friendship that arises from their mutual treatment as successful comrades in arms provides the basis for the phenomenon of right. On the other hand, by bringing into play other types of authority Kojève manages in *The Notion of Authority* to broaden the sources of recognition significantly. Particularly relevant in this respect, as Frost states, is the *leader* type of authority. The recognition as a leader of one of its members implies the readiness of the rest of the group to submit their specific beings to the political project envisioned by the former. Frost's chapter addresses two other important questions, namely, Kojève's treatment of Rousseau and Montesquieu in *The Notion* and the question of *contingency* in Kojève's "contingent writings." Regarding the first subject, Kojève seems to pit the Swiss thinker's *general will* against the French philosopher's separation of powers. For him, Rousseau's *general will* entails "permanence" and "harmony," and also refers to the political community taken as a whole, rather than as a sum of its parts—this idea of "wholeness" being incidentally crucial in Kojève's political thinking. Neither the "permanence" nor "harmony" of Rousseau's general will appear, moreover, to involve a break with the past. By way of contrast, Montesquieu's division of authority not only cuts off authority from its link to the past by eliminating the authority of the father but leads, subsequently, to the unceasing political instability characteristic of the bourgeois political order, or what amounts to the same, to Trotsky's "permanent revolution." As to Kojève's "contingent writings," Frost coins this accurate expression to refer to the practical connotations of some of Kojève's writings. Such connotations, as Frost further suggests, may reflect a tension in Kojève's political thought between its final goal embodied in a forever stable Universal and Homogeneous State and the "current affairs" of the transient present. Without ever losing sight of the first, Kojève, abhorring utopian advice that ignores both past and present, adapts his own political action to whatever the present has in store for him, be it Pétain's "national revolution," be it the role of De Gaulle's authority in a postnational France, be it the success of Monnet-Schuman's plans for Europe against his own. In his *The Emperor Julian and His Art of Writing,* Kojève may refer to such an adaptation when he calls to pay heed to the trustworthiness of "the testimonies of the cities."

CHAPTER 10: "THE SPECULAR PHILOSOPHER: ALEXANDRE KOJÈVE AND JACQUES LACAN"

"For Kojève who was my master (truly the only)" so reads, Trevor Wilson states in his chapter, the inscription on the cover of the first issue of *La Psychanalyse*, the review founded by Lacan in 1956, a copy of which he gave to Kojève as a gift. Wilson also informs us that among the table of contents of this first edition there was "a discussion of negation or 'Verneinung' in Hegel," as if a Lacan then aged fifty-six was keen on doubling the tribute that he paid to Kojève. This recognition of the Russo-French thinker as his master is not the only one. As late as 1972, at the age of seventy-one, he writes in a footnote in *L'Étourdi* (*Bewilderment*) that he "considers Kojève as his master, the one that initiated him into Hegel."[27] Lacan was in the 1930s an active and assiduous attendee at Kojève's lectures on Hegel. In 1935, or maybe even earlier, the French psychiatrist started organizing workshops at his house. He not only invited Kojève to them but showed himself ready to change the date if that allowed Kojève to attend the meetings.[28] Such a recognition was rather one-sided for there is no evidence of reciprocity on the part of Kojève. As Wilson points out in his chapter, their similar age notwithstanding, "it would notably be Kojève who took the status of intellectual mentor to Lacan." The connotations of the word "master," into which such mentorship can be translated, make it reasonable to raise the question about the real reach of Kojève's influence over Lacan, who since the 1930s had established himself as a psychiatrist in the 16th arrondissement in Paris and whose influence on the formation of the soul of contemporary man is arguably not negligible. Wilson explores in his essay "the pivotal role played by Kojève in shaping the direction of Lacan's work" and he does so by placing the focus of his analysis on Lacan's article, "Family Complexes in the Formation of the Individual." Lacan was already engaged in this writing in 1935, and he and Kojève discussed it in their correspondence. Based on said writing, Lacan gave a conference at the 14th International Congress of Psychoanalysis in 1936 in Marienbad, which can be considered as "the first formal presentation of Lacan's theory of the mirror-stage in early childhood development." Not without controversy, the original French edition of the article was finally published under the title "La Famille" in *Encyclopédie Française* in 1938. As Wilson explains, Lacan will further elaborate on the same topic in a speech he gave at the 16th International Congress of Psychoanalysis in 1949 in Zurich. Interestingly, Lacan rates in this speech his own historical moment as one "that tips the whole of human knowledge into being mediated by the desire of the other." One can hardly ignore the Kojèvian reminiscences latent in such a mediation and such a desire. Wilson's analysis of *Family Complexes in the Formation of the Individual* also highlights the distinction that Lacan makes between *Complex* and *Instinct*. *Complex* refers to the set of cultural habits that is formed within the family and that humanizes the newborn. The term *Instinct*, for its part, refers to the biological elements that constitute the child. *Complexes* are formed at the expense of *instincts*, the cultural aspect implying the negation of the biological one. But this negation proceeds dialectically, each negated and now missing vital function being replaced by a positive nonbiological or social one that leads to "the vital dependence of the individual in respect to the group." Besides determining the first stages of individuation, namely, the primeval negation of instinct that the baby's weaning off breastmilk implies, the *complex-instinct* dialectic also reflects "the inclination to death, which is particular to the human psyche" and lies at the root of mental formations that will accompany the subject throughout his life. By "losing contact with its sustenance"—the mother's breast—the *weaning complex* makes the baby aware that "it is what its mother's breast is not." Wilson explains that these first Lacanian notions are traceable both to Kojève's dualist ontology nature/mental and to his conception of death as making up the core of human self-consciousness. Still, if going beyond these elementary stages of psychic development, one tackles, as Wilson does, more developed Lacanian *complexes* that have to do with the shape that the social element takes in the infant, one equally encounters Kojève's clear influence on the French psychiatrist's early thought. In this sense the *intrusion complex* and its counterpart the *mirror stage* can be read as a transposition into the formation process of the infant's mind of Kojève's twin rivals in the anthropogenic fight.

CHAPTER 11: "ALEXANDRE KOJÈVE'S ECONOMIC UNDERTAKINGS"

The last chapter of the volume focuses on Kojève's activities as a high civil servant for the French Ministry of Economic Affairs. The chapter's scope is to capture the link between Kojève's theoretical corpus and his practical initiatives as what we may call a *statesman*. We would be wrong to think *statesman* is too weighty a term for someone whose job was inside a rather obscure directorate of said Ministry. The theoretical motivation that underlay his actions and his own voluntarism led Kojève to foster his own economic ideas beyond the comparatively modest position he held. In addition, the French administration was still rebuilding itself after WWII and was permeable to influences that did not strictly correspond with the meritocratic controls that one expects from a consolidated bureaucracy. The fact is that besides the need to coordinate its activities with higher instances, the Directorate of External Economic Relations (DREE) for which Kojève worked lacked competences in matters such as the distribution of the Marshall funds. Still, many of the ministerial notes that Kojève wrote and circulated among the heads of the different organisms in charge of France's external commercial policy dealt with such and related matters. Moreover, only "a mandarin of the high French administration"[29] would have been able to summon up the necessary confidence, as well as to gather enough support from his colleagues, to lead a *counterattack* against Schuman and Monnet's designs for Europe, as Kojève did in 1950. Even if it finally did not prosper, the move cannot but be held as highly significant. The French historian Gerard Bossuat talks in this context about "the D.R.E.E .,and its group of experts in which Kojève sets the tone."[30] But Kojève's setting the tone did not limit itself to his written advice. Almost from the outset he began attending economic summits around the world, trying to translate into effective action that which he wrote in his ministerial proposals. It is worth noting in this regard that Kojève's strong sense of contingency allowed him, as a negotiator, to adapt his long-term goals to the circumstances of each moment by creating each time the best possible outcome of an eventually bad one. Besides, his theoretical reflections were usually taken very seriously by people with high decision-making power within the French state apparatus. At the root of some of these theoretical reflections lie two premises, namely that the total solution to the world economic imbalances could be reached only if it was tackled at a global level, that is, if it counted with the previous blessing of the United States as the world leader, and that such a solution was meant to solve the "English problem" once and for all. This problem, for its part, is already sketched in Kojève's 1945 "Outline of a Doctrine of French Policy," and it reaches its peak between 1961 and 1963. The year 1961 is both when Kojève drafts an idiosyncratic note on the EEC's Common Agricultural Policy where he devises a total solution to the world's economic predicament that entails the United Kingdom having to turn its agricultural system on its head, as well as the year in which Great Britain makes its first application to join the EEC. January 14, 1963, for its part, is the date on which de Gaulle definitively vetoes the first British application to join the EEC in a highly controversial press conference. As the chapter shows, Kojève was one of the French representatives in Brussels whose negotiating skills were deployed to wreak havoc on the British aspirations. It is also more than likely that Kojève's total perspective on the agricultural problem of the world was part of the incompatibility thesis that the French delegation put forward to end the negotiations.

NOTES

1. Alexandre Kojève, *Tagebuch eines Philosophen* (Berlin: Matthes & Seitz, 2015), 69.

2. Alexandre Kojève, *L'Empereur Julien et son art d'écrire* (Paris: Fourbis, 1989), 6.

3. Raymond Nart, "Alexandre Kojevnikov dit Kojève," *Commentaire* 161 (2018): 221.

4. Juan Pablo Lucchelli. "Kojève, la politique et la philosophie, à propos de la dernière biographie d'Alexandre Kojève par Marco Filoni," *Revue du MAUSS permanente*, 7 octobre 2021 [en ligne]. https://www.journaldumauss.net/./?Kojeve-la -politique-et-la-philosophie

5. Nart, *Kojevnikov*, 224.

6. Leo Strauss, *On Tyranny: Corrected and Expanded Edition, Including the Strauss-Kojève Correspondence* (Chicago: University of Chicago Press, 2013) 175.

7. Allan Bloom, *The Closing of The American Mind* (New York: Simon & Schuster, 2008) 222, n.6.

8. Kojève, *On Tyranny,* 166.

9. Alexandre Kojève, *La Notion de L'autorité* (Paris: Gallimard, 2004), 144–146.

10. Alexandre Kojève, *Kant* (Paris: Gallimard, 1973), 50.

11. Alexandre Kojève, *Esquisse, d'une Phénoménologue du Droit* (Paris: Gallimard, 1981), 585, n.1.

12. Kojève, *Kant,* 49.

13. Kojève, *Esquisse,* 500.

14. Ibid, 34.

15. Alexandre Kojève, *Introduction à la lecture de Hegel* (Paris: Gallimard, 1968), 498.

16. Ibid, 400.

17. Carl Schmitt, "Der Begriff des Politischen" (Berlin: Duncker & Humboldt, 2002).

18. Ibid.

19. Kojève, *Kant,* 51.

20. Kojève, *Introduction,* 522.

21. Kojève, *On Tyranny,* 165–167.

22. Kojève, *Introduction,* 33.

23. Alexandre Kojève, "Outline of a Doctrine of French Policy," translation Erik de Vries. *Policy Review.* August & September (2004): 28. https://www. hoover.org/research/outline-doctrine-french- policy.

24. Alexandre Kojève, "Moscou: Août 1957," *Commentair* 62 (1993): 274.

25. Kojève, *On Tyranny,* 162 n. 6.

26. Kojève, *La Notion,* 146.

27. Jacques Lacan, *L'Étourdit* (Paris: Seuil, 1973), 6.
28. Juan Pablo Lucchelli, "Le premier Lacan: cinq lettres inédites de Lacan à Kojève," *Cliniques méditerranéennes* 2, no. 94 (2016): 297–308. DOI: 10.3917/cm.094.0297. URL: https://www.cairn.info/revue-cliniques-mediterraneennes-2016-2-page-297.htm.
29. Christoph Kletzer, p. 133.
30. Bossuat, vol II, p. 70.

BIBLIOGRAPHY

Bloom, Allan. *The Closing of the American Mind.* New York: Simon & Schuster, 2008.

Bossuat, Gérard, *La France, l'aide américaine et la construction européenne 1944–1954. Volume II.* Vincennes: Institut de la gestion publique et du développement économique,1997. http://books.openedition. org/ igpde/2786, 70.

Kletzer, Christoph. Alexandre Kojève's Hegelianism and the formation of Europe. *Cambridge Yearbook of European Legal Studies 8* (2006): 133–151.

Kojève, Alexandre.*Tagebuch eines Philosophen.* Berlin: Matthes & Seitz, 2015.

———. *L'Empereur Julien et son art d'écrire.* Paris: Fourbis, 1989.

———. *La Notion de l'autorité.* Paris: Gallimard, 2004.

———. *Kant.* Paris: Gallimard, 1973.

———. *Esquisse, d'une Phénoménologue du Droit.* Paris: Gallimard, 1981.

———. *Introduction à la lecture de Hegel.* Paris: Gallimard, 1968.

———. "Outline of a Doctrine of French Policy," Translation Erik de Vries. *Policy Review* August & September (2004). https://www. hoover.org/research/outline-doctrine-french- policy.

———. "Moscou: Août 1957." *Commentaire* 62 (Été 1993).

Lucchelli, Juan Pablo. "Kojève, la politique et la philosophie, à propos de la dernière biographie d'Alexandre Kojève par Marco Filoni." *Revue du MAUSS permanente* (7 octobre 2021). [en ligne] https://www.journaldumauss.net/./?Kojeve-la-politique-et-la-philosophie

———. "Le premier Lacan: cinq lettres inédites de Lacan à Kojève." *Cliniques méditerranéennes* 2, no, 94 (2016): 297–308. DOI: 10.3917/cm.094.0297. URL: https://www.cairn.info/revue-cliniques-mediterraneennes-2016-2-page-297.htm

Nart, Raymond. "Alexandre Kojevnikov dit Kojève." *Commentaire* 161 (2018).

Schmitt, Carl. "Der Begriff des Politischen." Berlin: Duncker & Humboldt, 2002.

Strauss, Leo. *On Tyranny: Corrected and Expanded Edition, Including the Strauss-Kojève Correspondence.* Chicago: University of Chicago Press, 2013.

PART I

Three Sources of Influence

Art, Religion, and Philosophy

Chapter One

From the Inexistent to the Concrete

Kojève after Kandinsky

Isabel Jacobs

In 1912, ten-year-old Aleksandr "Lula" Kozhevnikov, later known as the French Hegelian philosopher Alexandre Kojève, received a small watercolor.[1] On *Aquarell für Kojève*, patches of inky black contrast with colorful figures. It's almost nightfall. In a splash of royal blue there sails a boat with a fuming dragon's head. Above, the sinking sun in dark red. Birds and horses rush from a hilly city. Inside its walls, a church reminiscent of Moscow's Ivan the Great Bell Tower. Towards the left, a Russian orthodox monk in dark solemnity. On the right, a young warrior, holding a shield with the image of Saint George. He talks to a sorceress who resembles Baba Yaga, the famous witch of Slavic folklore. The watercolor, assembling some archetypal motifs of Lula's native Russia, was painted by his uncle, none other than the famous painter and theorist Wassily Kandinsky (1866–1944). Kandinsky was the half-brother of Kojève's father, Vladimir Kozhevnikov, whose life had been cut short in Manchuria during the Russo-Japanese war. Kandinsky's drawing offers a last glimpse of fin-de-siècle Russia, the backdrop to Kojève's childhood that would vanish with the October Revolution. The watercolor playfully alludes to Kandinsky's visual philosophy—as seen through the eyes of a child. It is probably the first document of Kojève and Kandinsky's fruitful relationship that was to last until Kandinsky's death in 1944. In exile, first in Germany, then France, their paths would cross time and again; in the meantime, they correspond extensively.[2] In his apartment in Vanves, Kojève kept Kandinsky's painting *Drei Elemente* (1925), the *Aquarell für Kojève*, three watercolors, and one ink drawing.[3] Their dialogue culminated in the collaborative essay,

"Les peintures concrètes de Kandinsky," written by Kojève between July 23 and 25, 1936, and later annotated by Kandinsky himself.[4]

In 1966, on the occasion of Kandinsky's centenary, an abbreviated version of the essay appeared as "Pourquoi concret" in Gualtieri di San Lazzaro's *XXᵉ siècle.*[5] The significance of Kandinsky's work, and visual art and aesthetics more broadly, for Kojève's philosophy is still relatively little explored.[6] Is it mere coincidence that one of the most influential twentieth-century philosophers was closely related to the pioneer of abstract art? In Christine Baudillon and François Lagarde's recent Kojève documentary, his niece Nina Kousnetzoff recalls her uncle repeatedly stating that "life is worth living because, from time to time, there are extraordinary moments, but you have to prepare for them."[7] Living an examined life, for Kojève, meant appreciating what one is looking for. Wisdom, in this regard, is inextricably entwined with *taste*. Or, in Kousnetzoff's words:

> In fact, the satisfactions he organized for himself were very well prepared because, for example, from an aesthetic point of view, he knew a lot. So he knew how to appreciate things "knowingly," that's an expression he often used, "knowingly" [*en connaissance de cause*]. That's typical of him, because it's not just a matter of looking, no, you have to know what to look for, and then you can appreciate it.[8]

And who was the philosopher Kojève if not precisely that posthistorical *connoisseur* who knew what to look for and how to appreciate it? While the documentary might give some anecdotal testimony to his appreciation for visual art, my essay examines in detail some elements of Kojève's aesthetics. In several close readings, I provide textual and historical evidence for a new reading of his multifaceted work through the lens of visual art. First, I will explore Kojève's early writings on inexistence and emptiness, uncovering how they already bear the hallmarks of his mature philosophy. I will then retrace the significance of these notes into his photographic practice, the work on Kandinsky's concrete paintings, and his late theory of the State. In my analysis of Kojève's aesthetics, I will focus on how a unique concept of *concreteness* pervades not only his Hegel interpretation in the 1930s but also his late ontology and political theory. The main goal of my reading is to unveil how Kojève developed, alongside Kandinsky's artistic project, a unique philosophical *style*, shaped by emptiness, repetition, and exhaustion. To conclude, I aim to demonstrate that visual art was the laboratory in which he experimented with the ingredients of what was to become his famous posthistorical reading of Hegel.

AESTHETICS OF INEXISTENCE

Shortly after the October Revolution, Kojève was forced to leave Russia. In 1920, he went on a spectacular journey through Russia and Poland to Germany. In Heidelberg, Kojève studied Eastern languages and philosophy. In 1923, in Berlin, he immersed himself in the capital's bohème. During these years, at the height of German Expressionism, photography became a central part of Kojève's life. His early photographs portray a life of luxury and leisure between Dahlem and the summer house in Beaulieu. In Paris, Kojève would share an apartment with his compatriot, the fashion photographer Eugène Rubin (also known under his pseudonym Evgenii Reis).[9] Photography remained Kojève's lifelong passion. On his extensive travels and diplomatic missions through Asia, Russia, and Europe in the 1950 and 1960s, Kojève took several thousands of photographs.[10] These strikingly empty images, at first sight touristic snapshots, depict life in a posthistorical world. Kojève's lens captured countless monuments, temples, churches, landmarks, and statues. If these empty landscapes are inhabited by people, only as fleeting fragments that vanish toward the image's margins. They seem withdrawn from both their environment and the spectator. Constructing an ideal point of view on human existence, Kojève's photographs mirror an impersonal gaze. The phenomenon of emptiness already haunts Kojève's *Journal of a Philosopher*, written during the 1920s.[11] Like his late photographs, these adolescent notebooks are mostly concerned with emptiness, or what Kojève calls his "philosophy of the inexistent" [*философия несуществующего*].[12] On October 26, 1920, Kojève describes his notes in German as "*Handarbeiten*," suggesting the idea of intellectual craftsmanship.[13] In the *Journal*, visual art plays a key role, culminating in Kojève's aesthetics of inexistence. The first sketches of this aesthetics can be found in the short dialogue, "Descartes and Buddha," dated June 12, 1920. Deconstructing Descartes's *cogito ergo sum*—the proposition that the act of thinking proves the cogito's existence—Buddha states:

> If we accept the homogeneity of the thinking process, then we are able to say that any thought whatsoever is, as it is, adequate to the concept of being [bytie]. Only reasoned being becomes reality [real'nost']; in other words, any thought potentially holds within itself the realization of the thinkable. Consequently, if thought, thinking being, concretizes and realizes it, and with that reveals itself to be, then the same thought, thinking nonbeing, as the non-real antithesis to being, itself becomes nonexistent.[14]

Through Buddha, Kojève makes the paradoxical suggestion that, if we accept the premise that thought realizes existence, thinking ultimately results in inexistence. We can only grasp this paradox if we understand Kojève's argument as a dialectical one. If existence is concretized thought, the thinking process always contains some unrealized potentiality—nonbeing. Thus, the dialectical tension between being and nonbeing produces the *inexistent* as a mode of absence.[15] Kojève distinguishes two types of thought: thinking being that realizes itself, and thinking nonbeing as "the non-real antithesis to being." Thinking nonbeing, or unrealized thought, "abstracts itself" and becomes inexistent.[16] With Kojève's later philosophy of art in mind, it is remarkable that existence and inexistence are paired already here with concreteness and abstraction: The concretized thought is real, the abstract one inexistent.[17] Accordingly, abstract being is inexistent while concrete being becomes real. Yet, for Kojève both potentials of the thinking process are interrelated:

> For if thought is real, then real too are the products of thought. In other words, the understanding of nonbeing—as a product of thought—is also real as such. But the concepts of being and nonbeing may be thought only as contrary or opposed concepts. Ergo—either thought thinks the concept of nonbeing as non-existence and thereby becomes nonexistent itself the moment that the concept of nonexistence is introduced, or else thought thinks all as real, and thereby creates itself as an existent.[18]

Interestingly, Kojève distinguishes between nonbeing and inexistence, the latter as the "unrealization" of the former. The nonexistent—or inexistent—is described by the Russian term *несуществующий*.[19] Both modes of absence are introduced as Concepts [*Begriff*], a Hegelian term that would become pivotal in Kojève's later work where it is identified with Time. When the concept of nonbeing is realized in thought, it becomes nonexistent, as does the thinking process itself. In other words, if existence is a product of thought, thinking as such becomes inexistent. Ultimately, for Kojève's Buddha, any rationalist attempt at proving existence must lead into an infinite regress. In this experimental dialogue, an early confessional text, the young émigré playfully explores how Buddhist conceptions of inexistence reduce Western rationalism ad absurdum. On his way into a forced exile, Kojève found himself vacillating between East and West, on the search for new forms of expression. In the summer of 1921, he began to study Buddhist philosophy with the famous Indologist Max Walleser in Heidelberg. Besides learning Sanskrit, Tibetan, and Chinese, Kojève focused on classical texts of Mahāyāna Buddhism, especially the work of Indian thinker Nāgārjuna (ca. 150–250 CE). Translating Nāgārjuna's works in Walleser's seminar, Kojève encountered the concept of *śūnyatā* that refers to emptiness, boundlessness, absence, and non-self.[20] Under the influence of Buddhist and other non-Western ontologies, Kojève's early philosophy is centered around inexistence, aiming to negatively capture existence through absence.

But what can visual art tell us about inexistence? As the *Journal* suggests, art, in its intricate relation to form, provides a unique access to inexistence. The origin of art, Kojève tentatively suggests in one of the fragmentary outlines of his system, is "thinking of the realized world as non-existent" or "the representation of sensations?? [sic]."[21] In the phenomenon of art, issues of representation, existence, and form fall into one. Shortly after "Descartes and Buddha," in an early journal entry, Kojève suggests that thought does not exist before it realizes itself as form. Echoing popular Buddhist scriptures, such as the Heart Sūtra, Kojève argues that the antithesis of the thinkable is "thought without form, outside of form."[22] On August 12, 1920, during a trip to Rome, Kojève wrote a longer section in his diary titled "On the Inexistent in Art and the Art of the Inexistent." In the Italian capital, dividing his time between the Vatican Museums and the Villa Borghese, Kojève claims:

> The only thing of value in art, that which distinguishes art from other creations of human thought, is the element of the non-existent, the non-thinkable, rather it is the sensual understanding of the pure idea of thought and the attempt to express it in such forms that concretize and limit it least.[23]

Unlike religion or science, art provides a *sensual* understanding of the inexistent. The purer the artwork, the less concretized it is; this means, "the less one perceives the material, the means, and the more one feels the pure idea." Art concretizes ideas through words, sound, form, or color. The pure idea, however, "does not exist in the image, but it is perceptible as that nothingness which lies behind the real creation." There are two ways in which art relates to reality. The first one, capturing "the inexistent in art," uses reality as a starting point and represents it by creating an "idea of being." One example of this mode of art—which we can call representational—is photography. Only retroactively, photography introduces the element of the inexistent. In contrast, the second mode, the *art of the inexistent*, does not reproduce reality at all. Unlike photography, it does not aim to capture "a thought about a thought" but to express the pure idea—of inexistence—itself.[24] Interestingly, in these early fragments, Kojève does not yet associate the art of the inexistent with any particular artistic medium or art form. However, he would later address this gap in his essay on Kandinsky's concrete paintings. While in the *Journal* artistic representation is introduced through different modes of inexistence, it resurfaces in the essay on Kandinsky as the dichotomy between abstract and concrete painting. The first, abstracting beauty from reality, is the way of representational and subjective art. The second, creating a concrete expression of beauty, is the way of Kandinsky's nonrepresentational and objective paintings.

Before delving into Kojève's essay on Kandinsky, I would like to highlight one last aspect in these early fragments on inexistence: Kojève's reflection on photography and mechanical reproduction that foreshadows Walter Benjamin's famous 1935 "The Work of Art in the Age of Mechanical Reproduction."[25] Analyzing a copy of Leonardo's *Mona Lisa*, Kojève states that "strangely enough, however good a reproduction is, it always lacks something."[26] Neither feeling "the antiquity nor the hand of the master," the reproduction lacks its original *aura*. Mona Lisa's eyes are not human but express "the gaze of the non-existent, cold as the very idea of being."[27] It is somewhat ironic to read these lines in a book that is itself nothing but a copy of a lost original. In fact, throughout his life, Kojève was to shift his perspective on reproduction. As Groys points out, Kojève maintained that he never attempted to say anything new; instead, refusing originality, he "claimed simply to repeat and reproduce the text of Hegel's *Phenomenology of the Spirit* without adding anything to it."[28] We might argue that this gesture of "radical philosophical unoriginality"[29] stems from being a passionate photographer and collector. In his apartment in Vanves, Kousnetzoff remembers, the only original works were some watercolors by Kandinsky. Kojève's office resembled a private museum of Catholic religious paintings in reproduction.[30] Besides his photographic practice, Kojève collected thousands of postcards and mass-produced images.[31] Fascinated by the loss of aura in the age of Warhol's pop art, Kojève's serial photographs mimic the reproduction's impersonal gaze. Capturing inexistence itself, Kojève's photographs were, in Groys's words, "a kind of continuation of Hegelian phenomenology."[32] Mediating between "an individual gaze (the subjectivity) and the universal spirit," the photographs neutralize, or rather synthesize, multiple perspectives. From the late 1920s onward, engaging with avant-garde art, Kojève's interest in the art of the inexistent led him to abstract painting: art without an object. It comes as no surprise that Kojève's main interlocutor became his famous uncle. In their correspondence, Kojève's reflections on inexistence increasingly refer to non-figurative painting. In a letter from September 20, 1931, Kojève describes his reaction to Kandinsky's recent watercolor *Fleckig*. For Kojève, in *Fleckig*, less geometric than previous compositions, something entirely new happened. Here, the structure "is not organically derived from the artistic content, but that it replaces this content." As a result, the painting looks "like a combination (very remarkable and fine, but without genius) of ready-made forms."[33] Again, Kojève plays here with the idea of radical unoriginality; objectless art, a kind of pictorial ready-made, comes into existence without artistic genius. Kojève continues:

> Here we can see the "justification" and the understanding of the appearance of "objectless" painting (excuse me, I can't write "abstract"). But this

understanding is still very superficial. I seem to have found something deeper. In connection with my book on Atheism, I was thinking about the essence of art (the difference between art and religion). It seems to me that art without an object has some metaphysical basis. But I can't write about it now, it's too complicated. We'll talk about it when we meet.[34]

Refusing to call his uncle's paintings "abstract," the young Kojève remains puzzled by the problem of visually representing inexistence. Soon Kojève would meet his uncle again—the result of their encounter would be one of the most remarkable theories of abstract art.

KANDINSKY'S CONCRETE PAINTINGS

While his nephew, oriented to the East, was developing an aesthetics of inexistence, Kandinsky turned his head westward. Returning to Germany, Kandinsky took up a position at the newly founded Bauhaus in 1921. Throughout the 1920s, along with fellow Bauhaus artists Paul Klee and László Moholy-Nagy, Kandinsky radically reinvented painting. After the Nazis shut down the Bauhaus, Kandinsky was forced to leave Germany. He found refuge in Paris, at that time the center of the Russian diaspora. Among those émigrés was Kojève, now teaching at the École pratique des hautes études. Between 1933–1939, Kojève held his legendary seminar on Hegel's *Phenomenology of the Spirit*, attended by, among others, Jacques Lacan, Georges Bataille, André Breton, and Raymond Queneau. Kojève's eclectic reading of Hegel was to shape major discourses of the time, from psychoanalysis and phenomenology to Surrealism. When Kandinsky arrived in Paris in 1934, he was virtually unknown in France. The Parisian art scene at the time was dominated by Surrealism and Cubism. While Surrealist works distorted reality, they never fully abandoned figurative representation. Gradually, abstract art began taking roots in the French capital. *Abstraction-Création*, a group of abstract artists, joined by Kandinsky, was founded as a reaction against Surrealist domination. Together with the journal *Cahiers d'Art*, it became the new mouthpiece of abstract painting.

In his extensive theoretical work, Kandinsky never developed a coherent theory of abstraction. However, the abstract—later called the concrete—pervades Kandinsky's work from *Concerning the Spiritual in Art* until his late writings from the 1940s. Throughout his career, Kandinsky's own understanding of abstraction remained ambivalent.[35] While we often refer to abstract art as nonfigurative or nonrepresentational—беспредметный in Russian—Kandinsky continually reinterpreted what abstraction meant. Rather than simply painting nonfiguratively, Kandinsky aimed to create works that were abstract in their essence.[36] In his early writings, most prominently *Concerning the Spiritual in Art*, the abstract is still associated with spirituality, inner experience, and nonobjectivity.[37] Strikingly akin to Kojève's aesthetics of inexistence, Kandinsky states here that the artwork with the highest spirituality is the one least dependent on materiality.[38] While it was previously argued that Kandinsky derived the term "Spirit" [*Geist*] from occult sources,[39] Lisa Florman convincingly pointed to its Hegelian roots.[40] It is also worth mentioning that *concreteness* was an emerging concept in Soviet Marxism which Kandinsky might have encountered during the first years after the Revolution, when he was involved in Soviet cultural politics as a member of IZO-Narkompros in Moscow.[41] In these years, under the influence of Marxism and Russian constructivism, Kandinsky's radically antimaterialist stance gave way to a dialectical understanding of abstraction as one moment in a process of dematerialization—or concretization.

Kandinsky's transformed understanding of abstraction is reflected in his subsequent writings. In *Point and Line to Plane*, published in 1926 at the Bauhaus, Kandinsky is no longer occupied with the "spiritual"; instead, the material elements of abstract painting—point, line, color, and plane—become concrete forces.[42] Increasingly, Kandinsky refers to his paintings as concrete. But why this shift *vers le concret*? In his "Reflections on Abstract Art," published in *Cahiers d'Art* in 1931, Kandinsky claimed that abstract artists had to "prove that painting without an 'object' [. . .] has the right to exist."[43] Admitting that the label *abstract* might be "misleading and detrimental" when taken literally, Kandinsky seems yet unable to offer a convincing alternative. The same conceptual dilemma plagued his 1936 essay "Abstract Painting."[44] Diagnosing the "confusing effect" of the term *abstract* when used in its ordinary meaning, Kandinsky calls for replacing it. Paradoxically, the inventor of abstract art was compelled to free his creation from the specters of abstraction. To get rid of the "detrimental" *abstract* meant to overthrow it—or, in Hegelian jargon, to sublate it—with its dialectical counterpart: the *concrete*. Kandinsky's Hegelian conversion was certainly catalyzed, if not induced, by Kojève whose Hegel lectures galvanized the French capital at the time. With Kojève, his nephew and lifelong friend, Kandinsky had in-depth discussions of his practice and conceptual difficulties. Only with Kojève's help was Kandinsky able to develop a more coherent understanding of abstraction; this is, one that rethinks abstraction as concrete reality.[45]

The manifesto of this new concrete art, replacing the outdated pamphlet *On the Spiritual in Art*, was Kojève's 1936 essay "Les peintures concrètes de Kandinsky," proofread and annotated by Kandinsky himself. In a chapter of her study on Kandinsky's concrete art, Florman examines Kojève's essay in dialogue with Hegel, Kandinsky, and Solovyov's aesthetics.[46] While convincingly situating the essay in a Hegelian tradition, Florman omits both Kojève's earlier aesthetics of inexistence and the crucial historical context framing the essay, particularly Russian and French discourses on concreteness in the 1930s. One example is Jean Wahl's *Vers le concret*, an exploration of contemporary philosophy in light of concreteness.[47] Wahl describes a tendency toward the concrete which is defined as an ideal, opening up a mediating space between language and reality. The concrete was also a key notion in Russian Hegelian philosopher Ivan Ilyin's 1918 groundbreaking study *The Philosophy of Hegel as a Doctrine of the Concreteness of God and Humanity*.[48] Prefiguring, and arguably directly influencing, Kojève's reading, Ilyin presents Hegel's system in light of concrete universality.[49] Finally, the concrete, already surfacing in Kojève's early writings on inexistence, becomes a cornerstone of Kojève's—and before that Koyré's—interpretation of Hegel, traversing both the lectures and his late *System of Knowledge*.[50] In short, concreteness was a philosophical leitmotif in early twentieth-century Hegelianism, infused with religious philosophy, Marxism, and existential phenomenology. Against this backdrop, Florman's claim that the essay was not aimed at Kojève's circle but "at a wider, less philosophically oriented audience—Kandinsky's audience" is slightly misleading.[51] I argue that, on the contrary, Kojève's essay clearly transmitted a philosophical subtext. The essay serves multiple functions: it is an intimate tribute to Kandinsky; it expands and revises early writings on the aesthetics of inexistence; and it reflects on and intervenes into dominant tendencies of contemporary philosophy. In this transitional text, Kojève comes to terms with the ontological foundations of both Kandinsky's art and his own system.

In my reading of the essay, I focus on two main constellations. First, the relevance of a distinctly Hegelian, and yet idiosyncratically Kojèvian, understanding of abstraction and concreteness. Second, Kojève's notion of the Beautiful as a variation on the Hegelian idea of *Concept [Begriff]*[52] or what I call "concrete totality." Recalling its etymology, we can define abstraction—deriving from the Latin verb *abstrahere*, to withdraw—as both *extraction* and *removal*.[53] In contrast, the concrete—from *concrescere*, to grow together—refers to actuality and totality. The pivotal role that concreteness played in Kojève's lectures from 1934–1935, held just a year before the essay was written, cannot be overemphasized. In his seminar "The Dialectic of the Real and the Phenomenological Method in Hegel," Kojève frames Hegel's method as the dialectical movement toward and the revelation of concrete reality. Revealed reality for Kojève is always concrete; it is a totality or undivided whole.[54] Taken separately, subject and object are abstract, the totality, however, is concrete. Referring to Hegel's *Encyclopaedia*, Kojève further argues that only the concrete Real is dialectical, while abstractions are not.[55] The "naive man, the vulgar scientist or the pre-Hegelian philosopher" are not concerned with the concrete totality as the dialectical Real but with mere abstractions. Kojève most likely had here another text in mind, namely Hegel's well-known pamphlet, "Who Thinks Abstractly?" in which he argues that philosophical thought is not abstract but in fact concrete.[56] For Hegel, the development of thought is the dialectical movement from the abstract to the concrete, culminating in "the Absolute Idea as the highest degree of concreteness."[57] Abstraction, however, as Jamila Mascat wonderfully elaborated, is as pivotal for Hegel's speculative project as concreteness. The abstract as the separate (*abs-tractum*) is "the result of a reflective process that produces opposition and crystallises the terms of division."[58] The faculty to think— paint—truly abstractly is distinct from "the accidental and ungrounded process of absolutisation of the particular into the universal."[59] In the process of thinking, abstraction turns into concreteness, mediating the particular and the universal. This concrete totality is the "immediate unity of the universal and the individual, [. . .] a work of art wherein no part separates itself from the whole."[60] Likewise, for Kojève, abstraction is not a purely negative term but has to be understood dialectically: the abstract is inextricably entwined with the concrete. In his seminars, paving the way for the Kandinsky essay, Kojève establishes concreteness as the dialectical movement itself:

> Let us consider a real table. This is not *Table* "in general," nor just *any* table, but always *this concrete* table right here. Now, when "naive man" or a representative of science or other speaks of *this* table, he isolates it from the rest of the universe: he speaks of *this* table without speaking of what is not this table. Now, *this* table does not float in empty space. It is on *this* floor, in *this* room, in *this* house, in *this* place on Earth [. . .]. To speak of *this* table without speaking of the rest, then, is *to abstract* from this rest, which in fact is just as real and concrete as this table itself.[61]

Naive man, or the pre-Hegelian philosopher, only speaks of this table not as a concrete reality, but as an abstraction, thereby separating it from the whole to which it belongs. Concrete reality, in Kojève's view, is "the spatial-temporal *totality* of the natural world: everything that is *isolated* from it is by that very fact an *abstraction*, which exists as isolated only and by the *thought* of the man who thinks about it."[62] The abstraction of the table is only a subjective, fragmentary view that does not represent the totality of concrete reality. In his text on Kandinsky, Kojève then develops a full-fledged theory of concreteness. The "naive man" reappears here as the representational painter. Kojève also renegotiates the ontological status of concreteness through analyzing Kandinsky's concrete paintings as objects. Before further exploring this argument, let us take a look at some key ideas of the essay. In the first part, Kojève distinguishes between two types of the *Beautiful* [*le Beau*]: beauty incarnated in real things—the beauty *of* the tree—and pure beauty, this is "the Beautiful 'in and for itself.'" This second type of beauty is incarnated in the artwork that does not serve any other purpose than being beautiful:

> Art is thus the art of extracting the Beautiful from its concrete incarnation, from this "other thing," which is—"also"—beautiful, and of preserving it [*et de le maintenir*] in its purity. In order to preserve it, art also incarnates the Beautiful, in a painting [*tableau*] for example.[63]

The painting extracts—or *abstracts*—the Beautiful which is incarnated in concrete things and maintains it in the sense of a Hegelian *Aufhebung*. Kojève calls this abstract Beautiful an "unreal value" serving no other purpose than itself. The Beautiful has only the value of being Beautiful. What might sound tautological at first, turns into Kojève's criterion to differentiate between art and non-art. Only by being beautiful is a painting is more than a "dirtied surface."[64] Self-sufficient beauty is art's only raison d'être. Art creates beauty that is sustained only by itself and detached from any concrete being that incarnates it. As Florman suggests, Kojève might be referring to Vladimir Solovyov's article, "The Meaning of Art," in which beauty is conceptualized as the embodied "good," a concretization of the highest ideal. In fact, for Solovyov artistic beauty is more than "the superficial materialization of the ideal," while also surpassing "the equally superficial spiritualization of matter."[65] Instead, the artwork strives towards a perfect mediation between form and content, a "spiritual corporeality" which prefigures what Kojève calls *concreteness*. Kojève argues that painting, as the art of vision, represents space; however, the tableau is only surface. Its beauty, realized by the balance of forms and colors on a flat plane, is independent from the space it represents. The surface of the tableau, Kojève writes, incarnates pure beauty when it is self-sufficient. Is has value only by and for itself.[66] While sculptural beauty never makes us see the *interior*, painting reveals the beauty of the surface itself; it is fully transparent of its own being. Kojève follows here Kandinsky who emphasizes the importance of *interiority* for painting and associates it with spiritual nature or true being.[67] And yet in Kojève's hands, interiority turns into a radically immanent process of *incarnation*. Again, Kojève might be alluding to the complex entanglements of matter and spirit envisioned in Solovyov's aesthetics.[68] However, for Kojève, unlike Solovyov, incarnation is less a materialization of the spiritual—or the Idea—then a concretization or *Aufhebung* of the Beautiful:

> The Beautiful is incarnated in the skin, which follows the form of the breast. But *this* Beautiful is absolutely independent of that form, which is why it can be

preserved as such [*être maintenu tel quel*] in being incarnated in a *flat* surface. And it is only this *flat* visual surface of the skin that is a *pictorial* value.[69]

Kojève distinguishes between the natural beauty of the human body and pictorial beauty—Beauty as such. In a painting, Beauty is not dependent on a particular form. Paintings that merely reproduce the shape of the breast do not embody the Beautiful. True painting, on the other hand, extracts—or *abstracts*—visual aspects from reality that are maintained—or *concretized*— in a flat surface. There are two types of paintings, "abstract and subjective," and "concrete and subjective" paintings.[70] While both types of paintings abstract beauty from reality, their modes of representation radically differ. Abstract and subjective paintings "[*extract*] the pictorial Beautiful from the *non*artistic real."[71] When speaking about *abstract* painting—in the same way that we already encountered in the Hegel lectures—Kojève refers to representational or figurative painting. This conceptual twist is crucial for the later reconceptualization of Kandinsky's art as *concrete*. In this sense, to paint abstractly means merely reproducing natural beauty and to therefore withdraw it from its original incarnation. Abstracting beauty is a process of *fragmentation*, destruction of the unity of the tree's beauty. A painting of a tree can only reproduce its "visual aspect" but not the beauty of "the entire concrete, real tree" with its smell, depth, and sound.[72] The painted tree is an abstraction that merely represents one fragment of the concrete totality of its being. As a fragment, the abstract painting necessarily remains subjective:

> The concrete Beautiful of nonartistic reality passes through this "subject"—the painter—before being incarnated, as the abstract Beautiful, in the tableau. The Beautiful of the tableau is thus a Beautiful transmitted by the subject—a Beautiful subjectivized in and by this transmission, it is a *subjective* Beautiful.[73]

The representational painting creates abstract beauty mediated by a limited subject-painter. The problem of representation already surfaces in a letter that Kojève wrote to Kandinsky on February 3, 1929. Here, Kojève argues that the only serious debate in painting is the question whether or not an artwork expresses purely subjective emotions or objective beauty.[74] Representative paintings—in the 1929 letter described as "idealist"—remain subjective, whereas nonrepresentative—"realist"—paintings are concrete objects.[75] Ultimately, all painting except Kandinsky's is therefore subjective. In the essay, redefining these notions, Kojève argues that the means of representational paintings are exhausted in four types, distinguished by their different grades of abstraction; symbolic, realist, impressionist, and expressionist.[76] As Hugh Gillis argues, Kojève's essay can be convincingly read in the light of his famous end of history thesis. In Gillis's view, Kojève examines "how

[Kandinsky's] abandonment of representation realizes the end, in both senses of the word, of painting." Echoing the famous Hegelian thesis of the end of art, Kojève considers Kandinsky's paintings the goal and conclusion of art history.[77] Kandinsky's art captures beauty in a posthistorical sense. The concrete and objective beauty of Kandinsky's paintings is "analogous to the achievement of absolute knowledge in the Hegelian system of science."[78] Both Kandinsky's art and Kojève's philosophy "represent an exhaustion of possibilities, a kind of limit situation beyond which it is impossible to go."[79] However, this shared aesthetics of exhaustion does not mean that no more paintings—or philosophy—can be created. It only means that no new artwork will go beyond what Kandinsky's concrete paintings have already achieved. Like philosophy after Hegel, painting after Kandinsky can only repeat itself. This posthistorical aesthetics is characterized by closure, emptiness, and exhaustion. Kandinsky's paintings, Gillis argues, are concrete because they are devoid of content, in short, *empty*.[80] What this means become clearer when we look at what Kojève considers the other extreme on the spectrum of representation: Picasso's abstract and subjective paintings which are most unlike Kandinsky's art.[81] Combining absolute abstraction with an enormous effort of subjective attitude—or *genius*—Picasso's paintings risk falling into pure subjectivism. Most of Picasso's paintings, Kojève claims, are merely "gaudy canvases."[82] In contrast to Picasso, Kandinsky creates the Beautiful ex nihilo. His beauty exists only within the paintings and nowhere else. Kojève claims that Kandinsky's paintings are truly *concrete* because their "Beautiful was not 'extracted' or 'abstracted' from a real, non artistic object, which would be— 'also'—beautiful, but—'primarily'—something else again." The Beautiful in Kandinsky's paintings is pure and immanent; it is as real, or even more real, as the Beautiful of the real tree. Referring back to his early aesthetics of inexistence, Kojève suggests that Kandinsky's paintings concretely express inexistence. Unlike photographs, Kandinsky's paintings are truly autonomous and depend on nothing beyond themselves. He elaborates further:

> Now, if the Beautiful was not *extracted* or *abstracted* but created whole cloth, it is—in its very *being*—not *abstract* but *concrete*. Being created whole cloth, that is entirely, it is as whole: nothing is missing from it, nothing was removed from it, since this Beautiful—nonexistent outside of the tableau—cannot be richer and more real than it is in the tableau or as the tableau.[83]

Again, it becomes clear how indebted the essay is to Kojève's early aesthetics in the *Journal*. Already there, he had claimed that art ought to be as little *concretized* as possible in order to capture inexistence or the pure idea. Now, art no longer strives toward expressing the inexistent but seems to fully affirm the absence of an object. Instead of inexistence, the concrete painting expresses a pure Beautiful that does exist but only in the tableau—and nowhere else. For Kojève, each of Kandinsky's paintings is a self-contained whole, a complete universe in itself. Each painting is a "uni-totality" that exists in the same way "as do trees, animals, rocks, men, States, [or] clouds."[84] As such, the concrete and total painting, representing no object, turns into an object itself. This pictorial object "*is* as objects *are*, that is, it *is* in an *absolute* and nonrelative way; it *is* independently of its *relations* with anything else; it *is*, like the Universe *is*. And that is why the 'total' tableau is also an 'absolute' tableau."[85] Unlike in the *Journal*, where the art of the inexistence does not refer to any particular art form, Kojève now ascribes painting a privileged position over other media. Not artworks in general, but only Kandinsky's paintings are objects as real as stones or trees. In 1932, in a book review on Roman Ingarden, Kojève claims that, for instance, a literary work can never be objective or concrete:

> The object described as (or more exactly, created by) a literary work can be infinitely rich, it can fascinate and move, it can influence a whole epoch and determine the evolution of a civilization;—and yet an impassable abyss will separate it from the humblest real, "objective" and concrete object.[86]

While the literary artwork only creates an illusion of reality—a "quasi-reality"— Kandinsky's concrete paintings *are* real objects, independent from both artist and spectator. However, these objects radically differ from Surrealist objects. Most likely referring to the 1936 International Surrealist exhibition, Kojève claims that the Surrealists "[pile] up real, nonartistic objects in order to create an artistic one."[87] Surrealist objects, Kojève claims, have "nothing to do with Art in the standard sense of the term, but at the very most with the art of deception, the art of those who succeed—in a pinch—at passing for mad—and even then only with the gullible (to be polite)—without really being mad (since the absence of common sense is simply foolishness, which is quite different from madness)."[88] For Kojève, only Kandinsky creates *Art* with a capital "A," defending objectless art against Surrealism's "madness." Kojève's manifesto of objectless art seemed to have a ripple effect on Kandinsky's practice. In the late 1930s, just after the essay, his paintings radically changed. At that time, Kandinsky increasingly used bright colors, hieroglyphs, and nongeometric, free-floating shapes.[89] In the last decade of his life, Kandinsky revisited images from Russian folklore reminiscent of the watercolor for the young Kojève. Increasingly, Kandinsky defined his art as *concrete*. In "The Value of a Concrete Work," Kandinsky directly responds to Kojève, dividing painting into either "representational" or "concrete." Where representational paintings use objects as pretexts, depending on the spectator, concrete paintings emerge independent from them.[90] Concrete art is "pure painting" whose possibilities are infinitely unlimited.[91] At the same time, echoing Kojève's essay, Kandinsky published "Abstract or Concrete?" in an exhibition catalogue at the Stedelijk Museum. Here, Kandinsky argues that abstract art is not expressed by a subject but rather expresses itself; a concrete artwork creates a world, just as real as the "world of nature." Kandinsky writes further:

> In every truly new work of art a new *world* is created that has never existed. Thus, every true work of art is a new discovery; next to the already known worlds, a new, previously unknown one is uncovered.[92]

For both Kandinsky and Kojève, art hence possesses a strong *ontological* force, creating universes that were inexistent before. While speaking of beauty, their aesthetics is mainly interested in what an artwork *is*. In Kojève's ontology, the artwork represents the totality of concrete reality itself; it is a self-contained unity of variety. The concrete painting is the opposite of false abstraction; is does not isolate particulars and universalizes them, but, on the contrary, creates its own concrete universality, or what Kojève calls, using Hegelian terms, a *Begriff* (Concept). The Beautiful of the concrete painting is, just like the Concept, a purely concrete totality. In the lectures of the years 1938–1939, Kojève transfers his reflections on concreteness and totality, emerging from the Kandinsky essay, into the realm of Hegelian "Science." It is striking how close the language of Kandinsky's paintings comes to how Kojève describes signification in Hegel's system. The concrete Concept of "dog," for instance, and the "real" dog, here and now, fall into one; the Concept—or Beautiful—embodies the whole of revealed reality.[93] And because the dog, as every living being and object, is mortal, the Concept can be *detached* from the dog—enabling the existence of an abstract Concept.[94] The concrete concept, on the other hand, is identical to reality itself. Kojève's philosophy of concreteness, originating from his dialogue with Kandinsky, culminates in *The Concept, Time and Discourse,* written in 1952 and published posthumously.[95] In what was supposed to become a central part of his system of knowledge, Kojève dedicates a crucial section to the relation between the abstract and the concrete. Distinguishing between *abstract Things* and *concrete Notions*, Kojève argues that "the only concrete Thing is *Totality*, which is as universal as individual and where the Particular coincides with the General."[96] This concrete totality is the uni-total Concept as Begriff. Concreteness eventually remained a *fil rouge* in Kojève's late system. A closer look reveals a compelling analogy between Kojève's analysis of Kandinsky's paintings and his later theory of the state. In the already mentioned 1929 letter, Kojève describes his impression of Kandinsky's painting *Einige Kreise* (1926). Analyzing the painting, Kojève observes:

[I] was struck by the lack of unity in this painting: the center is absent, the boundaries are quite coincidental, yet the different elements of the painting have a meaning only when they are linked together. [. . .] Since they are infinite they cannot have a "center" or, which is the same, each point of the painting becomes a "center."[97]

In short, every element only gains meaning through the totality of the painting. With no fixed center, every point, as peripheral it might be, turns into a potential center of the whole. More than twenty years later, in his debate with Leo Strauss on tyranny, Kojève develops a concept of posthistorical empire that strikingly mirrors these reflections on Kandinsky's concrete totality.[98] Kojève argues that the first such empire—what he calls the universal and homogenous State—was created by Alexander the Great. In contrast to his Greek predecessors, Alexander's political action "was guided by the idea of *empire*, that is to say, of a *universal* State, at least in the sense that this State had no *a priori given* limits (geographic, ethnic, or otherwise), no *pre-established* 'capital,' nor even a geographically and ethnically *fixed* center destined to exercise political dominion over its periphery."[99] Like Kandinsky's paintings, autonomous systems with no fixed center, Alexander's empire is a limitless State, held together only as concrete totality. The statesman "was clearly ready to [. . .] govern this unit from a geographical point he would have freely (rationally) chosen in terms of the new whole."[100] It cannot be overstated how significant this notion of concrete totality was for Kojève's political theory and his pivotal role as a French bureaucrat in constructing the foundations of what would eventually become the European Union.

In 1966, on the occasion of Kandinsky's centenary, Kojève publishes a précis of the unpublished manuscript on Kandinsky's concrete paintings in *XXe siècle*. Condensing the manuscript, the updated version is shorter, with some transformations, such as introducing the types of painting in reversed order.[101] Kojève also adds a footnotes in which he describes the historical evolution of painting as a dialectical progress towards concreteness; while the "subjectivist element" gradually increases, the degree of abstraction decreases. With Kandinsky's "*total* painting" this process comes to its conclusion.[102] Published thirty years later than the first version, the essay appears against the backdrop of poststructuralism emerging as the most powerful current in French postwar philosophy. Scathing criticism comes from none other than Jean-François Lyotard, the father of French postmodernism:

This is obviously the Hegelian speaking, a man of the nineteenth century, because he believes in a univocal, albeit complex movement of natural, cultural and spiritual realities toward their perfect elucidation. He is seeking to persuade you that with Kandinsky, the art of painting, by abandoning representation, passes from the subjective to the objective, and from the part to the whole, and that it is passing through a moment in its development as decisive as the one that brought about the transition from Kantian subjective criticism to Hegel's absolute idealism. I am saying that this way of placing things in perspective is out-of-date, even though it is of today and aims at extolling what is currently most up-to-date.[103]

For Lyotard, Kojève's text represents everything that is not contemporary, or what he calls postmodern. To become postmodern, Lyotard proclaims, we need to reject any "outdated"—Hegelian—ideal of circular system. Instead, philosophy explores artistic experiment, striving toward novelty, multiplicity, fragment, and opacity.[104] But does Lyotard not overlook the shared ground between postmodernism and Kojève's aesthetics? Is it not precisely the posthistorical condition that is at stake for Kojève? At the end of history, Kojève would reply to Lyotard, the philosopher must refrain from any attempt at novelty. Under the postmodern condition, the philosopher is nothing but a connoisseur—Kojève's dandyish kind of sage—who knows what to look for and how to enjoy it. Posthistorical men, becoming animals again, "would construct their edifices and works of art as birds build their nests and spiders spin their webs, would perform musical concerts in the manner of frogs and cicadas, would play like young animals, and would indulge in love like adult beasts."[105] The Kojèvian connoisseur-philosopher is at once a posthistorical and, in the Nietzschean sense, *untimely* figure. Like Lyotard, Kojève insists on repetition, ritual, and reproduction as the cornerstones of a posthistorical world that predisposes us to treat culture as emptied from its traditional content. However, unlike other postmodernists, Kojève was the only one who ultimately declared his own unoriginality—radically performing the death of the author that French theorists such as Barthes or Foucault merely proclaimed.[106] Hence, as "the only philosophical writer who can be compared to Duchamp [or] Warhol,"[107] Kojève occupied an exceptional position in deterritorializing philosophical aesthetics in the second half of the twentieth century. Realizing discourse to the end of its possibilities, while constantly navigating its limitations, Kojève's work is a singular attempt at posthistorical aesthetics that is simultaneously "out of date" and "up-to-date"—it marks the end both as prelude and conclusion.

EPILOGUE: WHO THINKS CONCRETELY?

On July 21, 1946, two years after Kandinsky's death, Kojève writes a belated, intimate obituary titled "Kandinsky's Personality":

What struck most about Kandinsky, in all who knew him intimately, was the extraordinary *harmony* of his whole life, as well as of the very personality that this life expressed. A life without conflicts, without clashes, without intimate or external upheavals. A personality without sharp corners, without apparent or real dissimilarities. An artistic and private life that flowed naturally, in its entirety and down to its smallest details, from a personality that was complete in itself. A personality that was able to express itself through life and through works of art, without this expression distorting him from what he really was.[108]

For Kojève, Kandinsky's life and art were uniquely classical, revealing "the balanced and serene calm of a contrapuntal and harmonious richness which remains concrete in its universality."[109] Just like his uncle, the philosopher and statesman Kojève synthesized theory and practice into one concrete *Gesamtkunstwerk.* As I aimed to unveil in this paper, visual art and aesthetics prepared the ground for Kojève's philosophy, including his interpretation of Hegel and political visions of a universal State. Different configurations of the inexistent and the concrete, emerging from his dialogue with Kandinsky, resurfaced in all his philosophical projects. Analogous to Kandinsky's concrete paintings, Kojève's oeuvre stems from his ability to think concretely, starting with the earliest explorations of inexistence in the *Journal,* and culminating in the late system of knowledge that accompanied his career as an administrator for the French government. Throughout his life, Kojève developed a unique style, the philosophical signature of our posthistorical age, shaped by radical exhaustion and unoriginality. As I aimed to work out in this paper, Kojève's style, aligned with aesthetic connoisseurship, was intricately linked to his dialogue with visual art, from Surrealism and photography to Kandinsky.

NOTES

1. Sers 2016, 132.
2. From the correspondence in Russian and German, forty-two letters and postcards from Kandinsky and eight from Kojève are published (Kandinsky 1992, 143–75).
3. *Drei Elemente* is currently located at the Musée d'Art moderne et contemporaine in Strasbourg. The *Aquarell für Kojève* belongs to a private collection in Paris. The three watercolors and the ink drawing are in the Centre Pompidou (inv. no. AM 2001/200–203) (Filoni 2005, 79).
4. The manuscript is preserved in the Fonds Vassily Kandinsky at the Centre Pompidou (inv. no. VK640). It was recently digitized, together with some drafts, letters, and a typescript. The initial title was "Les peintures objectives de Kandinsky"; the author crossed out "*objectives,*" replacing it with "*concrètes.*" Kojève wrote the essay based on interviews with his uncle which he recorded in a shorthand style on small

cards (five cards are kept in the collection of the Centre Pompidou). Kandinsky was actively involved in the revision and approved the article. The complete version of the essay was published in 1985 (Kojève 1985); the first English translation appeared in 2014 (Florman 2014, 149–71).

5. See Kojève 1966. This second version is a revised summary of the 1936 manuscript that introduces new interpretative avenues. The typescript was initially titled "Peintures concrètes et objectives. L'art de Kandinsky" (see VK640).

6. Lisa Florman's art historical study is the most extensive work on the relation between Kandinsky and Kojève (2014). While Florman wonderfully elaborates on the Hegelian influence on Kandinsky, Kojève's aesthetics play a minor role, neglecting both his earlier work on the inexistent and some important historical contexts. On Kojève's aesthetics, see Auffret 1990, 198ff.; Filoni 2005; 2010; Gillis 2016.

7. Baudillon and Lagarde 2021.

8. Ibid.

9. Reis later wrote a remarkable memoir on Kojève, offering some rare insights into his private life (Reis 2000).

10. Today preserved in the Département des Estampes et de la Photographie at the Bibliothèque nationale de France. A selection was shown in the 2012 exhibition *After History: Alexandre Kojève as a Photographer*, curated by Boris Groys at BAK in Utrecht. See Groys 2012a.

11. Written in Russian, the first version of the *Journal* got lost on the way to Germany; in 1920/1921, Kojève reconstructed the diary and added new entries. Since most entries are written retrospectively, their dates and order are naturally unreliable. Some loose fragments, excerpts, and notes, spanning as far as 1927, show the attempt at a philosophical system. On the *Journal* see Auffret 1990; Filoni 2021; Kojève 2005a; Weslati 2017.

12. Kojève 2015b, 63. This and all following quotations from Kojève's text are my translation of the German edition of the *Journal*, cross-reading it with the Russian manuscript in the "Fonds Kojève" at the BnF (NAF 28320, Boîte 1) and the Italian edition (Kojève 2013a).

13. Ibid., 92.

14. Kojève 2015b, 321f.

15. Kojève's terminology remarkably anticipates conceptions of nothingness in existentialist ontologies, such as by Jean-Paul Sartre. Not coincidentally, biographer Auffret calls Kojève's early philosophy a negative "In-Existentialism" (Auffret 1990, 94).

16. Kojève 2015a, 49.

17. In the manuscript, Kojève initially wrote "*skonkretiziruet*," later changing it with pencil to the imperfective aspect "*konkretiziruet*," signalling the *processuality* of concretization (NAF 28320).

18. Kojève 2015b, 322.

19. Kojève's terminology in the Russian original deserves some attention. Kojève uses, largely interchangeably, *sushechestvovanie* (existence), *bytie* (being) and *real'nost'* (reality). Different modes of absence are signalled by various negations; nonbeing is both spelled "ne bytie" and "nebytie," corresponding to "not being" and

"nonbeing" in English, the latter closer to *inexistence*. Inexistence seems to indicate a stronger, preconceptual mode of absence, foundational to any ontological attempt (NAF 28320).

20. In his guide to the Heart Sutra, Tanahashi analyzes the concept of *śūnyatā*, traditionally translated as *emptiness* (Tanahashi 2014, 15ff.). In fact, he retranslates *śūnyatā* as boundlessness or zeroness, not to be confused with inexistence. Rather than emptiness, Tanahashi argues, *śūnyatā* is the experience of nonduality and indicates unlimited freedom.

21. Kojève 2015a, 139.

22. Ibid., 51.

23. Ibid., 67.

24. Ibid., 68.

25. Benjamin 2008.

26. Kojève 2015a, 67.

27. Ibid., 102.

28. Groys 2021, 146.

29. Ibid., 147.

30. Baudillon and Lagarde 2021.

31. A few thousands of Kojève's postcards, including travel plans, are preserved in the BNF, in a system of boxes that were organized by Kojève himself.

32. Delamarre 2013.

33. Kandinsky 1992, 160.

34. Ibid., 162.

35. See Florman 2014; Kienzler 2020; Tupitsyn 2008; Zimmermann 2002a.

36. Kienzler 2020, 406.

37. Zimmermann 2002a, 238.

38. In fact, it is not impossible that Kandinsky read Kojève's journal. In 1935, Kandinsky published "Empty Canvas" in *Cahiers d'Art* (Kandinsky 1994c). Here, he expresses ideas astonishingly close to Kojève's reflection on emptiness. Kandinsky writes that the empty, "silent" canvas, full of expectations, is "more beautiful than some paintings" (780). While merely indicated in my paper, the relation between Kojève's meditations on inexistence and Kandinsky's objectless art deserves further research.

39. Sers 2016; Zimmermann 2002a.

40. Florman 2014.

41. On Kandinsky's Soviet period and the Visual Arts Department of the Commissariat for Education, see Podzemskaia 2019; Tupitsyn 2008.

42. Kandinsky 1994d.

43. Kandinsky 1994e, 756.

44. Kandinsky 1994f.

45. Florman similarly argues that Kojève's text is a kind of "corrective" to Kandinsky's earlier texts aiming to make Kandinsky's argument more accessible (Florman 2014, 45).

46. Florman 2014.

47. Wahl 1932.

48. Il'in 2010.
49. Acclaimed Hegel scholar and Ilyin translator, Philip T. Grier argues that Ilyin's original reading of Hegel's concrete doctrine had a significant impact on Kojève and other neo-Hegelians in 1930s France, such as Koyré, Hyppolite, and Wahl (Grier 2010, lvii–lxi.). As Grier rightly observes, the fact that Kojève does not credit Ilyin as a reference is rather typical. In fact, only in a letter to George Kline, written in 1967, does Kojève explain that he had "read Il'in's Hegel, but without comprehending much (I was too young then)" (quoted after Grier, lx).
50. Kojève 1969; 1990.
51. Florman, 45.
52. See Florman 2014, 48.
53. Florman, 52. On abstraction, see De Libera 2014 and Mascat 2018.
54. Kojève 1969, 173.
55. Ibid., 210.
56. Hegel 1966.
57. Mascat 2018, 33.
58. Ibid., 32.
59. Ibid., 36.
60. Ibid., 38.
61. Kojève 1969, 211.
62. Ibid.
63. Kojève 2014, 152.
64. Ibid., 153.
65. Solovyov 2001, 145.
66. Kojève 2014, 155.
67. See Zimmermann 2002a.
68. Smith 2011.
69. Kojève 2014, 156.
70. Ibid., 156ff.
71. Ibid., 156.
72. Ibid., 157.
73. Ibid., 159.
74. Kandinsky 1992, 143.
75. It is worth noting here that Kojève was a fervent commentator on the idealism-realism debate in German phenomenology of the 1920–1930s, publishing dozens of short book reviews. See for instance Kojève 1932/33.
76. Kojève 2014, 160.
77. As Kyle Moore convincingly argued in an email from January 6, 2022, a Kojèvian end of art seems almost diametrically opposed to the Hegelian one: "Whereas Hegel seems to argue that art's function was to a large degree to make the divine visible and, hence, bring representation to its highest level, Kojève sees the end of art in the realization of [the] non-representational."
78. Gillis, 157.
79. Ibid., 164.

80. In his analysis of Kojève's posthistorical aesthetics, Gillis explores how Kojève's concept of snobbery as pure form—devoid of any content—might have influenced Georges Bataille's notion of "unemployed negativity" (173). While not mentioning Kojève's aesthetics of inexistence, there is a clear continuity between his early reflections on emptiness and the later writings on snobbery and 'Japanization' (see Gillis, 165ff.). Kojève's idea of pure form is also related to *silence*, a phenomenon that is so central to his aesthetics that to do justice to it would go beyond the scope of this paper.

81. On Picasso, see Kojève's letter from 1931 (Kandinsky 1992, 160).

82. Ibid., 162.

83. Ibid., 163.

84. Ibid., 164.

85. Ibid., 166.

86. Kojève 1932/33, 481.

87. Kojève might refer here to another text written in 1936, André Breton's "Crisis of the Object." Drawing on Gaston Bachelard's notion of reality, Breton speaks about an "unprecedented *desire to objectify*," pairing the development of Surrealism with modern physics and its reliance on non-Euclidean geometry (Breton 2002b). It is highly likely that Kojève was familiar with recent developments in Surrealist writing on art, not least because Breton was regularly attending the Hegel seminar during these years.

88. Florman, 229.

89. Sers 2016, 298.

90. Kandinsky 1994h, 820.

91. Ibid., 821.

92. Kandinsky 1994i, 832.

93. Kojève 1969, 107.

94. Ibid., 141.

95. Kojève 1990.

96. Ibid., 118.

97. Kandinsky 1992, 144ff.

98. Interestingly, *concreteness* resurfaces here as an ideal of political leadership. To not "lose sight of *concrete* reality," Kojève argues, the man of action has to make abstractions; "he makes cuts and isolates certain parts or aspects by 'abstracting' them from the rest and treating them 'in themselves'" (Kojève 2013a, 149). These abstractions are—in Hegelian terminology—precisely not concepts but what "the 'uninititate' wrongly calls '*concrete* cases'" (ibid.). Just like the Hegelian philosopher, the statesman has to mediate the particular and the universal, striving from abstraction to concreteness.

99. Kojève 2013b, 170. Luis J. Pedrazuela directed me to this particular passage from *Tyranny and Wisdom* in an email from December 2, 2020.

100. Ibid.

101. Florman, 54.

102. Kojève, 1966, 65.

103. Lyotard 1993, 329.

104. Ibid., 335.
105. Kojève 1969, 159
106. Groys 2012a, 147.
107. Ibid.
108. Kojève, 2005b, 51. Posthumously edited text by Kojève, written in Vanves, 21 VII 1946. My translation is based on the Italian translation (Filoni 2005).
109. Ibid.

BIBLIOGRAPHY

Auffret, Dominique. *Alexandre Kojève: La philosophie, L'État, la fin de l'Histoire*. Paris: Bernard Grasset, 1990.
Baudillon, Christine, and François Lagarde, dir. *Alexandre Kojève, en connaissance de cause*. Marseille: Baldanders Films, 2021.
Benjamin, Walter. *The Work of Art in the Age of Mechanical Reproduction*. Trans. J.A. Underwood. London: Penguin, 2008.
Breton, André. "Kandinsky." In *Surrealism and Painting*. Trans. Simon Watson Taylor. Boston: MFA Publications, 2002a: 286.
———. "Crisis of the Object." In *Surrealism and Painting*. Trans. Simon Watson Taylor. Boston: MFA Publications, 2002b: 274–81.
Delamarre, Thomas. "Interview with Boris Groys on Alexandre Kojève." *French Culture*, 2013.
De Libera, Alain. "Abstraction." In *Dictionary of Untranslatables: A Philosophical Lexicon*, edited by Barbara Cassin, et al. New Jersey: Princeton University Press, 2014: 1–7.
Filoni, Marco. "Estetica dell'in-esistente: Il giovane Kojève e l'arte." In Kojève, Alexandre. *Kandinsky*, edited by Marco Filoni. Macerata: Quodlibet. 2005: 55–82.
———. *L'azione politica des filosofo: La vita e il pensiero di Alexandre Kojève*. Turin: Bollati Boringhieri, 2021.
Florman, Lisa. *Concerning the Spiritual and the Concrete in Kandinsky's Art*. Stanford: Stanford University Press, 2014.
Gillis, Hugh. "Art and Literature at the End of History: Kojève as Critic." In *Sojourns in the Western Twilight: Essays in Honor of Tom Darby*, edited by Janice Freamo and Robert Sibley. Québec: Fermentation Press, 2016: 155–77.
Grier, Philip T. "Translator's Introduction." In *The Philosophy of Hegel as a Doctrine of the Concreteness of God and Humanity*. Evanston, Illinois: Northwestern University Press, 2010: xxi–xciv.
Groys, Boris. *Introduction to Antiphilosophy*. Trans. David Fernbach. London; New York: Verso, 2012a.
———. "Alexandre Kojève: After History." Lecture at BAK, 2012b.
Hegel, G. W. F. "Who Thinks Abstractly?" In *Hegel: Texts and Commentary*, edited by Walter Kaufmann. New York: Anchor Books, 1966: 113–19.

Il'in, I. A. *The Philosophy of Hegel as a Doctrine of the Concreteness of God and Humanity*, edited and translated by Philip T. Grier. Evanston, Illinois: Northwestern University Press, 2010.

Kandinsky, Wassily. *Correspondances avec Zervos et Kojève*. Les Cahiers du musée national d'art moderne (hors-série/archives). Paris: Centre Georges-Pompidou, 1992: 143–75.

———. *Complete Writings on Art*. Ed. Kenneth C. Lindsay and Peter Vergo. New York: Da Capo Press, 1994a.

———. *On the Spiritual in Art*. In *Complete Writings on Art*, edited by Kenneth C. Lindsay and Peter Vergo, 1994b: 114–220.

———. "Line and Fish." In *Complete Writings on Art*, edited by Kenneth C. Lindsay and Peter Vergo, 1994c: 774–75.

———. "Empty Canvas." In *Complete Writings on Art*, edited by Kenneth C. Lindsay and Peter Vergo, 1994d: 780–3.

———. *Point and Line to Plane*. In *Complete Writings on Art*, edited by Kenneth C. Lindsay and Peter Vergo, 1994e: 524–699.

———. "Reflections on Abstract art." In *Complete Writings on Art*, edited by Kenneth C. Lindsay and Peter Vergo, 1994f: 755–60.

———. "Abstract Painting." In *Complete Writings on Art*, edited by Kenneth C. Lindsay and Peter Vergo, 1994g: 784–89.

———. "The Value of a Concrete Work." In *Complete Writings on Art*, edited by Kenneth C. Lindsay and Peter Vergo, 1994h: 820–28.

———. "Abstract or Concrete?" In *Complete Writings on Art*, edited by Kenneth C. Lindsay and Peter Vergo, 1994i: 831–32.

Kienzler, Klaus. *Cézanne, Klee, Kandinsky: Zur Phänomenologie der Kunst des Sehens*. Munich: Verlag Karl Alber, 2020.

Kojève, Alexandre. "Review: Roman Ingarden. Das Literarische Kunstwerk. Eine Untersuchung aus dem Grenzgebiet der Ontologie, Logik und Literaturwissenschaft (1931)."*Recherches philosophiques*, Vol. 2. 1932/33: 480–86.

———. "Pourquoi concret." *XXᵉ siècle*, no. 27, 1966: 63–65.

———. *Introduction to the Reading of Hegel*. Ed. Allan Bloom, trans. James H. Nichols, Jr. Ithaca; London: Cornell University Press, 1969.

———. "Les peintures concrètes de Kandinsky." *Revue de métaphysique et de morale* 90, no. 2, 1985: 149–71.

———. *Le Concept, le Temps et le Discours: Introduction au Système du Savoir*. Ed. Bernard Hesbois. Paris: Éditions Gallimard, 1990.

———. *Kandinsky*. Ed. Marco Filoni. Trans. Marco Filoni and Antonio Gnoli. Macerata: Quodlibet, 2005a.

———. "La personalità di Kandinsky." In *Kandinsky*, edited by Marco Filoni. Macerata: Quodlibet, 2005b: 49–53.

———. *Diario del Filosofo*. Ed. Marco Filoni. Trans. Claudia Zonghetti. Turin: Nino Aragno Editore, 2013a.

———. "Tyranny and Wisdom." In Strauss, Leo. *On Tyranny*, edited by Victor Gourevitch and Michael Roth. Chicago; London: The University of Chicago Press, 2013b: 135–76.

———. "The Concrete Paintings of Kandinsky." In *Concerning the Spiritual and the Concrete in Kandinsky's Art*, edited and translated by Lisa Florman. Stanford: Stanford University Press, 2014: 149–71.

———. *Tagebuch eines Philosophen*. Trans. Simon Missal. Berlin: Matthes & Seitz, 2015a.

———. "Descartes and Buddha." Trans. Mikhail A. Pozdniakov. *Critical Research on Religion* 3, no. 3, 2015b: 320–2.

Lyotard, Jean-François. "Philosophy and Painting in the Age of Their Experimentation: Contribution to an Idea of Postmodernity." In *The Merleau-Ponty Aesthetics Reader: Philosophy and Painting*, edited by Galen A. Johnson. Evanston: Northwestern University Press, 1993: 323–35.

Mascat, Jamila M. H. "Hegel and the Advent of Modernity." *Radical Philosophy* 2.01, 2018: 29–46.

Podzemskaia, Nadia. "Vasilij Kandinskij et la Section IZO (1918–1920): Notes sur la fondation des Ateliers nationaux d'art libres." *Revue des études slaves* XC 1–2, 2019: 215–30.

Reis, Evgenii. *Kozhevnikov, kto vy?* Moscow: Russkii put',' 2000.

Sers, Philippe. *Kandinsky: The Elements of Art*. London: Thames & Hudson, 2016.

Smith, Oliver. *Vladimir Soloviev and the Spiritualization of Matter*. Boston: Academic Studies Press, 2011.

Solovyov, Vladimir. "The Meaning of Art." In A Solovyov Anthology, edited by S. L. Frank. London: The Saint Austin Press, 2001: 139–49.

Tanahashi, Kazuaki. *The Heart Sutra: A Comprehensive Guide to the Classic of Mahayana Buddhism*. Boston; London: Shambala, 2014.

Tupitsyn, Margarita. *Against Kandinsky*. Stuttgart: Hatje Cantz Verlag, 2008.

Wahl, Jean. *Vers le Concret: Études d'histoire de la philosophie contemporaine*. Paris: Vrin, 1932.

Weslati, Hager. "The Inexistent in the Ontology of Alexandre Kojève." *China Media Research* 13, no. 4, 2017: 48–56.

Zimmermann, Reinhard. *Die Kunsttheorie von Wassily Kandinsky I. Darstellung.* Berlin: Gebr. Mann Verlag, 2002a.

———. *Die Kunsttheorie von Wassily Kandinsky II. Dokumentation.* Berlin: Gebr. Mann Verlag, 2002b.

Chapter Two

Between Kant and Hegel

Alexandre Kojève and the Absolute State

Jeff Love

Human existence is a mediated suicide.

—Kojève[1]

One surrenders oneself in the process of making one's truth universal; the victorious revolution overcomes the revolutionary.

—Kosma Prutkov

My title refers to a pervasive tension in Alexandre Kojève's work. On the one hand, there is the Hegelian Kojève, the famous and enigmatic lecturer who exercised enormous influence on French intellectual life in the inter- and postwar periods, declaring the end of history and its expression in the universal and homogeneous state, the state akin to what was taking form in the Soviet Union under Stalin at the time. On the other hand, there is a strikingly Kantian Kojève who puts the question as to whether history can ever come to an end and thus whether the universal and homogeneous state—a state no longer needing laws to address disputes or differences among its citizens—would ever be realizable or is, in his own words, not rather a "limit case for homogeneity is in fact never absolute."[2]

In this chapter, I present these two sides of Kojève's thought in the manner of an overview: I first present an account of the Hegelian Kojève with reference to the lectures he gave in the 1930s that were published, under the editorial guidance of Raymond Queneau, as *Introduction to the Reading of Hegel* (*Introduction à la lecture de Hegel*) in 1947. I then present the more elusively Kantian Kojève with reference to a large manuscript (over 900 pages in the autograph copy) on law, entitled *Outline of a Phenomenology of Right* (*Esquisse d'une phénoménologie du droit*) written in 1943 but published posthumously at the request of Raymond Aron in 1981. I conclude with some speculative comments regarding the relation of these two different aspects of Kojève's thought.

I

I begin with the Hegelian Kojève, by referring to Kojève's mordant claim that the highest form of emancipation is suicide, a claim made clearly in an unpublished Russian manuscript from 1931 entitled *Atheism* (finally published in French in 1999) and repeatedly in the Hegel lectures.[3] This claim sounds so outrageous, so contrary to good sense, that many are tempted simply to dismiss Kojève on that account, unless, of course, they are acolytes of Schopenhauer, and it is not at all clear that Schopenhauer has many acolytes outside of the artistic *milieux* where his thought once flourished. It is no accident that I mention Schopenhauer, however. Kojève's thought reflects some of Schopenhauer's most basic doctrines, a point all the more interesting given Kojève's status as a commentator on Hegel. But, as we shall see, Kojève's commentary contains many layers showing many influences, and the affinity with Schopenhauer plays out against other important affinities.[4]

If Schopenhauer bids us to free ourselves from the will, Kojève urges us to free ourselves from the most pernicious restriction on our freedom: the imperative to self-preservation (a way to freedom, I might add, itself determined by what it opposes). This may sound very much like Schopenhauer, if we ignore the striking dualism that Kojève constructs. This dualism establishes a basic difference between what Kojève refers to as animal desire and distinctively human desire, the former being wholly dominated by the imperative to self-preservation, the latter expressing itself primarily through resistance to that imperative. For Kojève, we become truly human when we risk our security knowingly, and the greatest risk that we can take in that respect is knowingly to offer up our own lives. The primary example he provides is familiar—the contest for recognition or supremacy Kojève reads into the famous discussion of the master-slave relation in subdivision A of chapter IV of the *Phenomenology of the Spirit*. The master is the one who faces death without flinching, and his opponent, if he flinches, becomes the slave. The master shows no fear of death; the slave is defined by that fear. Mastery is a kind of freedom understood precisely as the absence of concern for self-preservation. The slave is of course only a slave, the vanquished, and becomes the creature of suffering that turns its entire existence into an attempt to be free from suffering, to negate suffering by negating the causes of suffering.

But why does a fight take place? Kojève's explanation is crucial to his thinking. The fight takes place as a result of human, not animal, desire. For Kojève, desire is profoundly negative. Kojève illustrates this point with homely examples. He describes animal desire as simple appetite, the desire for food to satisfy hunger. Kojève claims that this desire negates its object. It does so by ingesting or transforming the object in the process of ingestion. The plant is thus transformed by ingestion into nutrients that maintain the animal's existence. All animal desire is transformative in this way; the animal negates by transforming for the sake of self-preservation. Kojève insists, however, that distinctively human desire is different from animal desire. The difference comes clear if we consider the object of desire. The animal takes for an object whatever can satisfy its hunger—the animal's desire is material. Human desire is distinguished by the fact that it is not directly material but the desire of the desire of another. This clumsy locution describes a fundamental shift: human desire does not relate to an object but to another human being as a being with its own desires. Moreover, human desire is distinguished by the difference in the type of negation involved. Rather than negating the material object in an act of ingestion, human desire negates another desire by supplanting it or, as Kojève emphasizes, by forcing one party to recognize the desire of the other by adopting it as its own: I negate your desire by compelling you to recognize and adopt my own in its stead.

Human desire from this perspective is pure, brutal self-assertion or the assertion of one desire over another—human desire is in essence the desire for recognition (of desire). This desire cannot be satisfied until all desires other than mine—or ours—have been eliminated: the desire for the desire of the other is inherently hegemonic and universalist since nothing less than universal recognition can offer satisfaction: "Man can be *satisfied* only by being *recognized universally.*"[5]

Why is this so? Kojève holds that we cannot be sure of ourselves—that we are not mad—until we have eliminated all opposition to our own forms of desire.[6] This is an extraordinary claim, and it merits careful comment. Kojève creates an analogy between animal and human desire in this particular respect: rather ironically, at least in the latter case, both result from an overwhelming desire for self-preservation. For the animal, ingesting various foods is necessary for the continuation of the animal's existence, the basic motive of all animal activity that remains unquestioned. For the human, the desire for the desire of others is based on the need to assert one's own desires over those of others as a way of assuring one's "reality," that the way one lives is indeed the real and only way—that one comes into possession of the full and final truth.

The full and final truth is universal recognition: one kind of life prevails over all others such that no rival way of evaluating things remains. One kind of life becomes *universal and homogeneous*. The slave is emancipated by creating his own reality and by assuring that the reality so created be recognized and accepted by all. This is the slave revolt or revolution for Kojève, the final revolution that brings history to a close.[7]

II

This quest for freedom is what concerns Kojève. The master is a dead end or impasse. Freedom is not even an issue for the master. The peculiar irony is that the master's freedom from the fear of death leaves the master stagnant and unable to change. For Kojève this is not exactly a problem. Indeed, the problem is the slave, for it is the slave who begins and makes history. Put simply, history is precisely the narrative of the slave's attempt to attain emancipation from his servitude—or universal recognition.

Now, this history should trouble us to pause. Criticism of Kojève's focus on the master-slave relation is not lacking—Robert Pippin is one of Kojève's fiercest critiques precisely on account of what he sees as Kojève's extravagant simplification of and overemphasis on subdivision A of chapter IV.[8] Pippin may have a point. Kojève grants enormous significance to the master-slave relation: it is central to the narrative he constructs in his lectures and appears to be applied as the fundamental structure that emerges within the historical process. History for Kojève is struggle, though it would be too much to say that it is the history of class struggle. Nonetheless, history is constituted by a struggle that begins with the fear of death and ends with the vanquishing of that fear. As Kojève notes, if both parties to the initial struggle die, there is obviously no further struggle. This is the case as well if one party dies. Either possibility precludes further struggle. Only the *refusal* to engage in the original struggle to the death, creates a new struggle that is oriented precisely to overcome the fear of death that has imposed upon the slave his servile status.

This overcoming is quite curious, however. The mastery achieved by the slave seems to be an "ignoble" mastery because it is the highest expression of the imperative to self-preservation that defines the slave as slave in the first place. If the slave achieves final satisfaction or emancipation from nature and the fear of death, this achievement seems illusory since the slave has not conquered his own natural impulse to live—indeed, the irony of the slave's success is that it is at the same time a terrible failure, a bestialization. The slave in conquering nature allows himself to be conquered *by* nature, an irony that underscores that the slave does not free himself from the fear of death but chooses, rather, to be completely ruled by it to the point where the victorious slave has become nothing more than a beast enslaved to an appetite he cannot control. The slave's emancipation is at once the most complete enslavement—but, as we shall see, it is also a kind of suicide.

Any decent empirical historian would balk at the stunning reductiveness of this interpretation of history, which claims in essence that all history is oriented to salvation or "salvation history" (recall Heidegger's "Alle Geschichte wird zur Heilsgeschichte").[9] All history is aimed at emancipation from struggle, at an end of history, at overcoming history. History is the nightmare or reign of error or slaughter bank from which we seek shelter. Here another layer seems to emerge if we are wont to see in this pattern reflections of the Christian salvation narrative where one is thrust into the world only to seek in the final account to save oneself from and through it. Though, as with the other narratives woven into Kojève's commentary, the similarity is not exact or even ambiguous because Christian salvation tends to reject the narrative of mastery over nature as an expression of grotesque selfishness—of self-preservation grown into a horrific collective egoism.

It is indeed easy to overlook the strangeness of this interpretation of history since it seems so familiar to us. Why must history be oriented to salvation? Why must history be oriented in any particular way? Can we not conceive of history in other ways? Kojève's response to these questions is cryptic, to say the least, since one may infer from his focus on the first part of chapter IV only that history is born in the fear of death and has no other possible sense than as an attempt to overcome that fear, either metaphorically or quite literally in the doomed sort of technological revolution that Kojève assumes to be the final achievement of the slave having freed itself for good. The slave having freed itself from the fear of death is the curious "master of the world" (*le maître du Monde*) who through technology has overcome death itself (through bestialization).[10]

Ironies aside—Kojève affirms here, if anything, the importance of a teleological narrative of history and insists that this is the only possible narrative of history. No other view of history could possibly be maintained because for Kojève there is no other history than the history of philosophy, of philosophical attitudes to the world understood, as the cliché has it, as "shapes of consciousness." The historian's rejection of such an approach as reductive or "ideological" is itself ideological. The only refuge, then, for history is in emancipation, an emancipation that completes and thus negates history, ideology and, in its most ironic aspect, the human life itself. As Kojève notes in the *Outline*, "a purely human universe is inconceivable because without nature man is nothingness, pure and simple."[11] Emancipation as the full triumph over nature is nothingness, an emptiness, because full emancipation, final freedom, is itself nothingness—it cannot even be described as a state because any state presupposes nature or limitation, and, for Kojève, nature and limitation seem to be synonymous.

The slave's victory as bestialization is also a form of self-immolation, a trenchant irony given the slave's pursuit of self-preservation.

This brings me to the other main thread of this discussion—Kojève's notion of wisdom and its relation to the negative. If there are two principal narratives in Kojève's commentary on Hegel, these are the narrative of the master and slave and the narrative of the final accession to wisdom that, according to Kojève, is Hegel's most enduring and revolutionary contribution to philosophy. It is enduring and revolutionary because it brings an end to philosophy as the "love of wisdom." This second narrative has generated a great deal of controversy because Kojève suggests that all basic forms of thinking have been articulated such that there is nothing new to articulate: we have reached a final stage, that of wisdom, and we may go no further other than to repeat what has already been thought in some fashion. Kojève's famous claim that history has reached an end derives from this second narrative and is its culmination.

Let me describe this narrative in some detail before proceeding to ask a simple but important question: How does the accession to wisdom fit with the narrative of master and slave? Are these two versions of the same underlying narrative or are they markedly different expressions of a different underlying narrative? The question is important in grasping Kojève's peculiar challenge to philosophy, but it is also important because the reception of Kojève's commentary has tended to focus on the master-slave relation as against the arguably far more unusual interpretation of wisdom that emerges in the 1938–1939 lectures. The reasons for this are obvious. The claim to omniscience that accompanies Kojève's interpretation of wisdom is provocative and has generally been considered unconvincing or perhaps even facile irony.

III

The wisdom narrative starts with an uncompromising definition: wisdom is complete or absolute knowledge. Wisdom has already been achieved with the achievement of absolute knowledge in the sage. The latter is defined as follows:

> In regard to the *definition* of the Sage—all philosophers are in agreement. It is indeed very simple and can be set out in a single phrase: The Sage is one capable of responding in a *comprehensive*, indeed, satisfying manner, to *all* questions that one may pose to him in regard to his acts, and to respond in such a way that

the *whole* of his responses form a *coherent* discourse. Or even—what amounts to the same thing: the Sage is the man *completely and perfectly conscious of himself.*[12]

The sage or wise man is omniscient. There is no question that he cannot answer, and no answer that he gives may contradict any other answer he gives to other questions: his discourse must be complete and completely consistent. In the interpretation of chapter VIII of the *Phenomenology* that follows this definition, Kojève attempts to show that Hegel achieves this wisdom not only by answering all questions that can be posed in history (questions regarding action) but by showing also that no further questions may be asked—or, what is the same thing, that all other questions that may be asked lack sense or are in *error.*

Kojève provides "justification" of his claim regarding Hegel in the 1938–1939 lectures by reference to yet another narrative. Kojève claims this narrative should prove conclusively that wisdom is at hand and that no other narrative can possibly be conceived unless it is conceived in error. Kojève borrows this narrative from the rich Russian theological tradition (though affinities with Ludwig Feuerbach and Bruno Bauer are also evident): it is the orthodox narrative of deification, of man having becoming god (θέωσις). By becoming God man frees himself of himself—man becomes nothing or discovers his proper identity as nothing. Kojève seems to reverse the traditional emphasis, however—his deification turns god into man, as a finite deity, ending up in a most peculiar combination, that of finite omniscience, and, as Kojève tries to convince us, the only possible omniscience is finite. For Kojève Hegel's *Phenomenology* expresses and overcomes the theological narrative and, as such, is a profoundly *atheist* text.

Kojève's claim then turns out to be that Hegel has in fact become wise by realizing and developing the only possible form of omniscience or absolute finality that we can imagine—that of the finite god. Kojève expresses his view in a remarkable passage from the fourth of the 1938–1939 lectures (a text, I note, that is not included in the English translation):

It suffices to read a manual of Christian theology (I emphasize: Christian), where God is effectively a total and infinite being, and to say after having read the manual: the being in question—that's me. This is simple, of course. Yet, even today, this seems to us to be an absurdity, an "enormity" without equal. And we label as mad anyone who openly makes the affirmation. This means that it is extremely difficult to affirm (that is, seriously). And it is a fact that millennia of philosophical thought have passed before Hegel finally dared to say it. It's simply that it was not easy to come to the concept of a Christian God. And, then, having come to it, it was not easy to identify oneself with this concept, to apply it to oneself. Hegel tells us that this is possible only for the Citizen

of the universal and homogeneous State. . . . It is only this Citizen who may
affirm the identity with God without being mad, who may affirm it by being a
Sage, who may affirm it in revealing thus a reality, that is by proclaiming an
absolute Truth.[13]

While laced with a certain irony, this passage brings together several of the
main strands of Kojève's argument as it leads into a more detailed account of
the possibility of finite omniscience. The sage is not merely the end of philosophy, the sage must also bring to an end the theological position, and this
is only possible if the sage assumes the identity of God.

The obvious question is: How may the sage, the finite being, assume the
identity of God without contradiction? In other words, how does God become
man or how does man become atheist?

Kojève's answer to this question is quite complicated—hardly surprising
given the nature of the question itself. Indeed, Kojève would expend more
effort on attempting to prove that all possible basic shapes of consciousness
(as such, shapes of action as well) have been passed through than on any
other aspect of his interpretation of Hegel. The posthumous publication of his
extensive attempts to bring Hegel's thought up to date attest both to this enormous effort and to a pervasive sense of failure that emerges in the increasing
technical complexity and ironical stance of his later work—in a word, Kojève
sensed how fragile or absurd his insistence on an end having already come
into view might seem, and he struggled for many years to answer his crit-
ics and his own doubts. Like Kant, whose twelve categories have invited so
much resistance, Kojève's attempt to show that all possible modes of thought
have been articulated has been received with skepticism.[14]

To discuss Kojève's technical arguments is an absorbing, though ultimately
disappointing, topic, and not one I want to develop here. Let me provide a
short answer: the sage emerges when the world has become completely a
product of human labor—when the world has become fully a human creation
as evinced by the historical unfolding of human self-creation in time. One
could argue that the chief importance of Hegel for Kojève lies in the compre-
hensiveness of the Hegelian system—its devotion to a complete and seamless
interpretation of reality as beholden to the concept (defined as time or history)
and thus to a final construction of reality as distinctively human.

This sounds like a radical constructivism, and, in a sense, it is. Kojève
argues that distinctively human activity—the basic action of history—is
aimed at negating nature as that which is different from or threatening to the
human—the distinctively human core of reality is to transform nature into
a product of human activity thereby assimilating it or, in other terms, fully
anthropomorphizing it. Where Kojève departs from the constructivist model
is in his emphasis on negation. In this respect, Kojève adopts a key Hegelian

trope, the so-called "monstrous power of the negative" (*die ungeheure Macht des Negativen*)[15] to describe both the essential movement toward emancipation of the slave and the assent to wisdom. Freedom results from the negation of all limitations on human activity—that is to say, negation becomes complete when nature has been abolished as the regulating power. The slave and the sage replace nature by a negation that is equivalent to the completely free self-production of the new human being—a being that is distinctively human because it has consciously overcome death.

IV

It should be obvious, however, that this new being is deeply problematic. Has the slave truly achieved emancipation from nature? And, if so, does this emancipation amount to much more than a form of collective suicide or extreme form of self-abnegation in the universal and homogeneous state? We have already addressed these questions rather quickly in passing. For Kojève, they are crucial. I quote from the final paragraphs of the final lecture of the 1938–1939 cycle, the very end of the Hegel lectures:

> The entire sphere of finitude, by the fact that it is itself something, belonging to the senses—collapses into the true-or-truthful faith before the thought and intuition (*Anschauung*) of the eternal, [the thought and intuition] becoming here one and the same thing. All the gnats of subjectivity are burned up in this devouring fire; and *even the conscience* of this giving of oneself (*Hingebens*) and of this annihilation (*Vernichtens*) is annihilated (*vernichtet*). Hegel knows it and says it. But he also says in one of his letters that this knowledge has cost him dearly. He speaks of a period of total depression that he lived through between the twenty-fifth and thirtieth year of his life, of a "hyperchondria" that went "bis zur Erlähmung aller Kräfte," "to the point of a paralysis of all his forces" and which arose precisely from the fact that he could not accept the necessary abandonment of individuality, that is in fact of humanity, that the idea of absolute Knowledge demands. But, finally, he overcame this "hyperchondria." And, becoming wise through this last acceptance of death, he published, few years later, the first part of the "System of Knowledge," titled, "Science of the Phenomenology of the Spirit," where he reconciles himself with all that is and has been, by declaring that there will never again be anything new on earth.[16]

The end of history is an "abandonment of individuality, that is in fact of humanity" and thus, of death as well. If Kojève seeks to cultivate revolutionary ardor in his students, this final comment is certainly bracing, if not rather devastating. The post-historical state is one of "living bodies with human form, but emptied of spirit," another image Kojève offers to describe what is left in the final state.[17]

The question is: What does Kojève intend to do to his audience? He provides a drastic account of a humanity bereft of individuality that is nothing more than a grouping of bodies. But this account is consistent. The accession to a post-historical state for Kojève requires the separation of human and animal desire. The human being has become a point that interrupts the repetition of the animal world, a repetition that maintains a "system" of reliable continuances. Indeed, animals seek self-preservation as part of a larger economy of continuities that sustains the natural system.

To the extent the slave overcomes his fear of death, he interrupts this natural system, and he does so through work. The final end of that work is to create a world in which the human being is master. But this world cannot be the natural system—indeed, the slave's final desire to overcome the given is a desire to overcome the natural system *in toto*. How might *we*, entrenched as we are in the natural system, possibly come to understand a state that has no narrative and can have no narrative, a state that is in many respects similar to that of the master, albeit with the major difference that the master faces death by risk whereas the slave does so fundamentally through work? We may understand this state only *subtractively* or *negatively*. The progress of the slave is subtractive in so far as the slave peels off the layers of natural being that afflict and enslave it—the slave's progress is a freedom from predication.

Hence, Kojève's claim about individuality is not so difficult to understand in this context. Arguably more difficult to understand is the dark image of bodies without spirit. But, indeed, what is left after the human leaves? Bodies, "pure" materiality—whatever that might be. How can we grasp these bodies in any other way, even as a figure of speech? Kojève's radicality is to describe the end of history as an essentially post-predicative state. Bodies without spirit in this sense are nothing else than matter, pure matter, and no one has succeeded in explaining what matter in itself might be.

Kojève has in effect separated form from matter; he has reversed the progress of philosophy from Parmenides to Hegel—or he has fully outlined what it must entail. For Kojève argues that the narrative of the slave is one in which time and the concept become one—it is the progressive infiltration of time into the concept.[18] What Kojève does not say so directly is that this identification is only possible in the universal and homogeneous—absolute—end state where time and concept become one, an identification that in its silence equals the beginning of philosophy with Parmenides, thereby providing the necessary circularity and closure to history.[19]

But, if this is the case, Kojève cannot explain how he is able to declare that time and the concept have become one. To do so implies that time and the concept have not become one because there is a discursive position that allows one to describe that unity—a position at once in- and "outside the circle." If this position were not so, it would no longer be able to declare itself as such. In other words—and this is a crucial point—the unity of time and concept eliminates reflection or consciousness "of" any X. Neither philosophy nor any speech at all is possible.[20]

V

Kojève proclaims the abandonment of individuality as the proper culmination or perfection of human action and thought as well as the achievement of the most complete freedom. The central narrative of master and slave ends with the establishment of the universal and homogeneous state in which all citizens recognize themselves seamlessly in their fellow citizens. The universal and homogeneous state in fact arises only where the "I" has become "We" to such an extent that there is truly no difference between citizens: they resemble mathematical points on a grid, qualitatively identical though numerically distinct. The equation of human freedom with the abandonment of individuality is of course nothing new, a number of religious traditions depend on it. Kojève is avowedly atheist, and abandonment of individuality for him, though bearing an obvious structural similarity to the abandonment of individuality in communion with God, is much closer to certain currents in the Buddhist tradition, which Kojève refers to as an atheistic religion, both in his early work entitled *Atheism* from 1931 and in his book on Kant from 1952.[21]

Before addressing this Buddhist context in the book on Kant, another important aspect of the abandonment of individuality and its connection with freedom needs to be brought into focus—namely, Kojève's notion that the ultimate proof of human freedom is the willingness to commit suicide and thereby to relinquish any further concern for one's individual—hence, material—existence. Suicide is the most distinctively human act of emancipation, for it is the rejection of any hold nature, as the supposed instinct for self-preservation, may have on us.[22] No animal contemplates suicide, and a human being who is unwilling to commit suicide, or at least to realize his capacity to commit suicide at any moment, is for Kojève not truly human but still in thrall, still very much the slave unable to come to complete or genuine emancipation. In *Atheism* as well as in the Hegel lectures, Kojève underscores the importance of suicide to the expression of freedom as freedom from the dictates of nature.

> The "human being in the world" is given to herself "from without" in self-consciousness, and in self-consciousness she is given to herself as free or, more accurately, self-consciousness is freedom. In self-consciousness she is

given to herself as finite, in self-consciousness she is free, i.e., the one who at
any minute can freely kill herself. And, thus, at any minute she lives merely by
virtue of the free refusal of suicide, i.e., she is free not only at the moment of
suicide but at any moment of her existence.[23]

In a note on this section, Kojève adds that the "human being should not end
her life in order to be free; on the contrary, suicide, as the realization of freedom, is by the same token its annihilation."[24] While Kojève seems to caution
that suicide is not indeed the proper expression of freedom, it is only so as
long as it is a possibility that one may actualize at any given point. The problem here is, however, that the failure to actualize the possibility of suicide
may just as easily pass for an unwillingness to do so that is surely far stronger
evidence of servitude than of freedom, and this ambiguity cannot easily be
dismissed. For the point of suicide is to emancipate oneself from the tyranny
of nature understood as the tyranny of self-preservation or the will to live
itself, the very will that creates the slave in opposition to the master at the
supposed dawn of history.

The will to live as natural or as instinct is precisely that which holds the
slave in servitude, and if the slave cannot deliver himself from that servitude,
then freedom is impossible. Instinct is the decisive term because instinct
describes a natural disposition that, by analogy with the animal world, cannot
be varied. Instinct is thus the most basic expression of necessity as the "way
of nature." Hence, for Kojève to claim that human beings act in accordance
with this instinct is to claim that they are not human—they are nothing more
than animals living according to a natural system that has nothing to do with
the human or with history, that is, with the capacity to alter or resist nature
itself. To act in accordance with the instinct for self-preservation is precisely
a form of servitude though it is not recognized as such. Recognition comes
with the combat which initiates the master and slave relation.

Here is the problem, however, that affects Kojève's thinking as a whole:
to prove or give adequate proof of one's own freedom requires not merely
that one may or may not at any given point commit suicide but a positive act,
and not merely an ambiguous omission, that risks life in a basic way. Such
a risk must indeed become the decisive criterion of proof that differentiates
the master from the slave. For, without such an act, there is simply no way
to know whether one is dealing with a master or a slave because a slave may
content himself with the notion that he has the capacity to commit suicide
even though he is not willing to do so or in fact fears to do so, thus perpetuat-
ing his servitude: inaction in this respect is indistinguishable from servitude,
and the notion that one may at any given time commit suicide could function
as a sort of deception or illusion upon which the slave relies in order to turn
away from his servitude or pretend that his servitude is not as complete or dire

as it may well be. The slave terrified of death and thus in thrall to the will to live or the natural instinct for self-preservation cannot free himself merely by thinking about a possibility that he is unwilling to actualize. Freedom is not merely the capacity to be free of nature but equally, if not more so, the proven or active willingness to be free of nature.

Whether Kojève changed his mind from *Atheism* to the Hegel lectures is of little moment. It is sufficiently clear from the latter, that he recognizes the necessity of risk—and this of course means the risk of one's life—to express freedom and that risk is effectively the only adequate proof of the human capacity for freedom. Otherwise, the human being—the slave—who is unable to risk remains a slave, virtually an animal for whom self-preservation is a natural dictate that cannot be overcome, either for want of courage or due to the recognition, noted above, that the realization of freedom can be equivalent to annihilation or the surrender of one's self-awareness or self-consciousness (both originally resulting from the slave's refusal to risk his life). Moreover, the refusal of risk, the indignity of such a refusal, may be submerged in precisely the forms of justification that Kojève has brought forth in terms of the mere capacity to think of committing suicide at any moment or the various forms of discipline of "animal impulse" that are found in many religious traditions as vain attempts at mortification or punishment of the flesh which leave the animal perhaps weakened but do not risk its life in the total manner that the combat between master and slave does.

In his book on Kant from 1952, Kojève engages in an extended discussion of Buddhism in precisely this regard. There Kojève seems to advocate a more radical position than the one presented in *Atheism* and, indeed, arguably more radical than the Hegel lectures as well. For Kojève affirms in his discussion of Buddhism that to continue living is not compatible with genuine freedom— the foremost choice is between inaction leading to death and final extinction or action that cannot but continue life, and thus servitude:

> For the Buddhist, the *natural* life is *eternal* (or, at least, co-eternal with Time); it is sufficient to act in any way whatsoever (to act from Desire; Karma) to be re-*born* and thus to *live* indefinitely; on the contrary, one must do something special in order to *extinguish oneself* (Nirvana) after one's natural death; to wit, (i.e. to acquaint oneself with the "dogma" [Dharma] and) to apply the "Discipline" (Vinaya) which consists moreover in doing nothing or doing "nothing" (eg. the *Wei wu-wei* of the Daoists: "to do non-doing"), that is, to suppress the "Desire" (Ràga) that leads necessarily to Action (Karma) determining (even if "moral") a future *life*. Now, as far as he is Religious, the Buddhist admits the impossibility of Satisfaction in this "worldly" *life*. Religious "Satisfaction" or "Salvation" can only consist in Extinction (since, even if he is reborn, which is possible if one applies a certain "moral," as Buddha or the supreme God, he lives a "worldly" life and cannot obtain the religious Satisfaction that is the only

true value for him. [What is truly remarkable is that the Buddha advises against the supreme "morality" that "divinizes" man because, having become God, that is, perfectly *happy* or "blessed," he is no longer able to recognize the *unworthy* character of this "blessedness," in such a manner that the very idea of genuine Satisfaction (=happiness of which he is worthy) becomes forever inaccessible to him, in such a manner that he is condemned to eternal life (or co-eternal with Time). Of course, Satisfaction is only "lived" during the life of the Buddha, that is, of the "accomplished" Buddhist, and it is nothing else, in the final account, but Faith, in the sense of a subjective *certitude* concerning the *expectation* of death at some point (close for the Buddha and deliberately far way, indeed indefinite, for the Boddhisattva) definitely and for the good.[25]

According to this passage, no life can be free—the "worldly" life of the individual is not only senseless (provided the true sense of life is nirvāna) but base as well, no matter how well disguised that baseness may be. To remain living means servitude to the basic necessities of life: one must eat and drink, sleep and defecate. In other words, one remains a slave to one's own material, individual self, a necessarily selfish self to the extent that other beings must be harmed to sustain this self. Those who think that they become blessed, selfless or otherwise free through adherence to a discipline, morality, the law or the truth are simply blind to the "unworthy" character of their lives because they deceive themselves effectively. And they deceive themselves effectively because they refuse to admit that there can be no manner of freedom available to a being that still holds on to its life or that cannot articulate how genuine freedom can be compatible with the animal natural necessity of prolonging life by maintaining at some level the well-being of the material, individual self. Rather than cultivating the possibility of freedom through suicide, the slave by continuing to live continues to express not only the primacy of self-preservation or the will to live but also his own primacy over others, if only potentially where scarcity does not bring conflict.

VI

If this is so, then what sort of state can the final state be, the universal and homogeneous state or, to put it with mild irony, Kantian purgatory? While this state plays an important teleological role in the Hegel lectures, Kojève's most expansive treatment of its structure is the *Outline of a Phenomenology of Right*. This long text offers an overview of the basic elements that pertain to the universal and homogeneous state as legal structures or structures of what Kojève refers to as a system of *droit*, right, or *Recht*. The system of right creates a calculus or "logic" of action that is explicitly hegemonic, permitting no remainder of custom or justice external to the system of right it proposes. It is thus universalist and final or, at the very least, points to a final system of regulation in the universal and homogeneous state from which there can exist no possibility of departure or variance that is not itself error or crime.

The first section of the treatise provides an account of the basic unit that ties the entire text together: the "juridical situation." This is a formal relation among three parties, two agents in potential conflict with each other, A and B, and a third, intervening figure, C, which carries a twofold responsibility: to police and to adjudicate any actual conflicts. Kojève indicates that this relation is not an abstraction but identifies the most simple possible relation that may give rise to intervention or adjudication by the third, C. Kojève holds that there is no "juridical situation" when there are only two parties involved (the minimum for any relation whatsoever) simply because there is no possibility for adjudication but rather only conflict that has no secure form of resolution.[26]

Adjudication is the fundamental notion in the treatise. Adjudication presupposes a conflict for which there is an established and universally agreed resolution procedure, the final product presumably of the struggle between master and slave set out in the Hegel lectures and reiterated (with significant modifications) in the *Outline*. For, in a conflict having only two parties, there can be no assumed resolution procedure; indeed, the assumed resolution procedure is, according to Kojève, the trajectory of history itself as the history of the master-slave relation. Therefore, a resolution procedure is only possible at the end of history when the conflict between master and slave has concluded. Kojève does not put it this way in the opening section of the treatise. Instead, he addresses the distinction between the political and the juridical relation by arguing that the former presupposes conflict between friend and enemy whereas the latter presupposes a more general amity.[27] In other words, the juridical relation presupposes general agreement among the parties as to the procedures and institutions of conflict resolution; it thus assumes that the desire for recognition which gives rise to conflicts has been satisfied.

A nagging concern emerges here. If the universal and homogeneous state represents the final overcoming of individuality, why would there be any need for a juridical apparatus? Surely, the abolition of individuality would bring with it the abolition of selfish desire (as in recognition) that is the perennial source of conflict, of the temptation to place one's own over others? The universal and homogeneous state as a system of right would seem to involve a contradiction. Kojève's treatise on right qualifies this obvious implication somewhat by suggesting that the universal and homogeneous state in its "purity" is a "limit case," as such possible to think but impossible to achieve in action.[28]

Nonetheless, the comprehensive teaching of the treatise makes no sense without another firm presupposition: that the juridical signals the ultimate end of the political, of struggle, of history, individuality as such. Where the political finally ends, the juridical truly comes into its own as the authoritative ordering of action in the universal and homogeneous state. Conflict has come to an end, the juridical system becomes a sort of surrogate "instinct," a new or "second" nature to correct the error that conflict represents and to create the groundwork for a terminal condition in which individuality, understood as error, will be definitively overcome. Viewed in this light, individuality is a deviation (or "error") to be suppressed via a juridical system, an administrative state, and this suppression is essential to the universal and homogeneous state that thereby offers the most radical emancipation from the fear of death itself. For if one no longer seeks to preserve one's individuality, one is no longer afraid to die, for only individuals die.

VII

The mere existence of the treatise and the system it outlines expresses a thoroughgoing skepticism about the end of history that goes directly against the narratives that originate in the Hegel lectures. This skepticism is much closer, as I have already suggested, to a Kantian position that regards history as interminable. In terms of individuality, the elaborate judicial structure of the universal and homogeneous state presupposes the difficulty of adequately suppressing individuality so as to bring about the truly final state that needs no judicial structure to contain individuality or individual inclination (in Kantian terms). The judicial structure of the universal and homogeneous state is the starkest admission that history has not and does not end because the transference of individuality to the collective is precarious.

Here is the correlate to Kojève's comment about Buddhism. For as long as the individual maintains itself, the possibility of deviation exists and true homogeneity remains an ever-distant goal.[29] The reason for this is that the mere act of maintaining oneself alive is an egoistic, individual act, and thus an act that undermines the collective because it affirms the ineradicable priority of individual self-interest over that of the whole. To give oneself truly over to the whole is thus impossible as long as one remains alive, the distinctively Kantian sense that universal duty shall not vanquish individual inclination retains its capacity to bring into doubt the Hegelian consummation of individual and collective expressed in the I becoming we and the reverse. This relation of I and we cannot become fully, seamlessly reciprocal. To the contrary, the individual, as such, cannot but remain a reproach to complete reciprocity (which would, in any case, collapse or overcome the distinction on which it is based).

The *Outline* is thus a radical departure from the project of the Hegel lectures, and it even brings their confident end, as an end to history, into question. One may counter, however, that there is nothing inherently temporary—or nonfinal—in the judicial structure of the universal and homogeneous state, that there is also no reason to measure such a state against the standard of the state that withers away completely, requiring no laws and no judicial machinery at all since disputes are rendered impossible. This argument ignores, however, the striking potential for a resurgence of the political in resistance to judicial domination, the administrative state, because as long as individual inclination cannot be eradicated, a secure and permanent final state cannot be guaranteed, much less durably established.

VIII

The eradication of the individual ends up as the decisive factor in the end of history and the creation of a truly universal and homogeneous state. If the individual, as such, cannot be successfully eradicated, finality is impossible. Here it may be worthwhile to return to the beginning and Kojève's affirmation of suicide as the completely emancipatory act. For complete emancipation has to be the emancipation from individuality in the sense of emancipation from servitude to the body and its material needs which are always individual needs. The corollary to the well-known claim that only individuals die is of course that it is only they who live as well, and as long as they live—necessarily in thrall to the "will to live" itself—they are in servitude. But Kojève also states, in the *Outline*, that complete emancipation for human beings is impossible, for as soon as the animal—the body—has been overcome, so has the human:

> The human being, therefore, is just as *real* and *objective* as the natural being. And he is just as *actual* (or active) as the latter. One cannot say, however, that there is a dualism here in the ordinary sense of the word: man is not a *substance* opposed to natural substance. For man is only the *negation* of Nature: he is *Negativity* and not *Identity* or Substantiality. If the Universe is a ring, and if Nature *is* like the metal of which this ring is made, Man *is* only like the hole of this ring. For the Universe to be a ring and not something else, there must be a hole in the same way as the metal which surrounds it. But the metal can exist without the hole, and the Universe would be something without being a ring. The hole, by contrast, would be nothing without the metal, and there is no Universe that would only be a hole. Thus, Nature can exist without Man, and a purely natural Universe is perfectly conceivable (although its conception in

actuality presupposes in fact the existence of man who conceives it and whom the Universe involves). A purely human Universe, by contrast, is inconceivable, for without Nature, Man is nothingness pure and simple.[30]

There could hardly be clearer evidence of Kojève's Kantian stance, at least in the *Outline*. The true end of history is the annihilation of the human, no doubt a possibility now that may not have been contemplated by Kojève in 1943. Thus, the universal and homogeneous state cannot be an end state in the way I have suggested: the precondition of the state's withering away is in fact the end of humanity *in toto*. Barring such a radical final result, the universal and homogeneous state can be nothing more than an ideal unrealizable in any other way than through the eradication of humanity itself. More than that, the ostensibly *final* state cannot guarantee its own perpetuity because there is always the risk of recidivism, a falling back into the assertion of self-interest over the collective whole. We might recall the state described so well by Evgeny Zamyatin in *We*, where base self-interest and the enjoyment of self-interest comes to mock the One State and its pretensions of holism and finality—the empire of reason gives way to self-interest and personal inclination that cannot even define themselves adequately within the mathematical reason that takes priority in the One State. We might thus also recall the pertinent questions that Dostoevsky's underground man poses to the rational state, anticipating both Kojève, an avid and attentive reader of Dostoevsky, and Zemyatin.

Dostoevsky suggests that human beings would prefer to preserve their own possibility of wishing whatever might occur to them—a whim—over the "perfection" of the final, "rational" state:

> But I repeat to you for the hundredth time, there is only one case, one only, when man may purposely, consciously wish for himself even the harmful, the stupid, even what is stupidest of all: namely, so as to have the right to wish for himself even what is stupidest of all and not be bound by an obligation to wish for himself only what is intelligent. For this stupidest of all, this caprice of ours, gentlemen, may in fact be the most profitable of anything on earth for our sort, especially in certain cases. And in particular it may be more profitable than all other profits even in the case when it is obviously harmful and contradicts the most sensible conclusions of our reason concerning profits . . .[31]

This statement is an affirmation that crime (or "error") is ineradicable: the inclination to reject a (any) given order is in fact at the essence of the human being. Within Kojève's terms, the admission that there can be no human being without Nature, that the ring structure he describes is fundamental to the very definition of human existence, is an admission of the inevitable failure of the Hegelian project. If in a famous article Kojève acknowledges that "Hegelian philosophy is not a truth in the proper sense of the term: it is less the adequate discursive revelation of totality than an idea or ideal, that is to say, a 'project' which is to be realized," he also remarks that Hegelian philosophy "because it is not yet true . . . alone is capable of becoming true one day."[32] Yet, this "one day" must remain infinitely distant unless, of course, the human being succeeds in destroying itself en masse through the destruction of nature, what would seem to be the proper goal of the activity of negation that is so central as the truly humanizing activity in the Hegel lectures.

What are we to make of this admission of failure, of the potential impossibility of the realization of the Hegelian project other than through mass suicide? Far from asserting the advent of the universal and homogeneous state, Kojève asserts its likely impossibility or even absurdity, should we take the idea of its complete realization seriously. If Kojève appears as more Kantian than Hegelian, perhaps, he also appears to affirm in a negative sense the katechontic view of history important to his exoteric antipode, Carl Schmitt.[33] If that is indeed so, we still must ask why Kojève adopts such a contradictory stance, on the one hand, repeatedly affirming the end of history as a fact (whether with Napoleon or Stalin), while admitting, on the other, that this end is hardly a fact and indeed *cannot* ever be such since the end of history brings with it the end of the consciousness that knowingly grasps things as facts. Where is the "real" Kojève?

This question is perfectly appropriate because the contradiction invites resolution of the "either-or" type: either Kojève is a committed, if radical, Hegelian or a Kantian who hides his skepticism as to finality under the guise of an ostensibly attractive ideal—the universal and homogeneous state. Each opposition ironizes the other, for the Hegelian cannot respect the compromise—the skepticism—of the Kantian who promotes impossibility as a positive goad to "progressive" action, while the Kantian cannot accept the extremity of the Hegelian resolution of history in the eradication of the human but recognizes the salubrious consequences of the universal ideal provided one does not think too carefully about it. What we may be left with, however, is an unstable alternation of these opposed possibilities which cannot end up in final resolution or whose alternation is in fact a terminal one, the finality of the impossibility of finality enacted in the perpetualized opposition of Hegel to Kant that ends up favoring Kant as long as it continues: "fail again, fail better."

NOTES

1. Alexandre Kojève, *Introduction à la lecture de Hegel,* ed. Raymond Queneau (Paris: Gallimard, 1968), 93. I follow the French text (which I translate myself) where

that text is not included in the considerably abridged English translation: *Introduction to the Reading of Hegel,* trans. James H. Nichols, Jr. (Ithaca: Cornell University Press, 1969). Otherwise, I cite the English translation. The French text is referred to hereinafter as ILH and the English as IRH.

2. Alexandre Kojève, *Outline of a Phenomenology of* Right, trans. Bryan-Paul Frost and Robert Howse (Lanham, MD: Rowman & Littlefield, 2008), 141, hereinafter referred to as OPR.

3. Kojève, IRH, 54, 226, 247, 248; ILH 93.

4. Some of these, such as Martin Heidegger and Karl Marx, are well known, while others, such as Fyodor Dostoevsky, Nikolai Fedorov, and Vladimir Soloviev, are more recondite. And there is the Buddhist subtext as well that is explicit in *Atheism* (1931) and in Kojève's book on Kant, completed in 1952 but first published posthumously in 1973.

5. Kojève, *IRH*, 80.

6. Kojève makes this argument most clearly in his essay "Tyranny and Wisdom." See Alexandre Kojève, "Tyranny and Wisdom" in *On Tyranny* eds. Victor Gourevitch and Michael S. Roth (Chicago: The University of Chicago Press, 2000), 150–154.

7. Kojève claims this revolution will be "bloody" (*sanglante*) and one in which the slave risks his life finally relinquishing his status as slave. *ILH*, 113.

8. Robert Pippin, *Hegel on Self-Consciousness: Desire and Death in the* Phenomenology of the Spirit (Princeton: Princeton University Press, 2010), 11.

9. Martin Heidegger, *Nietzsche* 2 vols. (Pfullingen: Neske, 1961), II/133.

10. Kojève, ILH, 33.

11. Kojève, OPR 141.

12. Ibid., ILH, 317.

13. Ibid., ILH, 373.

14. See, for example, Stanley Rosen, *Hermeneutics as Politics* (Oxford: Oxford University Press, 1987), 95–107.

15. W. G. F. Hegel, *Die Phänomenologie des Geistes* eds. Hans-Friedrich Wessels and Heinrich Clairmont (Hamburg: Felix Meiner, 1988), 26.

16. Kojève, *IRH*, 168.

17. Ibid., *ILH*, 388.

18. Kojève, IRH, 130–132.

19. Ibid., IRH, 134–151.

20. On this point see Kojève's manuscript, published only after his death, called *The Concept, Time and Discourse.* Alexandre Kojève, *Le Concept, Le Temps et Le Discours,* ed. Bernard Hesbois (Paris: Gallimard, 1990), 54–55. Kojève writes: "Now, the aim of philosophical pedagogy is to proceed toward wisdom and, thus, the progressive elimination of all Reflection no matter of what kind" (my translation). The final unity of time and concept brings about the achievement of this wisdom.

21. See Alexandre Kojève, *Atheism,* trans. Jeff Love (New York: Columbia University Press, 2018), 1; and Alexandre Kojève, *Kant* (Paris: Gallimard, 1973), 46–49.

22. Not surprisingly this is a point emphasized by the leading Japanese philosopher of the twentieth century, Nishida Kitarō, who weaves elements of Buddhist thought together with Western philosophy, and primarily Hegel. In his essay, "Logic and

Life," Nishida writes: "Only humans are aware of death, only humans commit suicide." Not only does Nishida connect suicide with freedom but with freedom as distinctively human. See, Nishida Kitarō, *Place and Dialectic,* trans. John W. M. Krummel and Shigenori Nagatomo (Oxford: Oxford University Press, 2012), 109.

23. See Kojève, *Atheism,* 85.

24. Ibid., 155 (note 136).

25. Kojève, *Kant* 47. My translation. Like most of Kojève's writings, this book was published posthumously (in 1973). I have closed the round bracket that begins on line 10 and ends on line 12, though the round bracket is left open both in the printed text and the original manuscript. Moreover, I make no claims as to the correctness of Kojève's account of Buddhist thinking nor his use of it in this context. The paradoxes (i.e., seeking or desiring extinction as liberation from desire) are indeed characteristic of discussions of nirvana, nonetheless. For an admirably clear and concise account of the problem, see Mark Siderits, *Buddhism as Philosophy* 2nd ed. (Indianapolis: Hackett Publishing, 2021), 36–41.

26. Kojève, OPR, 37, 38, 40.

27. Ibid., 134. In this case, the reliance on Schmitt is explicitly avowed by Kojève.

28. Ibid., 141.

29. See Rosen, 105. Rosen compares Kojève not only to Kant but to Plato as well.

30. Ibid., 214 (translation slightly modified).

31. Fyodor Dostoevsky, *Notes from Underground,* trans. Richard Pevear and Larissa Volokhonsky (New York: Vintage, 1993), 28.

32. Alexandre Kojève, "Hegel, Marx and Christianity," trans. Hilail Gildin in *Interpretation* 1 (summer 1970): 42.

33. On Carl Schmitt and the *katechon,* see Julia Hell, *The Conquest of Ruins: The Third Reich and the Fall of Rome* (Chicago: The University of Chicago Press, 2019), 403–430. Whereas Schmitt welcomes the katechon as restraining the end, Kojève is considerably more equivocal.

BIBLIOGRAPHY

Dostoevsky, F. M. *Notes from Underground.* Translated by Richard Pevear and Larissa Volokhonsky. New York: Vintage, 1993.

Hegel, G. W. F. *Die Phänomenologie des Geistes.* Edited by Hans-Friedrich Wessels and Heinrich Clairmont. Hamburg, Felix Meiner, 1988.

Heidegger, Martin. *Nietzsche.* 2 vols. Pfullingen: Neske, 1961.

Hell, Julia. *The Conquest of Ruins: The Third Reich and the Fall of Rome.* Chicago: The University of Chicago Press, 2019.

Kojève, Alexandre. *Atheism.* Translated by Jeff Love. New York: Columbia, 2018.

———. "Hegel, Marx and Christianity." *Interpretation* 1 (summer 1970): 21–42.

———. *Introduction à la lecture de Hegel.* Edited by Raymond Queneau. Paris, Gallimard: 1968.

———. *Introduction to the Reading of Hegel.* Translated by James H. Nichols, Jr. Ithaca: Cornell University Press, 1969.

————. *Kant*. Paris: Gallimard, 1973.

————. *Le concept, le temps et le discours*. Edited by Bernard Hesbois. Paris: Gallimard, 1990.

————. *Outline of a Phenomenology of Right*. Translated by Bryan-Paul Frost and Robert Howse. Lanham, MD: Rowman and Littlefield, 2008.

————. "Tyranny and Wisdom." In *On Tyranny*, edited by Victor Gourevitch and Michael S. Roth, 135–76. Chicago: The University of Chicago Press, 2000.

Nishida, Kitarō. *Place and Dialectic*. Translated by John W. M. Krummel and Shigenori Nagatomo. Oxford: Oxford University Press, 2012.

Pippin, Robert. *Hegel on Self-Consciousness: Desire and Death in the* Phenomenology of the Spirit. Princeton: Princeton University Press, 2010.

Rosen, Stanley. *Hermeneutics as Politics*. Oxford: Oxford University Press, 1987.

Siderits, Mark. *Buddhism as Philosophy*. 2nd ed. Indianapolis: Hackett Publishing, 2021.

Chapter Three

Kojève and Christianity

José María Carabante

INTRODUCTION

The whole work of Alexandre Kojève can be interpreted as a peculiar settling of scores on philosophy's part with Christianity, following a long period in which faith and philosophy, precisely due to the interpretation made of the latter by the first Christian thinkers, had remained undifferentiated. The purpose of the present text is to show the extent to which such an interpretation is viable. Undoubtedly—if as has been shown by Leo Strauss, one of the most eminent Kojèvians of the twentieth century—history is but a conflict between Athens and Jerusalem, Kojève applied the full extent of his radicality to think about the struggle between thought and revelation. Like Hegel, the Russian thinker certainly assumes that the conflict has dissipated because the Revelation has indeed been fulfilled, ultimately certifying its own futility. Indeed, at the very moment in which philosophy, its name having been deposed, presents itself laid bare, as a "science,"[1] there is no longer any room for any revealed content. It is hardly surprising that Kojève should have been cast in the role of a prophet, although ultimately, in the posthistorical age in which he appears to be located when he writes, there cannot strictly speaking be any prophets, as there are no gods nor, for that matter, any messages to be conveyed. If anything, Kojève functions as a notary in charge of drawing up the record of the consummation—or death—of Christianity.[2]

It does not take much in-depth knowledge of Kojève's work for even the least insightful reader of *Introduction to the Reading of Hegel* to realize that his purpose is not so much a detailed exposition of the history of consciousness or an uncritical recapitulation of Hegel as something seemingly far more modest. And it is here that the work's religious interest, which is sometimes ignored, emerges. Kojève seeks to continue the lessons given by his friend, A. Koyré, before he was forced to abandon his academic obligations. He thus sees in his lessons that the main objective is that of dealing with Hegel's religious philosophy[3] which, in addition to responding to a pragmatic purpose, may be of use to the present author to support the hypothesis of this contribution, to wit, that Kojève's philosophy is defined by a peculiar understanding of Christianity and by a radical inversion of theology.

Kojève is interested in Hegel's religion for reasons of principle or system. First of all, Hegel presented himself initially as a theologian and sought in his early works to carry out a philosophical translation of Christ's teachings[4] before he decided to supplant them in a definitive way by inserting finitude into the center of the Absolute. Secondly, although he does not expressly state it, Kojève's recurring concern with the problem of God, atheism, and death shows that he thought that the dialectic between transcendence and immanence constituted the philosophical question par excellence. Moreover, this concern turns up in his doctoral thesis, in a manuscript that he began in 1931 but subsequently subjected to repeated revisions and rewritings, and which did not surface until decades after his death. In this text, Kojève concludes that mankind, as a being that is "communal" with the world—ultimately, as a *Dasein*—is unable to relate to transcendence.[5] Thirdly and finally, a few years before starting his lessons at the *École des Hautes Études*, Kojève had published his study on Solovyov's theistic metaphysics[6] in detail, and this initial work is also relevant for exploring the extent to which the affirmation of a supreme being seems to him to contradict man's freedom and autonomy, that is to say, the notion of a self-engendering being immersed in history.[7] However, be that as it may, following his initial interest, it would be erroneous to conclude that he regarded religion as something intrinsically relevant: if he deals with it as a subject for study it is because it can be integrated as an inseparable part of Absolute Knowledge.[8]

As we shall show below, the true interlocutor of Kojève's work, his true opponent is not Hegel but Christianity. Only on this basis can it be understood that he turned an exiguous chapter, barely taking up a couple of pages in the canonical edition of Hegel's works, into an exegetical key of Absolute Idealism. This is the Master-Slave dialectic. If he did so, that is because this dialectic not only reflects the struggle for recognition of one man before another, but also the ambition of the human being to set himself up as God. That is to say that Kojève's work reflects the dialectic between his own ideas and Christian principles. My purpose here is therefore to show that Kojève's philosophy takes the form of an inverted Christianity. To this end, I have divided the work into several sections. In the first one, I shall show the relevance of the Master-Slave dialectic and the emergence of the unhappy consciousness. Secondly, I shall highlight the relationship between this consciousness and the notion of anthropogenesis, glimpsing the end of the struggle for recognition in the death of God. Prior to analyzing the end of history, I shall examine what is entailed in the reaffirmation of the negative and the reflection of man as the sole being that can bring about the death of himself. Finally, an epigraph with the conclusions will be added.

DIALECTIC AND RELIGIOUS CONSCIOUSNESS

There is a marked reciprocity between Kojève's famous idea of the end of history and the end of Christianity, as well as between these two events and the conclusion/fulfillment of philosophical knowledge. Hegel would seem to have realized that he could not rid himself of theology until he could do so with philosophy. Within the complex relations between faith and reason, which some authors have identified with the motor of history, Christianity acts as an attenuating factor, unlike other religions, such as the Jewish faith, as long as it does not deviate from a certain orthodoxy. The question here is whether religion and philosophy can coexist.

In opposition to the attempt of Absolute Knowledge to bring about the disappearance of differences, including the duality between subject and object, the separate contribution of theology and philosophy has the effect, within Christian culture, of getting in the way of understanding the unity of the whole.[9] As interpreted by the first Christian thinkers, philosophy remained as a nonknowledge, as a longing, meaning that it attained compatibility with theology thanks to the latter being, in a way, the transcendent consummation of an immanent nonknowledge. What Hegel was able to see, if one examines his thought in greater depth, was that the core of theology includes the possibility of its own disappearance. Therefore, what Hegel, as a philosopher of absolute knowledge, as a sage, one might say, aimed at was to fulfill the promise of wisdom. Indeed, as Kojève points out, placing the overcoming of philosophical knowledge in historical perspective, that is, within the framework of the "Master-Slave" dialectic, "the whole evolution of the Christian World is nothing but a progress toward the atheistic awareness of the essential finiteness of human existence. Only thus, only by 'overcoming,' Christian theology, will Man definitively cease to be a Slave."[10]

Before we go on to unravel Kojève's peculiar understanding of Christianity, it is important to distinguish the two ways of understanding dialectics. This can be conceived in an external, historical way, or from an internal, more anthropological point of view. As per the first approach, God is the Master, with man taking on the role of the slave. Hegel's Master reflects the nature attributed to God by philosophers—more specifically, by Christian philosophers—to such an extent that one could almost say that he amounts to an exact copy. The Master is the Being of pure enjoyment.[11] As such, the Christian faith represents a hindrance: if, as Hegel explains, the slave is historically "liberated" through struggle—that is, through action and work—the advent of Christian teachings shackles the redeemed slave once again, but in an absolute way insofar as it places the Master in transcendence, beyond history and time.[12] Hegel takes on the role of redeemer, of a new Christ: his mission is thus to reopen the path that leads once again to emancipatory self-consciousness, inaugurating the journey of liberation that will make it possible for man to free himself from God, his ultimate master. The relevance that Kojève gives to the past—irrespective of whether it is in accordance with Hegel's intentions or not, which need not trouble us now—is also, to my mind, the main means that he finds to explain the inversion of Christianity which the construction of the Hegel–Kojève system points to, an inversion that, through the force of dialectics, at the same time constitutes the overcoming (*Aufhebung*) of the last form of religion.[13] Emancipation, in any case, takes a very specific form, that of the immanentization of transcendence and the inexorable death of God, since the self-transformation of man into Master puts an end to the dialectic, or to history, which amounts to the same thing.

It is unquestionably Hegel who first caught a glimpse of what atheistic understanding entails, of its roots. This is not a matter of interpreting some of the motifs of contemporary philosophy on the basis of the logic of secularization, as has been done by those who write in the wake of *The Phenomenology of Spirit*. The process is a much deeper one, as what is truly decisive is to become aware both of the fact that the possibility of a finite Absolute requires Christianity's promises being carried out to the fullest extent and of the double face of historical Christianity. The Christian God, its Absolute, constitutes a kind of catalyst: he is an obstacle for liberation (as the Master), but is also the necessary opportunity for the Spirit to successfully turn in on itself and thus close the circle of history. In this sense, Hegel's opinion is revealing, as he holds that religion is the "consciousness of the absolute essence," but not "self-consciousness" as yet.[14] It is not superfluous in this context to remember the various figures under which Hegel develops his philosophy of religion. He devotes himself to this question already in the prescriptive part of the *Phenomenology,* even if later, in his *Lectures on the Philosophy of Religion* he returns to differentiating between philosophy and religion. In the history of religious worldviews, Christianity amounts to as much as an absolute, that is to say, the synthesis between natural or immediate religiousness (in which God is an object) and artistic religion (in which anthropomorphized deities acquire a subjectivity). In the evolution of self-consciousness, the faith in Christ also signifies an advance as it is now an intuition, within the theological sphere, of the unity between subject and object, of immanence and transcendence, which emerges as the end—and the beginning—of the itinerary of the Spirit.

But let us go a little further back. At what point did religion make its appearance? For Hegel—as explained in detail by Kojève—religion constitutes the first appearance of the Absolute, albeit at a lower level: that of representation (*Vorstellung*). But it entails a move toward thought, without being a definitive achievement. As a system of finitude, everything in the Hegel–Kojève approach tends toward transience as well as toward consummation at a later phase. Similarly, religious representation is subject to dialectics, to the three phases of temporality. A differentiation is made, in the first place, between religious conscience in its universality (ancient religiosity), its particularity (Judaism) and the overcoming synthesis, in the unity of the divine and the human, represented by Christianity. Kojève may have first learned of the Christian unity that Hegel captures from reading Solovyov. Whatever the case, in Christianity the substance becomes the subject.[15] Even though it is a representation, what is idiosyncratic about Christianity is the fact that the spirit turns in on itself. Thus, it presupposes both a return and an "anticipation" of the journey of consciousness itself, although it never definitively overcomes alterity and presents itself, as we shall see, as an unhappy consciousness, opening another phase of history.

However, before we go on to consider this last phase, it is worth giving some thought to the subjective experience of the dialectic. Indeed: how does the subject experience the struggle? The "Master–Slave" dialectic is closely connected with unhappy consciousness, since, although Hegel does not make the relationship explicit, the inexorability of the desire for recognition is obvious. By means of the figure of the Unhappy Consciousness, the German thinker confronts the inner duality that entraps subjectivity. The link between the two parts of the *Phenomenology*, which strikes one as extremely important, has gained very little attention from commentators—whether of Hegel or of Kojève—despite the fact that the misfortune of consciousness constitutes both the counterpart of the worldly victory of the Slave against the Master and the means through which this apparently historical dialectic is internalized as a phase of the subjective consciousness itself. According to Kojève's anthropological conception, the desire for recognition urges man, enjoining and goading him into a fight or confrontation against the other consciousness. Unlike the thing, which is consumed as soon as negativity (action) comes its way, the desire that deals with another desire, with another consciousness, is not possible to annihilate in the same way. Such is the fundament of the dualism—the natural desire for a thing, on the one hand, and the human desire for another desire, on the other—with which Kojève believes to contribute to a better understanding of Hegel's system, thinking in parallel to Hegel and beyond Hegel.

We know that the struggle for recognition ends with the victory of the Master, that is, of he who overcomes the fear of death and, thanks to the Slave's intermediation, achieves self-consciousness.[16] The paradox, of which the Master becomes aware when it is too late and cannot be remedied, is that the recognition achieved by the Slave winds up being more objective than the one achieved by the Master. And this is so because the latter is not satisfied by the recognition of those inferior to him. As the Slave has been objectified, instrumentalized by the desire of the Master, it could be said that the recognition the Master obtains from the Slave is ironically none other than that of being recognized by a mere object: for this reason, because it is not the recognition that comes from a self-conscience, the Master's desire for recognition is not based on the Slave. The Master finds himself facing the impossibility of being recognized because he can only obtain recognition if he is recognized by somebody else akin to him, if he ceases to be a Master. He will therefore never be in a position to fulfil his desire. According to Kojève, for this to be a possibility, "he would have to be recognized by another Master. But this is impossible, since—by definition—the Master prefers death to slavish recognition of another's superiority. In short, the Master never succeeds in realizing his end, the end for which he risks his very life."[17]

As we shall see, this is also the case with God, the Master is likewise a factor that contributes to the production of the Slave, of the consciousness that will liquidate him: taking over nature by means of work, also another form of negating action, the Slave will suppress his own servitude, becoming, in the world of work, in that of culture, the absolute Master.

The fundamental difference between the Master and the Slave lies in the possibility in one—and the impossibility in the other—of the truth of independent consciousness, as Hegel points out. In the Slave's position, this is possible, but the Master will never be able to attain it. But let us accept the following: the Slave, by means of his work, is making his way towards the Master's position. Now, does this save the Slave, who has become the Master by virtue of the transforming action of his work, from misfortune? And if this is not the case, then when and why does unhappy consciousness turn up in his case? From the answer to these questions, one must conclude that the dialectic of consciousness and self-consciousness does not definitively conclude with the victory of the Slave and the death of the Master; rather, it undergoes the "unhappy consciousness" phase of the former. This precision is not an idle one and, if I have chosen to dwell on it, it is because it reflects the characteristic form of consciousness of Christianity, following the development of stoicism and skepticism.

Christian religiosity is also devastated by this figure of consciousness. By virtue of its denial, it acknowledges its existence. Christian consciousness is an unhappy consciousness because the split, the verification of the negation makes its appearance in the subject. Hegel specifies this as the consciousness of a "contradiction"[18] since, although it is on the way (*in via*), the unity of the in-itself and the for-itself has not yet been reached in this phase. Unhappiness arises when man understands himself as torn between two worlds (transcendence and immanence) and feels split, as if located at the inexorable crossroads to be found between the changeable and the immutable. Unhappy consciousness is the clear discernment of the disarticulation between the real and the ideal, and Hegel links it closely to the possibility of religion because it postpones the solution of that duality until a transcendent future. According to Kojève, it is at this moment that the human being becomes the Slave of another Master, in this case, of God. Unlike the skeptic, the Christian, the unhappy consciousness, accepts the inner duality, but this is precisely the cause of his unhappiness. According to Kojève, religion is only viable in misfortune and is maintained in it.[19]

SLAVERY OF GOD AND ANTHROPOGENESIS

The unhappy conscience thus transforms the dialectic between Master and Slave, which will no longer be regarded as a confrontation between one consciousness and another, or as a fight, but as a relationship between God and Man. It is here that the decisive key for separating Hegel's understanding of Christianity from Kojève's is to be found. To what extent can Hegel be regarded as the founder of an "atheistic humanism," as Kojève suggests, if Christian theology is the basis of his thought? Be that as it may, the fruit yielded by the figure of unhappy consciousness is the establishment of a link between transcendence and immanence, which is felt within consciousness itself as a break, a duality. It is thus explained by Hegel: "Here, then, we have a struggle against an enemy, victory over whom is rather a defeat, where attainment of the one is rather the loss of it in its contrary. Consciousness of life, of its Being-there and activity, is only grief over this Being-there and activity, for it has in this only the consciousness of its contrary as the essence and of its own nothingness."[20]

But the very consciousness of unhappiness, the verification of its duality, also operates as the agent that motivates overcoming, makes consciousness turn in on itself, after seeing itself reflected in the consciousness of the other. It must be explained, however, how the reconciliation takes place. In order to clarify the path from self-certainty and self-consciousness to the higher sphere of reason, the Phenomenology of Spirit resorts to reviewing the historical forms of religion. First of all, in the Old Testament, conscience is opposed to the singular under the figure of the immutable; secondly, in the mystery of the incarnate God, the singular and the immutable, God and man, are united. Finally, the realm of the Spirit appears. Although it points toward unity, there is still an inner conflict, an apparently insurmountable duality within the framework of religiosity. And man can only free himself from that duality—ultimately, from God—through his action, through struggle or work. If I insist on this explanation, it is because, to my mind, it is apparent here that a faithful reading of the letter of Hegel's text departs, so to speak, from the spirit that informs Kojève's exegesis of Hegel. In Hegel, religion is presented as a gateway to the absolute, in the same way that philosophy is. Although it is clear that, as a contingent figure of consciousness, it inevitably demands to be overcome during the development of the Spirit, religion is already a moment of the Absolute. Even in the form of representation, it is the antechamber or the gateway that leads to science, which is none other than the exposition of Hegel's actual system, the manifestation of its truth. However, Kojève does not read the text in so direct a way, but rather, in keeping with the legacy of left-wing Hegelianism and, specifically, of Marx, he attends to the human dynamics of work, to the contribution of man to the development of historical finitude.

There would thus appear to be two possible interpretations, whose apparent similarity must not lead one to overlook the fact that they have diametrically opposed consequences, as shown, in fact, by the history of reactions to Hegel's philosophy.[21] On the one hand, one might interpret Hegelianism as an attempt to consummate the immanentization of the Absolute, in which case, as an initial step, it could be favorably viewed. But it could also be maintained, as would seem to be the case with Kojève, that the main ambition of Hegel's system is to attend to the progressive humanization of God, to his anthropomorphization, which would confirm Hegel as a strictly atheistic thinker. In accordance with this exegesis, the road to self-consciousness, whose landmarks are gradually achieved thanks to the role played in time by struggle and by work, leads inexorably to an overcoming of transcendence, which is reached in a posthistory anchored in the recognition and acceptance of finitude. Along with the influence of one of Hegel's flanks, Kojève also reveals the influence of the philosophy of V. Solovyov: if Marx turned Hegel on his head, it must be said that Kojève, with their help, thoroughly altered Solovyov's theandric conception, meaning that God is not the Absolute that unifies everything[22]; rather, it is man and his work, as Absolutes, that determine the finite reflection of eternity to which history opens.

Kojève parts company with Hegel—with Hegel's understanding of Christianity—when he accuses him of being insufficiently radical when it comes to accepting the duality between Nature and History. This perception suggests that Hegel is still too much under the influence of theistic prejudices, especially the scheme of Christian theology. Kojève detects a kind of break between the work in which he invests his hermeneutic skills, the *Phenomenology*, and Hegel's subsequent writings, especially the *Encyclopaedia*. It is here, as is well known, that Hegel puts forward the principles of his philosophy of nature—which Kojève finds ludicrous—submitting it to the cosmic concept of time to the detriment of the historical perspective he had so uncontestably inaugurated in his reflections on the trajectory of consciousness.[23] What is obvious is that, if Nature ceases to be something given—the thing that is there—and, like the human sphere, turns into a becoming—in the world of work, of culture, of the artificial—it is mandatory to see God as the subject of the dialectic and that would mean submitting to the idea of a transcendent and creative being. It is undoubtedly this part of his philosophy that is taken into account by those who view Hegel as a theologian, forgetting the duality and the fact that the fight between Master and Slave, as it appears in the Phenomenology, is, as Kojève points out, the premise for a completely atheistic philosophical system.[24]

Although Kojève's philosophy—and even Hegel's[25]—has often been referred to as anthropotheism, it cannot actually be said that man is presented in it as a substitute that takes God's place. This would reduce the radicality of his position and refute what I believe: that Kojève is the thinker who has thought about atheism with the most consistency and rigor, to the point of offering, as opposed to theism, a philosophy of death. The nihilism resulting from the disappearance of the idea of God in the human horizon does not oblige him, in any way, to palliate the lack of meaning of nothingness by means of a spurious replacement for transcendence, or to postulate an immanent paradise, as is typical of political religions.[26] An atheist is not someone who postulates that there is no transcendent entity, but strictly speaking, someone who does not conceive of the possibility of a relationship with it: someone who, ultimately, distances himself from the problem of God because he denies everything that goes beyond the immanent.[27] How does one, in any case, reach such a position of radical acceptance of nihilism, this absolute philosophy of death? In order to better understand the difference of degree that separates Kojève's view from Hegel's, it should be noted that, although Hegel offers an apparently atheistic but surreptitiously theistic philosophy, Kojève detaches Hegelianism from all its theological adherences. Making a literary analogy, which may not have displeased Kojève himself, he could be called the "philosophical Kirillov," since it is indeed this character from *Demons* who best represents the liberation from God, which, as Kojève explains, is simply the possibility of definitively overcoming the fear of death. Thus, the most refined expression of atheism is self-destruction, suicide.

Let us momentarily return to the question of the unhappy conscience. Retrospectively, that is to say, from the position of the wise man who, having settled in posthistory, thinks about the phases that consciousness has gone through on its way to the Absolute, the unhappiness of he who notices the duality between the fleeting and the permanent is the condition of his complete freedom,[28] which brings back the Master-Slave dialectic. There is therefore a coincidence between the emancipation from religion and the attainment of consciousness in anthropogenesis, for self-consciousness and self-creation are terms of reciprocal implication. From this viewpoint, neither Hegel nor Kojève rule out the modern approach, as they both take the modern anthropogenetic project to its ultimate consequences.

The "man of reason," who attains historical existence once the phase of unhappy consciousness is overcome, has no religion because he realizes that the only reality is that which stems from his action, which only manifests itself in the only space-time dimensions that exist: those that are immanent.[29] Pushing into the background or getting rid of the idea of God, an enslaving notion in Kojève's opinion, as explained at the beginning of this contribution, requires the complete transformation of the anthropological conception and a move away from the notion of man, as a given, created being, predestined to a supraterrestrial perfection, to another notion, in which man is a self-created or self-engendered being.

But it is theological knowledge itself actually that, regarding God as the Lord/Master of man, ends up leading inexorably to his liquidation, to his death. Indeed, God is like the Lord who stands above nature, absolutely free, but while he indulges in passive, joyous self-reflection, he finds no consciousness that is equal to him on which to base his lordship. The tragedy of God results from the impossibility of the Absolute to be recognized by another Absolute, from the dissatisfaction with the recognition of a consciousness that is not equal to his, from the misfortune of only being recognized through the human virtue of "piety." Facing this paradoxical situation of the Master, we find man and the anthropogenic capacity of slavery, as well as the emancipatory power of action. What separates God from man is that the former cannot be more but less, while the latter can be more and never less. The Master-Slave dialectic is specified here in another way, another mode: as a struggle between the "humanization of God" and the "divinization of man." Because if, from the viewpoint of Hegel's philosophy, one insists on the parallel process between a God who becomes a man, as in Christianity, and a man who becomes God, this is because herein resides the main or most relevant historical figure of the Master-Slave dialectic. Man manages to rid himself of the weight of the Master—of God—thanks to work: taking over nature through technology, subjugating the natural world, subjecting it to his wishes. It is thus that he reigns afterward as Absolute Master.

Technology implies the overcoming of necessity and work also implies the overcoming of fear or anguish in the face of death, which is one of the factors leading to theism. "Man achieves his true autonomy, his authentic freedom, only after passing through Slavery, after surmounting fear of death by work performed in the service of another (who, for him, is the incarnation of that fear),"[30] says Kojève. The dialectic in which God loses is also the path that Christianity takes toward overcoming itself, toward atheism. Thus, Kojève's conception of Christianity points not only to posthistory, but also to a post-Christian world, as if the mystery of the Incarnation—in which God becomes man—led inevitably to the human overcoming of transcendence. Indeed, as B. Cooper indicates, the movement advances toward atheism, which means that there is a reciprocity between a greater degree of humanization and an increasingly forceful distancing from the supernatural, as Hegel makes clear in his succinct review of the history of religious representations.[31]

For Kojève, therefore, the possibility of living in the world as a truly autonomous and free being—ultimately, as a man—requires overcoming natural necessity and this is achieved through struggle and work. Atheism is the condition of this anthropology. Now, what does the abandonment of transcendence truly imply? According to Kojève's dualism—and taking into account that in his scheme God is a notion that has been overcome in history—what remains is finitude, that is, death and annihilation. From the prism of the fulfilled Absolute, of post-temporality, the history of Christianity is conceived as a continuous progress toward the fulfillment of the freedom gained due to the disappearance of God, whose death is already *in nuce* in the Christian worldview. As I have shown, Christianity is the true interlocutor of Kojève's work and his work aims to overcome the heritage of that faith, down to its latest adherences. This is why I believe it is wrong to understand Kojève's philosophy—and, in fact, Hegel's or, at any rate, Kojève's interpretation of the Hegelian system—as a mere secularization of the Christian eschaton. There is no hint of transcendence: just a finite universe. Kojève's radical atheism carries the impossibility of God to its ultimate consequences. Once again in the manner of Kirillov, Kojève regards nothingness as an absolute absence of being, without substantivizing it, as is common in philosophical reflection and in the most superficial treatments of nihilism.[32] It is thus that, between the lines, he confronts both Christian fideism and secular fideism which, even when abandoning the idea of the afterlife, replaces transcendent redemption with an attainable end in the world. It is apposite here to remember, however much in passing, that the intellectual is the figure of this psuedo-religious movement. "When the Christian becomes a Christian atheist, he remains confined to himself and does not interact. He is disinterested in all kinds of political and social activity."[33] Such an atheism is frivolous—it still being Christian—as it cannot assume the exigencies of finitude. The Revolution, the task that the intellectual is in charge of, is interpreted as a kind of atheistic fulfilment of the Christian dream.

In order to demarcate the figure of the atheist proper and the theist, we have to resort to the different way that both have of facing the inescapable fact of death. Unlike the believer, the atheist has to deal not with something, but with nothing. In the first case, death is the end or the antithesis of life, but for the atheist the opposition of the living is, strictly speaking, nothing. Acquiring a consciousness of mortality is presented as what is terrible; specifically, as the authentically Other, which somehow breaks the familiarity of the Dassein with the world. It is not surprising that this experience of otherness has been the usual path to transcendence since God is the last form to which the human being clings in order to avert death. To be precise, as Kojève rightly points out, the atheist does not deal with death as a step, but with the complete annihilation of his existence. Hence, as with Dostoevsky's character, Kojève can also interpret suicide as a free self-consciousness of finitude, that is, one of the ways in which freedom is expressed.[34]

THE REAFFIRMATION OF THE NEGATIVE

The fulfillment of freedom therefore involves two phases: on the one hand, the freedom of the origin and, on the other hand, the freedom of the end. In the first case, man owes his existence to himself: the initial deicide autonomizes man from the source of the transcendent being as the final phase of the "Master-Slave" dialectic. Once God has been superseded as the Master, man creates himself and creates the world. "To realize Freedom and to live in the World as a human being, autonomous and free-all this is possible only on the condition that one accept the idea of death and, consequently, atheism."[35] In the second case, in relation to the end, man emancipates himself from necessity by killing himself. Thus, as we shall see below, the circle is closed, and the superiority of the human is reaffirmed.

Kojève's dualism yields a key anthropological teaching. Contrary to what happens with other philosophers, anthropogenesis in Kojève's case implies a reaffirmation of the negative. It is on this negativity that "the anthropogenic value of the action"[36] is based. Man is not fulfilled through action, since that would imply a fixed and static nature that would lower the radicality of his free being. Ultimately, it would entail submission to theism, insofar as God appears as the creator. No: anthropogenesis requires that the human being create himself. Before Sartre alluded to the duality between essence and existence and explained that there is nothing defined prior to the latter, Kojève had alluded to the self-objectifying and emancipating consequences of technology. If, from the viewpoint of universal history, the dialectic between Man and God leads to the suppression of transcendence, it is work, struggle that makes self-consciousness possible. Prior to work, prior to technology, there is nothing and, therefore, prior to struggle there is no consciousness that can be known: there is only a pure desire. Technology can be viewed as anthropogenetic to the extent that it is through it that man objectifies himself and, therefore, creates himself. Technology and self-consciousness are thus correlative terms, as well as reciprocal since prior to action there is no self. For contemplation to be possible, the previous step is to interpose a creative act.

Without anthropogenesis, man would not advance toward self-consciousness nor, therefore, toward freedom. In the theistic framework, man submits to a supposedly transcendent superior will and, therefore, remains shackled in its providence. In other words: transcendence, by eliminating negativity, hinders the emergence of the human, whose creation becomes reality through technology, which is, under this prism, no more than the stubborn negation of the given. As a self-creating being, or one advancing toward his self-consciousness, man transcends the natural world and distinguishes himself from the animals. But anthropogenesis claims demand the counterpart of assuming the reality of death. Man is not the only self-created being; he is also, as Kojève himself insists in all his texts, the only being capable of bringing death to himself. Technology and death are the two faces of the reaffirmation of the negative. As a being of negation, man goes beyond what is given. Is there a supreme act of negativity, a determining fact of finitude? That would be the conscious and voluntary decision to kill oneself, which is the most powerful expression of an escape from the force of nature. Otherwise, the absence of God would only be apparent. In order for God to cease to be the "lord of life and death," it is necessary for Man to manifest his superiority over the transcendent Master by means of the negation of the given, which is work. Following the logic of the negative, the greatest act of negation—the greatest act of freedom—is death, as it is the way to completely transcend the horizon of the natural world.[37] When the struggle between the Master and the Slave is studied only at an anthropological level, it is difficult to conclude that history has an end. It is necessary to situate oneself on an anthropotheistic plane, from which it is possible to understand the historical cycle as the unceasing dialectic between Domination and Servitude. From this perspective, if the struggle between Master/God and Slave/Man ends with the triumph of the latter, history comes to an end. What Kojève does in this case is to tell of the victory of man over God as the consummation of time. The end of history—which for Kojève means nothing more than the history of the "working slave"—coincides with self-consciousness because it simultaneously implies the final stage of anthropogenesis: in effect, the fruit of the labor pains of finitude is none other than the victory of finite man over nature.[38]

The end of history, the arrival of the universal and homogeneous state, is possible when the course of action is already declining, which means that its arrival can happen only when the negativity has been cancelled. Thus, the end of history coincides with the suppression of differences: not only is there an annulment of the distinctions between Master and Slave, between Peace and War, but also between all antitheses, because it is the moment of reconciliation and recognition as the stopping of time requires the suppression of the desire for recognition. Ultimately, the end of time occurs not only when the Slave defeats the Lord through work, but also when his liberation is definitive because he becomes the absolute Master. Although Kojève does not consciously make the analogy, the reader cannot help but think of the—divine—satisfaction that overwhelms the First Man of posthistory, the same complacency that the Scripture attributes to God right at the moment of creation: ("And God saw that it was good"). As Kojève points out, "History stops when Man no longer acts in the full sense of the term—that is, when he no longer negates, no longer transforms the natural and social given through bloody Fighting and creative Work."[39] Only when man has taken possession of nature, freeing himself through work and struggle, does his own being transmute into the world, since he attains the quality of divine life, in accordance with which he abandons action and begins to contemplate himself. The end of history coincides with the civilization of technology because this implies the absolute submission of the natural given; it is the liquidation of dualism through the struggle of man against the environment and against those around him. It requires, in order to carry the argument to its ultimate consequences, the recognition of man by nature, a recognition that is expressed in the use he makes of it.

But what does reflective knowledge consist of? It is upon that knowledge about oneself—in that anthropology[40]—that Kojève bases wisdom, the knowledge of the whole that is achieved once history has been consummated and the difference between Subject and Object has disappeared. In reality, knowledge about oneself is knowledge of one's own self-genesis through action: Revelation therefore coincides with history. What is involved here is, in short, the absolutization of man, the identification of man with God, since in this way knowing about the absolute is not extrinsic to him, but rather it is his own being, his own process of generation: his self-engendering. Within this context, the specific way of understanding the move of history from the flank of knowledge brings us back to the theme of overcoming philosophy, with which we began. On the other hand, without the postulation of the Absolute in Immanence, it would not be possible to conceptualize the end of history, as Christian theology shows. The philosophical and theological implications are, at this point, important because they require, as Kojève knew well, the circularity of the system, as opposed to the notion of a linear time course. It has been said that the consciousness of historicity penetrates when the pagan cyclical time is called into question by the futurity opened by Judeo-Christian culture.[41] Kojève realizes, in fact, that a present can only be historical in relation to the future—specifically, as the Russian thinker explains, as long as the future enters in the present not immediately, but through the past, through an action.[42] It is obvious that the structure of Christian historicity entails the most successful embodiment of this conception, insofar as the Second Coming (Parousia) is the event par excellence, mediated by the First Coming (Incarnation). An intelligence as insightful and profound as Kojève's could not overlook any of this, and he fully realized that the culmination of history required not only accepting finitude, but the reflexivity of temporal consciousness; the return, thus, to a circular conception.

This does not mean, however, that man abandons himself to the relaxation of time or mitigates the possibilities of his action. On the contrary, taking circularity and anthropogenesis together, the awareness of finitude leads to a serious existence. "Because man dies fully and completely, with no 'afterlife' and no 'Beyond' where failures 'here below' could be redeemed, his actual participation in History is serious. Man alone, through his free individual acts, creates History, and he alone looks on, knowing he may fail, knowing he must die."[43] Finitude sharpens one's involvement in life and magnifies or ennobles the technical world to the point that man is compelled to exhaust all the possibilities available to him. That is why temporality can end, when further developments are no longer possible: "If, as Hegel argued, the end of History means human satisfaction, one can say that, by understanding fully his own death, and thereby knowing himself to be a free, historical individual, man becomes conscious of a self that has no desire to become other than as it is [. . .] history is over."[44]

DEATH AND INVERSION OF CHRISTIANITY

Marxist philosophy is usually interpreted as an inversion of Hegelianism, since Marx places the processes of reproduction and material life there where Hegel enhances the Spirit. Rather than by virtue of his relationship with Hegel, from what we have seen, we should choose to study Kojève's work as the radical inversion of Christianity, if only because of the obvious antithesis found between Christianity's appeal to redemption and the understanding of suicide as the supreme act of freedom. From this perspective, the true anti-Christian thinkers are neither Marx nor Nietzsche,[45] but the Russian philosopher who, paradoxical as this may seem, left his deepest reflections on the paradoxical end of the human verification of finitude unpublished. Kojève was able to think so radically about the demands of atheism thanks to his detailed theological knowledge and his familiarity with the most decisive problems of the Christian faith. More specifically, what left him intellectually dissatisfied was the contradiction between contingency and necessity. As he explains in his dissertation on Solovyov, it is difficult to speak of human freedom if, at the same time, one predicts the future of a redeemed humanity (or theo-humanity). Somehow this "religious" interest aroused by the compatibility between freedom and determination is also present in his interest in contemporary physics. In Kojève those interests are synthesized in his inclination for Hegelian philosophy, where he sees a solution to that paradox.[46]

As we have seen, then, the whole of Kojève's philosophy, as suggested at the beginning of these pages, could be interpreted both as a settling of scores with Christianity and as its most elaborate inversion. For the inversion of Christianity is, in Kojève, the way to put an end to that heritage. It is here that the teacher (Hegel) parts company from his disciple. Before concluding, let us summarize what has been stated. Kojève proposes a philosophy of radical finitude, both against Christianity's characteristic affirmation of transcendence and against the efforts to immanentize transcendence. Contrary to what is proposed by Christianity, which only redeems historicity in the afterlife, Kojève liquidates the passage of time by placing the moment of its definitive conclusion within history itself. From an anthropological point of view, Kojève conceives the desire for recognition as an anthropogenetic mechanism, meaning that, in his system, the idea of creation is superfluous. The end of history is not only self-consciousness, it does not even refer exclusively to the complete satisfaction of necessity, but rather, it constitutes the fruit of the combination of anthropogenesis and radical finitude. Finally, by conceiving suicide as the supreme act of freedom, Kojève puts an end to Christian hope. It is not paradoxical in any case that death should be the destiny of the satisfied man who has completed the cycle of history: the wise man is not he who has won in the struggle for recognition, but the slave who has had no choice but to lose his fear of death in order to overcome the complacent Master. If Kojève defined man as the animal that knows that he is going to die, going one step further, we can conclude that the wise man is he who fulfills the supreme ideal of freedom, suicide, evading the force of the natural given.

NOTES

1. G. W. Hegel, *The Phenomenology of Spirit* (Oxford: Oxford University Press, 2018), 5.

2. Alexandre Kojève, *Introduction à la lecture de Hegel* (Paris: Gallimard, 1968), 99.

3. Kojève, *Introduction à la lecture de Hegel*, 57.

4. G. W. F. Hegel, G. W. F., *Life of Jesus* (Manchester: University of Manchester Press, 1981), *passim*.

5. Alexandre Kojève, *Atheism* (New York: Columbia University Press, 2018), 29.

6. Alexander, Kojève, *The Religious Metaphysics of Vladimir Solovyov* (New York: Palgrave Pilot, 2019).

7. Vladimir Solovyov, *Lectures on Divine Humanity* (London: Lindisfarne Books, 1995).

8. Kojève, *Introduction à la lecture de Hegel*, 58.

9. Ibid., 515.

10. Alexander Kojève, *Introduction to the Reading of Hegel* (Ithaca and London: Cornell University Press, 1980), 57.

11. Kojève, *Atheism*, 66–67.

12. Ibid., 182–183.

13. Kojève, *Introduction à la lecture de Hegel*, 213.

14. Kojève, *Atheism*, 268.

15. Ibid., 295.

16. Kojève, *Introduction à la lecture de Hegel*, 22.

17. Kojève, *Introduction to the Reading of Hegel*, 46.

18. Hegel, *The Phenomenology of Spirit*, 82.

19. Kojève, *Introduction à la lecture de Hegel*, 67.

20. Hegel, *The Phenomenology of Spirit*, 87.

21. Vincent Descombes, *Le même et l'autre. Quarante-cinq ans de philosophie française (1933–1978)* (Paris: Editions de Minuit, 1979), 21.

22. Frederik Copleston, *Philosophy in Russia. From Herzen to Lenin and Berdyaev* (Notre Dame: University of Notre Dame Press, 1986), 221.

23. Kojève, *Introduction à la lecture de Hegel*, 378.

24. Ibid., 575.

25. Karl Löwith, *From Hegel to Nietzsche* (New York: Columbia University Press, 1991), 31.

26. Eric Voegelin, *Science, politics and Gnosticism. Two Essays* (Washington DC: Regnery, 1968), 35.

27. Kojève, *Atheism*, 20.

28. Kojève, *Introduction à la lecture de Hegel*, 72–73.

29. Ibid., 75.

30. Kojève, *Introduction to the Reading of Hegel*, 27.

31. Barry Cooper, *The End of History. An Essay on Modern Hegelianism* (Toronto: University of Toronto Press, 1984), 179.

32. Kojève, *Atheism*, 4.

33. Kojève, *Introduction à la lecture de Hegel*, 108.

34. Kojève, *Atheism*, 85.

35. Kojève, *Introduction to the Reading of Hegel*, 57.

36. Kojève, *Introduction à la lecture de Hegel*, 65.

37. Ibid., 566.

38. Kojève, *Introduction à la lecture de Hegel*, 18.

39. Kojève, *Introduction to the Reading of Hegel*, 191.

40. Kojève is talking about theology here, but does not overlook the fact that it is a very particular theology, because his God is the sage. However, it is really an

anthropology. If I have chosen this term, it is because it gives more clarity to the finite horizon within which the progress towards the end of history moves. In keeping with this interpretation, it has been said, for instance, that Kojève "De façon generale, Kojeve a donné une *version anthropologique* de la philosophie hegelienne" (Descombes).

41. Eric Voegelin, *Hitler and the Germans* (Columbia, MO: Missouri University Press, 1999), 70.

42. Kojève, *Introduction à la lecture de Hegel*, 369.

43. Cooper, *The End of History*, 74.

44. Ibid.

45. Karl Jaspers, *Nietzsche and Christianity* (Washington DC: Regnery, 1961).

46. James H. Nichols, *Alexandre Kojève. Wisdom and the End of History* (New York: Rowman, 2007), 11.

BIBLIOGRAPHY

Copleston, Frederik. *Philosophy in Russia. From Herzen to Lenin and Berdyaev.* Notre Dame: University of Notre Dame Press, 1986.

Cooper, Barry. *The End of History. An Essay on Modern Hegelianism.* Toronto: University of Toronto Press, 1984

Descombes, Vincent. *Le même et l' autre. Quarante-cinq ans de philosophie française (1933–1978).* Paris: Editions de Minuit, 1979

Hegel, G. W. F. *Life of Jesus.* Manchester: University of Manchester Press, 1981.

———. *The Phenomenology of Spirit.* Oxford: Oxford University Press, 2018.

Jaspers, Karl. *Nietzsche and Christianity.* Washington D.C: Regnery, 1961.

Kojève, Alexandre. *Introduction à la lecture de Hegel.* Paris: Gallimard, 1968.

———. *Introduction to the Reading of Hegel.* Ithaca and London: Cornell University Press,1980.

———. *Atheism.* New York: Columbia University Press,2018.

———. *The Religious Metaphysics of Vladimir Solovyov.* New York: Palgrave Pilot, 2019.

Lowith, Karl. *From Hegel to Nietzsche.* New York: Columbia University Press, 1991.

Nichols, James H. *Alexandre Kojève. Wisdom and the End of History.* New York: Rowman, 2007.

Solovyov, Vladimir. *Lectures on Divine Humanity.* London: Lindisfarne Books, 1995.

Voegelin, Eric. *Science, Politics and Gnosticism. Two Essays.* Washington, DC: Regnery, 1968.

———. *Hitler and the Germans.* Columbia, MO: Missouri University Press.,1999.

Chapter Four

History and Nothingness

*Kojève's Re-Leveraging of
Hegel's Dialectic of Freedom*

Waller R. Newell

I

Alexandre Kojève's reading of Hegel was originally influential among North American political theorists largely because of his debate with Leo Strauss regarding the meaning of modern tyranny and totalitarianism.[1] Today, now that interest in Strauss has been growing in Europe, a new generation of scholars is thinking about Kojève as well. I have argued elsewhere why I believe that Strauss did not agree with Kojève's interpretation of Hegel but assumed it to be true for the sake of argument in a single work, *On Tyranny*, where he referred to it pointedly as "Kojève's Hegel."[2] While I will summarize the main points of that argument as part of a concluding attempt to assess the general significance of Kojève's theoretical enterprise, my main purpose in this essay is not to revisit them at length. Instead, I want to emphasize some important differences between Kojève's transformation of Hegel and Hegel's own teaching that help to illuminate what Hegel was actually arguing. In particular, I want to stress that although Kojève's interpretation of Hegel is heavily Marxist-driven, it contains a dimension of Martin Heidegger's ontology of Being that is less directly evident, but which enables Kojève to create a new hybrid version of Hegel's historicism and its Marxist underpinning.

The key to understanding how Kojève's interpretation of Hegel departs from the Hegelian original is the centrality that he assigns to the Master-Slave dialectic, identifying it as the origin of man's negation and transformation of nature in the pursuit of freedom.[3] In reality, that encounter occupies a brief few pages well along into the *Phenomenology of Spirit*, is not identified by Hegel as being centrally important, and is arguably no more than, if as important as, the motif of the Unhappy Consciousness with which this section of the book ends. Indeed, in my view, the internalization of the Master-Slave encounter within the Unhappy Consciousness as the inner calling from God (the true Lord) to his servant man constitutes for Hegel a deepening and sublimation of self-consciousness that transcends the merely outward struggle between Master and Slave.

Moreover, this whole sequence of "shapes"—Master, Slave, Stoic, Skeptic, Unhappy Consciousness—is presented by Hegel at this stage in the *Phenomenology of Spirit* as still largely from within the viewpoint of "consciousness," in other words, from the perspective of the modern Cartesian self that assumes the priority of the individual and the distinction between the self and the other. After the full sweep of history has been introduced with the appearance of Spirit roughly halfway through the book, Hegel takes us back through the same sequence of shapes, but now within the broader context of the society and religion of the ancient polis, and culminating in the late Roman Empire. Hegel is explicit that this second account of the sequence of shapes is the fuller one, because the opposed selves of the earlier sequence are now thoroughly contextualized within the realm of the political community and customary ethical being (*Sittlichkeit*): "Earlier we saw the Stoical independence of pure thought pass through Scepticism and find its truth in the Unhappy Consciousness. . . . If this knowledge appeared then merely as the one-sided view of consciousness as consciousness, here the actual truth of that view has become apparent."[4] In Hegel's cumulative presentation, the "Master" morality, properly considered, was never literally reducible to that of an individual self, but emerged as a complex of communal historical forces from ancient Greek religion and society.

Kojève argues that, for Hegel, history progresses through the Slave, but this is by no means clear in Hegel's works. In the *Phenomenology of Spirit*, the first historical appearance of "freedom"—as opposed to the mere "independence" of the Master—comes not with the Slave, but with Stoicism, in many ways an aristocratic morality. Finally, for Hegel, modern man is not, as Kojève argues, simply a synthesis of Master and Slave as the Bourgeois, but of the entire "wealth of shapes" including Master, Slave, Stoic, Skeptic, and Unhappy Consciousness, an amalgam that is crystallized in the nineteenth-century cultural battle between science and Romanticism, or between Kant (the internalization of Jacobinism) and Goethe or Schiller (the Beautiful Soul)—a battle that will, once sublimated within Spirit, usher in the reappearance of God in History in a new era of mutual forgiveness.

Of course, in fairness to Kojève, he never claimed to be attempting to understand Hegel as Hegel understood himself, but is propounding a new reading for altered historical conditions in the twentieth century that might arguably make Hegel's philosophy more consistent with itself, by banishing the mystification of the concept of Spirit and replacing it with the historical action of man. That is a plausible rereading, but clearly a Left Hegelian or Marxist-derived one.

Kojève writes as if man is the "nihilator" in history, rather than Spirit—Hegel's name for the whole, which contains within itself, as "the labor of the negative," the transformative and destructive energy of historical creation actualized through its human avatars. Kojève, we might say, combines the reductionist materialism of Marx with the historical and cultural breadth of Hegel. Kojève sees sheer "nothingness" as the continuing historical essence of man, whereas for Hegel, history's accumulated "wealth of shapes" has enriched us teleologically through Bildung. Kojève in effect borrows the "nothingness" of Heidegger's concept of Dasein, the only being, as Heidegger argued in *Being and Time* directly touched by the innermost character of all Being: that it is not any fixed thing, that it "is" nothing or sheer finitude. But whereas Heidegger employed this concept to argue that, in its bottomless nothingness, Dasein could never be "filled up" by a doctrine of the progress of history like that of Hegel, Kojève maintains that this innermost nothingness is the very engine of historical progress itself.

For Kojève, the progress of history is purely anthropocentric, borrowing, as I have suggested, the nothingness of Dasein from Heidegger but uprooting it from any larger connection with Being (or with Hegelian Spirit). For Heidegger, the "notness" (*Nichtigkeit*) of Dasein is where Being as such touches human existence and radiates through it into a historical "clearing" through the reciprocal encounter between Dasein and Sein.[5] Kojève, however, turns Dasein into nothing more than a human subject, filling his inner void through the outward and literal conquest of nature. In an analogous manner, Spirit in its indeterminateness was for Hegel the source of our capacity to negate nature in the pursuit of freedom. But for Hegel, at bottom, the labor of the negative is not primarily human labor, but rather the subjective pole of Spirit (whose Concept is expressed as the unity of Subject and Substance), that is, "the Truth" about the whole that operates through its human avatars, progressively transforming the world as Spirit's own odyssey of self-actualization.

For Kojève, in stark contrast, man alone negates the sheer inert fodder of nature. Kojève identifies man with "self-consciousness," by which he means an individual human subject. It is man, initially the Slave, who creates history, art, and culture, including "ideologies" like Hegelian Spirit itself that legitimize the bourgeois status quo. But for Hegel, Spirit alone is truly self-conscious, progressively so as history unfolds teleologically—at bottom, the self of which I as a human being am conscious is the self-consciousness of Spirit operative through me. For Hegel, Spirit's longing for reconciliation (the Substance pole of the unity of Subject and Substance) and the negation of nature (the Subject pole of that interaction) operate in tandem through man, bringing about both greater freedom and greater harmony as history evolves, for Kojève, history is entirely an outward, positivistic, aggressive, and uniquely human transformation. In fact, I would argue that Kojève's closest philosophical cousin is not Hegel at all, but Fichte, the ultimate proponent of man's untrammeled will to conquer and reshape nature, with man, whose essence is will-power, having no intrinsic connection to nature itself, which is nothing more than "the material of our moral duty rendered sensuous." Hegel believed that his own ontology of the unity of Subject and Substance in Spirit had anticipated and headed off at the pass this voluntaristic extremism, which also fed the Jacobin tendency in modern politics to impose a rational pattern on human nature by direct action and revolutionary will, regardless of the constraints of precedent and tradition. As Fichte was to Jacobinism, so might we say Kojève was to Stalinism.

Perhaps the most fundamental divergence between Kojève's interpretation of Hegel and Hegel's own thought is over the status of revelation. In Hegel's formulation of the concept of Spirit in the preface to the *Phenomenology of Spirit*, under the pole of Subject is located the modern project for the conquest of nature, modern science and political liberalism, culminating in Kant's ethic of individual moral autonomy. Under the pole of Substance is located the contrary longing for reconciliation, love, beauty, community, and harmony between man and man and man and the world, characteristic of classical thought, but also including religious revelation, and culminating in Spinoza. The realms of Subject and Substance also crystallize respectively as "morality" (typified by Rousseau's General Will and Kant's Categorical Imperative) and communal or ethical being (*Sittlichkeit*), beginning with the chthonic and Olympian gods of the Greek polis. The conflict in Greek tragedy between the divine law of the gods and the human law of burgeoning philosophic rationality and universality is the first historical actualization of the interplay between Subject and Substance within the whole of Spirit. The divine law of the old hearth religion and "the community of the dead" is the welling up and evolution of "life" out of mere nature into the divine law, buttressing Strauss's criticism of Kojève for failing to realize that by "life" Hegel meant much more than the modern understanding of nature as matter in motion—it is more akin to the life-world of Spinoza. The welling up of "life" as the oldest chthonic religion of the ancestors displays a continuous evolution from nature into civilization. For Kojève, by contrast, the realm of the divine law and family life is nothing more than "biological" existence as an alien other pitted against the emergent rationalism of historical progress through the negation of nature. For Hegel, Spirit expresses itself both as the Divine Law and the Human Law. For Kojève, reason, actualized as the negation of nature, is exclusively on the side of the latter.

In my view, there is no way of establishing with certainty what kind of believer Hegel was. But there is no evidence at all for Kojève's characterization of his philosophy as atheistic. While Hegel's Christianity may have been a kind of deism or pantheism that was not in keeping with any traditional understanding of revelation, neither is it the case that, as Kojève asserts, "according to Hegel—to use the Marxist terminology—Religion is only an ideological superstructure that is born and exists solely in relation to a real superstructure," that is, a mere ideological justification for the class-based pursuit of power. Not only, as we earlier observed, is the religious deepening symbolized by the Unhappy Consciousness arguably more important for human development than the Master/Slave encounter over the conquest of nature, but the *Phenomenology of Spirit* as a whole culminates in a genealogy of religion from the most distant past down to the present. The way forward, in other words, is the way back—"God manifested" in History. The Marxist reductionism of Kojève's approach, reducing the realm of "life" to mere biological and physical stuff, is nowhere more evident than here.

One way of grasping the concept of Spirit, as I suggested earlier, is that into the lifeworld of Spinoza, emerging continuously out of nature toward the aspects of Godhead, and thus repudiating the dualism of Hobbes and Descartes, Hegel introduces the aggressive dimension of progressive historical transformation, the injection of "the labour of the negative" into Schelling's quietistic Spinoza-inspired "Absolute." Finally, whereas for Hegel, history fulfills itself as an irreducible plurality of distinct nation-states with their variety of windows on the world through their diverse educational cultures, the "foaming forth" of the Spinozist Kingdom of Spirits in Schiller's Ode to Joy with which the *Phenomenology of Spirit* upliftingly ends, Kojève forecasts an Orwellian coming world dystopian society of pedestrian materialism and uniform psychological emptiness ruled by a global tyrant, the Universal Homogeneous State—a variation, we might say, of Heidegger's understanding of the unstoppable spread of global technology, but without regrets.

II

Having traced Kojève's distinctive hybrid of Marx and Heidegger, let us now ask: How might one assess the over-all impact of Kojève's legacy? One way is to compare his thought with that of Georg Lukacs, who lived through roughly the same time period and witnessed some of the same political upheavals. Both were in the left-Hegelian camp, continuing what Feuerbach and Marx had begun. Both responded to the increasing bourgeoisification of the industrial proletariat—and therefore the disappearance of its potentially revolutionary character—with attempts to reinvigorate radical anticapitalist historicism. The Great Depression rekindled hopes for a proletarian uprising, but not for long—both liberal-democratic and fascist regimes employed monetarist mechanisms for redistributing income through massive public works projects so as to forestall a worker's rebellion.

The two men responded to what Kolakowski termed the predicament of "Marxism without a proletariat" in different ways. Like Kojève, Lukacs drew upon Hegel and Heidegger to enrich the Marxist understanding of history and to expand the meaning of modern alienation beyond the socioeconomic to include the psychological and aesthetic.[6] Lukacs became a Leninist dedicated to achieving socialism from above through a Vanguard Party of ideologues, building the productivity levels of capitalism through rapid industrialization and collectivization but without capitalistic profit or liberal bourgeois individual rights. He drew upon elements of Nietzschean Will to Power and Heideggerian "resolve" to turn the concept of the Party into a kind of collective of Supermen who would rebuild the world from scratch, absolutely unlimited by external, natural, or inherited conditions.[7] Ironically, he was called out by Lenin over this radical voluntarism on grounds of doctrinal purity for ignoring the objective "laws" of economic development proclaimed by orthodox Marxism, but in truth he was the theoretical distillation of Leninism itself. For in political reality none other than Lenin had abandoned the objective laws of socioeconomic development prescribed by Marx and gave history a sharp nudge to stage the Bolshevik coup, skipping the bourgeois stage of history.

While drawing upon Hegel for a historical, psychological, and cultural depth lacking in Marx as sources for a critique of the bourgeois capitalist order, Lukacs followed Marx to the letter in identifying the future with a world socialist order, not Hegel's emphasis on the nation-state. Kojève took a very different approach, perhaps reflective of the fact that Lukacs had been a real-life revolutionary actor (a commissar of the short-lived Hungarian Soviet Republic of 1919) while Kojève was a career civil servant in France. While Kojève also departed from Hegel's identification of the nation-state with the end of history and followed Marx in envisioning a new global order. It was not a socialist order in the Marxist sense, but a universal society in which the ideologies of capitalism and socialism would both fade away, a society in which an absolute state guaranteed everyone recognition of their equality and, through modern economic productivity, gratify their pedestrian desires and give them the leisure to beautify or adorn their private lives through the perfection of surface style (the BoBo snobbery of "Japanization"). The sense in which all previous ideological and regime distinctions would fade away in the Universal Homogeneous State was captured by his reportedly favorite saying of Heidegger, that as spearheads of global technology, America and Russia were "metaphysically the same." But even though both capitalism and communism were twin spearheads of the same process of global technology that would usher in the UHS and their own liquidation, temperamentally he favored the Soviet alternative, I believe because of its candor and lack of any kind of bourgeois window-dressing about morality and freedom characteristic of the capitalist powers in its ambition to transform the environment through rapid and ruthless industrial expansion. He remarked that he wept like a child the day he learned Stalin was dead. And it came to light in later years that, as a high-ranking civil servant, he passed information to the Soviets that may or may not have risen to the level of treason, but which certainly reflected his wish that America not outpace its main superpower competitor.

Kojève became known to my generation of Straussian political theorists through his famous debate with Leo Strauss on the character of modern tyranny and its rootedness or lack thereof in its ancient antecedents. These included my mentors Allan Bloom and Stanley Rosen, who, notwithstanding their profound admiration for Kojève, never equated Kojève's interpretation of Hegel with the proper understanding of Hegel. However, a number of my Straussian contemporaries, it is fair to say, tended to treat Kojève as a crib for Hegel, as if by reading *Introduction to the Reading of Hegel* they could skip reading Hegel's *Phenomenology of Spirit* or at least disregard other readings. Because of my own exposure to Emil Fackenheim's reading of Hegel, which stressed its religious dimension, and that of Kenneth Schmitz and Karsten Harries, which stressed its metaphysical core as the dialectic of Spirit, I never believed this, although I certainly recognized Kojève's thought as a brilliant appropriation of Hegel. On a psychological level it can perhaps be explained by Straussians feeling relieved that someone of Kojève's stature took Strauss so very seriously, enabling them to bask in a wider aura of intellectual acknowledgment than they were sometimes afforded.

It was in giving into this perhaps understandable sentiment, however, that my Straussian confreres overlooked two things. To reiterate: Kojève never claimed to be attempting to understand Hegel as he understood himself, the key Straussian hermeneutical principal. He was quite explicit that he was deconstructing and releveraging Hegel's thought to make its premises more consistent with themselves in light of the changed conditions of the twentieth century, especially by dismantling Hegel's concept of a transcendental historical dialectic and relocating the power to negate nature and advance freedom squarely in the hands of human actors. They also sometimes appeared to forget that Strauss disagreed with Kojève, that they had a debate, including over Kojève's interpretation of Hegel. As I have argued at length elsewhere, Strauss accepted Kojève's interpretation only for the purpose of that one debate, carefully distinguishing it as "Kojève's Hegel" because of his clear repudiation of it in his other writings, where he stressed Hegel's centrality to the "great counter-movement" sparked by German historicism against Cartesian rational individualism, credited Hegel with restoring the richness of "natural consciousness" as opposed to modern contentless rationalism as the starting point for making sense of human experience, and also credited him with restoring the study of religion to its central place in philosophy. According to Strauss, so far was Hegel's system from being atheistic, as Kojève argued, that no one had ever understood Aristophanes so profoundly as the apogee of the "art religion" of the ancient Greeks, while at the same time unambiguously asserting the superior status of "revealed religion" to even that ancient high point. He also criticized Kojève in a letter for jettison-ing Hegel's voluminous Philosophy of Nature, correctly arguing that without the teleological processes that Hegel found latent in nature before history began, the negation of nature by human freedom would have been hopelessly solipsistic, with no objective ground or basis beyond the positivism of its own anthropocentric historical domination. This points, again, to the subterranean Fichtean undertow in Kojève's appropriation of Hegel, specifically to Fichte's dismissal of nature as mere material fodder for untrammeled negation.

Ironically, despite the fundamental disagreements between Strauss and Kojève over the meaning of Hegel's philosophy, the legacy of Kojève reached perhaps its greatest celebrity through its adaptation by Francis Fukuyama in his famous essay and subsequent book claiming that the defeat of the Soviet Empire by the United States and the West amounted to Hegel's "end of his-tory" as explained by Kojève. Majid Yar captures the tenor of Fukuyama's argument very well, arguing that Fukuyama correctly sees Kojève's UHS as one in which "there are no more battles to be fought, no more experiments in social engineering to be attempted; the world has arrived at a homog-enized state . . . "[8] According to Yar, Fukuyama also correctly observes that in Kojève's view the capitalist economic system had triumphed in providing "the satisfaction of material human needs," and that "consumerism and the commodity" form "the primary mechanism for the provision of recogni-tion and values," presenting "the means by which recognition is mediated." Summing up the peculiar dystopian vision of Kojève's UHS, he writes: "Humans desire to be valued by others, and the means of appropriating that valuation is the appropriation of the things that others themselves value; hence lifestyle and fashion become the mechanisms of mutual esteem in a post-historical world . . . " Yar also argues that Fukuyama presents "a tri-umphal vindication of Kojève's supposedly prescient thesis that history has found its end in the global triumph of capitalism and liberal democracy"; that at the end of history, according to Fukuyama's take on Kojève, "the combination of capitalism and liberal democracy will reign supreme, and all other cultural and ideological systems will be consigned irretrievably to the past" in a "post-historical world governed by the logic of capitalist individualism."

This is an accurate depiction of what Fukuyama meant by Hegel's vision of the end of history filtered through Kojève. But in my view Fukuyama's understanding of the end of history constitutes an erroneous interpretation of both Hegel and Kojève. In truth, just as Kojève's interpretation of Hegel was (knowingly) a distortion of Hegel, Fukuyama's interpretation of Kojève was (I assume unknowingly) a distortion of Kojève, while at the same time, because he identified Kojève's Hegel with the truth about Hegel's teaching, a further distortion of Hegel as well. In other words, Fukuyama's Hegel was a distortion of a distortion. As Yar correctly relates, Fukuyama identified the end of history with the triumph of Lockean liberalism, individualism, and free markets over the ideology of communism. But in complete contrast with Fukuyama, Kojève had actually argued that the emergence of the end of history as the UHS would mean the eradication of both liberal and communist ideology, of both the capitalist and communist economic systems, along with their respective national hosts—the hammer and sickle would be put into mothballs at the same time as the Stars and Stripes. Kojève did not envision the end of history as a combination of liberalism and capitalism in a world governed by the logic of capitalist individualism, but instead their "withering away," to use Marx's famous formulation, along with their communist competitor.

In any event, the belief in the end of history, however one construed it, proved to be a brief celebration as the champagne was popped in front of the Berlin Wall in 1989 to the strains of Beethoven's "Ode to Joy," at least an indirect homage to the *Phenomenology of Spirit*. It was rapidly overtaken by events as the defeat of the Soviet empire proved not to spell the end of international conflict and ideological warfare but their intensification, as the national, ethnic, and religious minorities that the Soviet system falsely claimed to have been pacified by the brutal secularization of their tyranny—equally directed at religious faith and nationalistic "chauvinism"—re-emerged as vigorous as ever once the iron grip of communist rule was relaxed, revalorized as what Michael Ignatieff termed "road warrior" tribalism and sectarian religious violence, recrudescing again today as an increasingly worldwide conflict between "populism" and "global elitism." These are all forces and contradictions that Kojève would have readily recognized, and the historical jury is still out on whether his alternative to them—a new variation of the struggle between Masters and Slaves culminating in the UHS—will eventually prevail after all, and whether that will be to humankind's benefit or to its spiritual detriment.

NOTES

1. Leo Strauss, *On Tyranny* (Chicago: University of Chicago Press, 2000).
2. Waller R. Newell, "Kojève's Hegel, Hegel's Hegel, Strauss's Hegel: A Middle Range Approach to the Debate about Tyranny and Totalitarianism," in *Philosophy, History and Tyranny: Reexamining the Debate between Leo Strauss and Alexandre Kojève,* ed. Timothy Burns (Albany: SUNY Press, 2016).
3. Alexandre Kojève, *Introduction to the Reading of Hegel,* trans. Nichols (New York: Basic Books, 1969).
4. G.W.F. Hegel, *The Phenomenology of Spirit,* trans. Miller (Oxford: Oxford University Press), sec. 483.
5. Martin Heidegger, *Being and Time,* trans. Macquarrie (New York: Harper and Row, 1962).
6. Georg Lukacs, *History and Class Consciousness,* trans. Livingstone (Cambridge, MA: MIT Press, 1972).
7. Waller R. Newell, "Philosophy and the Perils of Commitment: A Comparison of Lukacs and Heidegger," *History of European Ideas,* 9 (1988).
8. Majid Yar, "Alexandre Kojève (1902–1968)," *Internet Encyclopedia of Philosophy,* https:iep.utm.edu.

BIBLIOGRAPHY

Hegel, G.W.F. *The Phenomenology of Spirit,* translated by James Miller. Oxford: Oxford University Press,1979.
Heidegger, Martin. *Being and Time,* translated by John Macquarrie. New York: Harper and Row, 1962.
Kojève, Alexandre. *Introduction to the Reading of Hegel,* translated by James Nichols. New York: Basic Books, 1969.
Lukacs, Georg. *History and Class Consciousness,* translated by Rodney Livingstone. Cambridge, MA: MIT Press, 1972.
Newell, Waller R. "Kojève's Hegel, Hegel's Hegel, Strauss's Hegel: A Middle Range Approach to the Debate about Tyranny and Totalitarianism." In *Philosophy, History and Tyranny: Reexamining the Debate Between Leo Strauss and Alexandre Kojève,* edited by Timothy Burns. Albany, SUNY Press, 2016.
———. "Philosophy and the Perils of Commitment: A Comparison of Lukacs and Heidegger." *History of European Ideas,* 9: 1988.
Strauss, Leo. *On Tyranny.* Chicago: University of Chicago Press, 2000.
Yar, Majid. "Alexandre Kojève (1902–1968)." *Internet Journal of Philosophy.* https: iep.utm.edu.

Chapter Five

Kojève and Marx

Elusive Affinities and Divergences

Igor Shoikhedbrod

Alexandre Kojève is usually regarded, by proponents and detractors alike, as a thoroughgoing Marxist, whose famous lectures on Hegel helped lay the groundwork for an existentialist Marxism that influenced such notable figures as Jean-Paul Sartre and Maurice Merleau-Ponty. Kojève's Marxism is routinely attributed to his militant atheism, his concern with nature and desire, and, most notably, his emphasis on the struggle for recognition, which receives its clearest expression in Hegel's account of the Master-Slave dialectic in the *Phenomenology of Spirit*.[1] Kojève helped popularize the view that Marx's treatment of estranged labor and his account of class struggle were inspired by Hegel's Master-Slave dialectic. With some notable exceptions, few Marx scholars have examined the veracity of Kojève's interpretive claims or his Marxist commitments. This chapter takes as its point of departure the elusive affinities and divergences between Kojève and Marx. It does so by examining Kojève's works (specifically, the *Introduction to the Reading of Hegel, Outline of a Phenomenology of Right, The Notion of Authority*, and, to a lesser extent, his correspondence with Leo Strauss) with the aim of comparing him and Marx on three fronts. Starting at the interpretive level, the chapter will compare the relative significance that Kojève and Marx attach to the modality of desire and the accompanying struggle for recognition. The second point of comparison will address the different ways that Kojève and Marx understand the relationship between labor/work, estrangement, and emancipation. The third and final point of comparison will focus on where history is tending according to Kojève and Marx and its implications for their respective end states (the Universal Homogeneous State/Socialist Empire and communism, respectively). Such a comparison will illuminate Kojève's originality as a thinker and specify the extent of his disagreements with Marx. These disagreements are often neglected when Kojève's work is classified under the unitary umbrella of Marxism—a tradition that is itself heterogeneous.

The classification of Kojève as a "Marxist" (or, if one prefers, a "Hegelian Marxist") is widely shared by political theorists across traditional political divides.[2] Allan Bloom famously referred to Kojève as a Marxist in his introduction to Kojève's *Introduction to the Reading of Hegel*. In retrospect, there is a rational kernel in Bloom's otherwise mystifying claim that Kojève was "the most thoughtful, the most learned, and the most profound of those Marxists who dissatisfied with the thinness of Marx's account of the human and the metaphysical grounds of his teaching, turned to Hegel as the truly philosophic source of that teaching."[3] If Marx's account of the human and the philosophical presuppositions of his thought were as thin as Bloom would have readers believe, why did he continue to regard Kojève as a Marxist in *any* meaningful sense of the term? The *esoteric* teaching that this chapter will seek to draw is that Kojève was, above all, an original thinker who cannot accurately be pigeonholed as a Marxist, although he was deeply influenced by Marx (as he was also by Hegel, Heidegger, and Soloviev) and actively contributed to his image as a Marxist.

Bloom was by no means the first commentator to categorize Kojève as a Marxist; this deed can be traced back to none other than Kojève himself, who routinely identified as a Marxist, and at least earlier in his career boldly referred to himself as a "strictly observant Stalinist."[4] While the task of comparing Kojève and Marx is made more challenging by Kojève's self-professed Marxism and Stalinism, one must take care to disentangle Marx from Stalin, while also separating Kojève's commitments to Marxism from his view of Stalin as a "political genius" on the international stage.[5] Otherwise, one risks succumbing to a superficial comparison of Kojève and Marx that would be a disservice to both thinkers. The chief aim of this chapter is to probe beneath surface affinities to discern substantive divergences between the two thinkers. Such an approach is necessary not least because Kojève saw his lectures on Hegel as serving a "propagandistic" purpose,[6] and the same is true with respect to his appropriation of Marx.

THE MASTER-SLAVE DIALECTIC AND ITS INTERPRETIVE IMPLICATIONS

It must be noted from the outset that Marx did not subscribe to the hierarchical distinction between labor and work that was articulated by Hannah Arendt, so the two terms will be treated as interchangeable throughout the chapter using a slash.[7] Kojève was not alone in emphasizing the connection between Hegel's "Master-Slave" dialectic and Marx's account of estranged labor. Sartre, Hyppolite, and Marcuse also noted the profound influence that Hegel's Master-Slave dialectic must have exerted on Marx's materialist conception of history and his theory of class struggle.[8] The essential difference between the interpretation of these thinkers and Kojève's lies in the weight that Kojève assigned to the Master-Slave dialectic, both in connection with his idiosyncratic reading of Marx and the broader trajectory of human history. With respect to Hegel's influence on Marx, he writes:

> Let us recall that this Hegelian theme ["the end of history"], among many others, was taken up by Marx. History properly so-called, in which men ("classes") fight among themselves for recognition and fight against Nature by work, is called in Marx "Realm of necessity" (*Reich der Notwendigkeit*); *beyond* (*jenseits*) is situated the "Realm of Freedom (*Reich der Freiheit*)," in which men (mutually recognizing one another without reservation) no longer fight, and work as little as possible (Nature having been definitively mastered—that is, harmonized with Man).[9]

Although Kojève refers primarily to the "end of history" in the aforementioned passage, the process by which history reaches its culmination is facilitated through the "struggle for recognition," which finds its earliest and clearest expression in the struggle between Master and Slave. Rather than referring to Marx's *Economic and Philosophical Manuscripts of 1844* in this context, Kojève cites the distinction in *Capital* between "the realm of necessity" and "the realm of freedom," likening the achievement of the latter to the generalized state of "happiness" that will obtain in the future Universal Homogeneous State/Socialist Empire (about which more later). While Marx certainly made the distinction identified by Kojève, he did not interpret class struggle exclusively or primarily through the prism of the struggle for recognition.

The most immediate point of contrast between Kojève and Marx concerns their different positions on the modality of desire and the relative significance that they each attach to the struggle for recognition. Kojève helped popularize the view that Marx's treatment of estranged labor and his account of class struggle were anchored in Hegel's Master-Slave dialectic. In the opening pages of his *Introduction to the Reading of Hegel*, Kojève cites a well-known passage from Marx's *Economic and Philosophical Manuscripts of 1844*, which reads as follows: "Hegel [. . .] Er erfaßt die *Arbeit* als das *Wesen*, als das sich bewährende Wesen des Menschen" (Hegel [. . .] grasps *labor* as the *essence*, as the self-confirming essence of man).[10] Kojève is suggesting here that Marx's reference to Hegel's account of labor/work was rooted in the latter's discussion of the Master-Slave dialectic. Despite its influence, the Kojèvian interpretation of Marx has not gone unchallenged. Chris Arthur is one of the few scholars in the Hegelian-Marxist tradition to have questioned the veracity of Kojève's interpretation of Marx's early manuscripts. Arthur maintains that there is no clear textual evidence to suggest that Marx's account of estranged labor was inspired by his reading of Hegel's Master-Slave dialectic. On the contrary, a careful reading of Marx's early manuscripts suggests that he credits Hegel for discerning Spirit's labor in the world through the process of estrangement, but then criticizes Hegel for focusing only on "intellectual" (i.e., abstract) labor. Arthur explains Marx's seemingly perplexing statements about Hegel as follows:

> When Marx says Hegel grasps labour as the essence, he is talking not about what Hegel *actually says about material labour* (hence the lack of reference to "Lordship and Bondage") but the esoteric significance of the dialectic negativity in spirit's entire self-positing movement (hence Marx's claim that the only labour Hegel knows is abstract mental labour). Marx sees in Hegel's dialectic of negativity the hypostatization into *abstract reflection* in philosophy of the *material process* whereby man produces himself through his own labour, a process which (Marx concurs with Hegel) must pass through a stage of estrangement.[11]

In other words, Marx's reference to Hegel's grasp of intellectual labor is not, as Kojève would have it, rooted in Hegel's Master-Slave dialectic; rather, when Hegel's name is mentioned in these manuscripts, he is given credit by Marx for recognizing the transformative side of labor only to be taken to task for focusing entirely on intellectual labor. If we follow the logic of Arthur's interpretation, Marx's point about intellectual labor is a reference to Spirit's labor/work in the world rather than the labor/work of the working slave.[12]

Arthur's interpretation is further supported by Marx's comments on James Mill, which were written around the same time as the *Economic and Philosophic Manuscripts of 1844,* with the important caveat that these comments feature explicit references to mastery and servitude.[13] When one turns to the comments on James Mill, it is evident that Marx has in mind a system of production and exchange that is defined by the generalized servitude of human beings to the power of commodities, as well as relations of mutual distrust and trickery among commodity owners in the market. At no point does Marx invoke Hegel's Master-Slave dialectic to make any of his substantive points. It is only in the *Grundrisse* (a work not taken up by Arthur) where Marx clearly invokes Hegel's Master-Slave dialectic as an analogue to the experience of the wage-laborer under capitalism. Marx writes:

> The recognition [Erkennung] of the products as its own, and the judgement that its separation from the conditions of its realization is improper—forcibly

imposed—is an enormous [advance in] awareness [Bewusstsein], itself the product of the mode of production resting on capital, and as much the knell to its doom as, with the slave's awareness that he cannot be the property of another, with his consciousness of himself as a person, the existence of slavery becomes a merely artificial, vegetative existence, and ceases to be able to prevail as the basis of production.[14]

At first sight, Marx's parallel between the situation of the wage-laborer and that of the slave seems to support Kojève's point about the profound influence that Hegel's Master-Slave dialectic had on Marx. On closer inspection, however, it becomes evident that Marx is referring to a profound cognitive awareness (as opposed to a "normative" recognition) on the part of the wage-laborer that is indispensable to their emancipation. While this insight still resonates with Hegel's account of the Slave's transformative experience through labor/work, it does not match the disproportionate emphasis that Kojève places on the modality of desire and the accompanying struggle for recognition in his idiosyncratic reading of Hegel's *Phenomenology of Spirit*. Returning to Marx's passing remarks in the *Grundrisse*, it is not the capitalist's recognition that the wage-laborer desires, nor is it the case that the capitalist desires the wage-laborer's recognition. Kojève knew far too well that the Master-Slave dialectic was but a rudimentary "moment" in the broader phenomenological odyssey. Nevertheless, in Kojève's hands—and this is a testament to his originality as a thinker—the modality of desire was transformed into an ontological starting point for human culture and civilization, while the enduring legacy of the struggle between Master and Slave would also precipitate the "end of history" in the Universal Homogeneous State/ Socialist Empire.

Contrary to prevailing interpretation, the centrality of desire and the struggle for pure prestige was the product of Kojève's original reading of Hegel's *Phenomenology of Spirit*, and not something that was implanted in his mind by Hegel, or for that matter by Marx's reading of Hegel's Master-Slave dialectic. The importance of the original struggle for pure prestige is elevated by Kojève to heights that are not recognizable anywhere in Marx's work (nor arguably in Hegel's). Early in his *Introduction to the Reading of Hegel*, Kojève writes: "Without this fight to the death for pure prestige, there would never have been human beings on earth. Indeed, the human being is formed only in terms of a Desire directed toward another Desire, that is—finally—in terms of a desire for recognition. Therefore, the human being can be formed only if at least two of these Desires confront one another."[15] While Kojève continued to emphasize his profound debt to Hegel, including praising his account of the struggle for pure prestige over Hobbes's treatment of vanity, which ignored the role of labor/work,[16] Kojève eventually registered his substantive disagreement with Marx over the modality of desire in the *Outline of a Phenomenology of Right*. In that work, Kojève argues that Marx and subsequent Marxists were wrong to overemphasize the "economic" side of labor/work at the expense of its spiritual side. It was this error, according to Kojève, that led Marx to neglect the underlying value of the struggle for pure prestige. In Kojève's words, "Marx was wrong to simplify and truncate the Hegelian conception [of labor/work]. For Hegel, the act of work presupposes another act, that of the fight for pure prestige, whose true value Marx does not appreciate."[17] Ironically, it is Kojève who puts to rest the interpretive claim that Marx's account of estranged labor was anchored in his reading of Hegel's Master-Slave dialectic. Had this been the case, Marx would surely have appreciated the value of the struggle for pure prestige. Although Marx would grant Kojève's insight that human beings are sensuous and therefore passionate beings,[18] his social-historical starting point is that of circumscribed *need* rather than a primordial *desire* for pure prestige that gives way to a struggle for recognition. Kojève, for his part, remains adamant that the struggle for pure prestige makes plain what one values and is willing to sacrifice in the face of death.

To be sure, it could be argued that revolutionary sacrifice is also central to Marx's account of class struggle, but Marx's account of revolutionary sacrifice does not share Kojève's existentialist hypostatization of the dyadic struggle for pure prestige. Instead, Marx emphasizes the background conditions (objective and subjective) that lead to revolution, or as Marx puts it, "the ideological forms in which men become conscious of this [class] conflict and fight it out. Just as our opinion of an individual is not based on what he thinks of himself, so can we not judge of such a period of transformation by its own consciousness; on the contrary, this consciousness must be explained rather from the contradictions of material life."[19] Therein lies the essential difference between the two thinkers on the modality of desire and the significance of the struggle for recognition.

LABOR/WORK, ESTRANGEMENT, AND
EMANCIPATION IN COMPARATIVE PERSPECTIVE

Kojève and Marx would agree that laboring activity sets human beings apart as "objective" beings with conscious knowledge of their history.[20] In other words, human beings have the distinctive capacity (relative to the most sophisticated nonhuman animals) to contemplate themselves in a world of their own making. Estranged labor is condemned by the young Marx in large part because it reduces laboring activity to physical survival and degrades human functions into purely animal functions, thereby robbing human beings of their distinctive capacities as objective beings. Notwithstanding these important affinities, which can be traced back to Hegel's and Kant's influences on both thinkers, Kojève and Marx diverge in their respective accounts of the value of labour/work in the *longue durée*. While Kojève is willing to affirm the formative activity of the working slave up to a point, Marx sees labor as becoming "life's prime want" under communism.[21] In contrast to Marx, Kojève consistently speaks of achieving "happiness" and the "cessation of action" at the end of history, which differs in important ways from Marx's understanding of labor becoming "life's prime want" under communism.[22] Consequently, while both Kojève and Marx value work/labor, they do so for different reasons and to different degrees.

Kojève values labor/work because it is central to the struggle for recognition, particularly the slave's awareness of their freedom as being-for-self, which proves indispensable for overturning slavery and achieving genuine relations of mutual recognition in the Universal Homogeneous State/Socialist Empire.[23] For Marx, on the other hand, neither generalized relations of mutual recognition nor improved contractual terms (i.e., a rise in wages) will "conquer either for the worker or for labour their human status and dignity."[24] Rather, only the revolutionary transformation ("positive transcendence") of capitalist private property and estranged labor will make possible "the real appropriation of the human essence by and for man."[25] While Marx's 1844 manuscripts may lead some interpreters to mistakenly infer that his early account of communism envisages the abolition not just of *estranged* labor but of labor/work altogether, this position cannot be sustained when his writings are considered cumulatively. It is important to stress the distinction between the emancipation from work/labor in its present form as wage labor, and emancipation from work/labor in general. This distinction is not a trivial one; it helps bring into relief the different ways that Marx and Kojève envision the role of labor/work in their respective "end states"—communism for Marx and the Universal Homogeneous State/Socialist Empire for Kojève. Although Marx looked forward to the reduction of necessary labor time with concomitant developments in technology, including automation, he differed from classical political economists like Adam Smith and early socialists such as Charles Fourier on the nature and value of labor/work. Smith regarded labor/work as a disutility under all conceivable circumstances, while Fourier associated emancipated labor/work with a state of play. While labour/work has traditionally been experienced as a repulsive activity, at least in its forms as slave labor, serf labor, and wage labor, Marx maintains that labor/work need not be experienced this way under all conceivable social arrangements, least of all under communism. In response to Smith, Marx writes:

Smith has no inkling whatever that this overcoming of obstacles [in and through labor] is in itself a liberating activity—and that, further, the external aims become stripped of the semblance of merely external natural urgencies and become posited as aims which the individual himself posits—hence as self-realization, objectification of the subject, hence real freedom, whose action is, precisely, labour.[26]

Against Fourier's equation of emancipated labor with "mere fun" and "amusement," Marx writes that "really free working, e.g., composing, is at the same time precisely the most damned seriousness, the most intense exertion."[27] Marx's opposition to Smith and Fourier is referenced in this context to register his nuanced disagreements with Kojève on the role and value of labor/work in the *longue durée*.

One possible way of bridging the divide between Marx and Kojève on labor/work is to argue that Kojève's conception of the Universal Homogeneous State/Socialist Empire and Marx's account of full communism converge around a shared vision of a "stationary state."[28] A stationary state is one where human desires are thoroughly fulfilled and the motivations for struggle are correspondingly eliminated. One may recall here Kojève's reference to Marx's distinction between the realm of freedom and the realm of necessity. On Kojève's interpretation, once the leap is made from the realm of necessity to the realm of freedom, a generalized state of happiness would obtain because everyone will be completely recognized in the Universal Homogeneous Empire/Socialist State. While this may be the case, Kojève's interpretation tells us far too little about what role, if any, there will be for labor/work once the realm necessity gives way to the realm of freedom. It is striking that Kojève omits Marx's view that the realm of freedom is grounded in the realm of necessity, and that "just as the savage must wrestle with Nature to satisfy his wants, to maintain and reproduce life, so must civilized man, and he must do so in all social formations and under *all possible* modes of production."[29] Rather than envisioning the transcendence of necessity (labor/work) under full communism, Marx sees the "true realm of freedom" as "blossoming" with the "realm of necessity as its basis."[30] Consequently, even if Marx and Kojève share a forward-looking vision of a "stationary state," Marx maintains that the realm of necessity cannot be transcended, and that labor would instead become life's prime want under communism. Communism eliminates the basis for class struggle, but it does not aim at transcending all forms of struggle, including in the domain of labor/work and the realm of necessity.

On the face of it, Marx would also welcome Kojève's claim that human history can be viewed as the successive "history of the working slave,"[31] provided that such a history tracks the extent to which human beings become conscious of their historical circumstances and emancipate themselves from the alien forces that previously held power or dominion over them. Thus Marx submits that "every emancipation is a *restoration* of the human world and of human relationships to *man himself*."[32] While historical struggles for emancipation can be viewed from the prism of the Master-Slave dialectic, it is not the case, as Kojève maintains, that the historical relationship of mastery and slavery is the "'first,' human, social, historical contract, not from the Master's point of view, but from the Slave's."[33] This would be a profoundly ahistorical outlook from the standpoint of Marx's materialist conception of history.[34] After all, the interchange between human beings and nature through labor has historically given rise to different forms of social intercourse (i.e., different historical "modes of production"), including but not limited to the so-called "ancient mode of production," in which slavery was the ruling principle and practice. Marx understands the heuristic concept of a mode of production in the following terms:

> This mode of production must not be considered simply as being the reproduction of the physical existence of the individuals. Rather it is a definite form of activity of these individuals, a definite form of expressing their life, a definite mode of life on their part. As individuals express their life, so they are. What they are, therefore, coincides with their production, both with *what* they produce and *how* they produce. The nature of individuals thus depends on the material conditions determining their production.[35]

Consequently, Marx would disagree with Kojève that the Master-Slave relation represents the first social contract, either from the standpoint of the Master or that of the Slave. He would also stress the importance of changing material conditions through class struggle to a far greater extent than Kojève, whose existentialist outlook places the emphasis on the dyadic struggle between Master and Slave. These divergences between Kojève and Marx also help inform their contrasting views on where history is tending and its broader implications for their respective end states.

THE END OF HISTORY AND RIGHT IN THE UNIVERSAL HOMOGENEOUS STATE/SOCIALIST EMPIRE

A comparison of Kojève and Marx would be incomplete without a discussion of the projected end of history and its implications for the future end state.[36] These topics are best approached when Kojève's *Outline of a Phenomenology of Right* is examined alongside *The Notion of Authority* and considered as contributions to a comprehensive legal and political theory.[37] For our purposes, Kojève's *Outline of a Phenomenology of Right* offers important insights into his understanding of the Universal Homogeneous State/Socialist Empire beyond the general sketch that is provided in the *Introduction to the Reading of Hegel*, where it is given credit for realizing human individuality to the fullest and bringing the historical process to a close.[38]

Although Kojève's conceptualization of the "end of history" in the Universal Homogeneous State/Empire remained largely unchanged between his *Introduction to the Reading of Hegel* and the *Outline of a Phenomenology of Right*, he modified his perspective on the precise trajectory of history's culmination, more specifically, the concrete institutional arrangements that would be conducive to its decisive realization. James H. Nichols has interpreted Kojève's changed outlook as follows:

> For the earlier Kojève, the standard Marxist (or, if you prefer, activist or heroic Hegelian) stance applies: the end of history is somehow basically known but actually achieving it lies in the future as our project, our task, our goal, the success in achieving which is of course contingent since the human future cannot be known. For the later Kojève: Hegel was right in the first place; history ended in 1806; what happens now is the working out of details of implementation that are of less than world-historical significance.[39]

Kojève's position on the precise working out of these details of implementation meant that he could refer ironically to Fordism in the United States as a more realistic harbinger of communism than the intentional political strivings towards communism undertaken in the Soviet Union. Whatever one makes of Kojève's provocative equation of American Fordism and Marxism, Nichols is correct to infer that the later Kojève adhered to a "convergence theory," according to which multiple roads would ultimately lead to the same destination, namely, the "end of history" in the Universal Homogeneous State/ Socialist Empire.

However, did Kojève and Marx agree about the ultimate "destination," both in terms of history's culmination and their preferred conceptions of the end state? As we have seen, Kojève associates the "end of history" with the cessation of "action" and the fulfillment of human happiness (understood in more expansive terms than conventional *hedonism*) through generalized relations of recognition in the Universal Homogeneous State/Socialist Empire. Much as Kojève's treatment of the "end of history" may appear to resemble Marx's position on the matter, Marx himself never refers to the "end of history" and explicitly disavows historical-philosophical theories that ignore contextual factors and specificities.[40] While the end-of-history thesis is routinely attributed to Marx for his seemingly "post-political" vision of communism, this interpretation loses its force when Marx's work is read with greater care. When Marx addresses the trajectory of human history in his 1859 preface with recourse to "ideal types," he writes:

> The bourgeois mode of production is the last antagonistic form of the social process of production—*antagonistic not in the sense of individual antagonism* but of an antagonism that emanates from the individuals' social conditions of existence—but the productive forces developing within bourgeois society create also the material conditions for a solution of this antagonism. The prehistory of human society accordingly closes with this social formation.[41]

Commenting on this precise passage, Georg Lukács correctly infers that "the term pre-history is chosen with care and has a double significance here. On the one hand, the implicit but still decisive rejection of any end of history. The expression used by Marx was however also designed, on the other hand, to directly demarcate the particular character of the new section of history."[42] On this interpretation, the end of prehistory, for Marx, signals the beginning of conscious human history. Consequently, there is no cessation of "action" or of the dialectic in Marx's work that is comparable to Kojève's formulation of the end of history in the Universal Homogeneous State/Socialist Empire. Nor is it the case that the end of class antagonisms would signal the end of individual antagonisms in all matters.

Kojève and Marx differ not only in their respective attitudes towards history; they also diverge in their accounts of the end state: the Universal Homogeneous State/Socialist Empire versus communism. Kojève's *Outline of a Phenomenology of Right* adopts a phenomenological approach to Right (*droit*). According to this approach, Right can be grasped as a strictly juridical phenomenon whenever A's action infringes on the rights of B and provokes a reaction by B, which requires intervention by an "impartial and disinterested" third, C.[43] Kojève criticizes those Marxists who dismiss the sphere of Right as an epiphenomenal extension of economic interests and relations.[44] Rather than linking the juridical form to historically specific relations of production, Kojève associates Right with the development and proliferation of exchange relations.[45] After making a thorough examination of juridical phenomena, Kojève outlines a series of sublations that accompany the historical transformation of right—more specifically, the movement from aristocratic right (inspired by mastery) to bourgeois right (inspired by slavery) through the future-oriented juridical standard of private socialist international right in the Universal Homogeneous State/Socialist Empire, which synthesizes elements of aristocratic right and bourgeois right through the transformation of equivalence into equity. Early in the *Outline,* Kojève explains that Right as justice can only be realized and made actual in the Universal Homogeneous

State/Socialist Empire, which provides an important supplement to his earlier formulation of this end state. Kojève writes:

> If a Society is *homogenous*, one can eliminate the words, "of an exclusive group." If it is *universal*, one can eliminate the words, "of a given society" [. . .]. The definition of the *essence* of *Droit* will also then be applied to the *existence* of *Droit,* precisely because existence and essence will be but one: the essence of *Droit* will be fully realized and the existence will be entirely penetrated by the fullness of the juridical essence. Justice will be fully realized in and by *Droit* because all human existence will be determined by Justice.[46]

Universal recognition is made possible in the Universal Homogeneous State/ Socialist Empire in virtue of the thoroughgoing application of justice and the fact that everyone can become an "impartial and disinterested" judge. History can come to an end because everyone will be recognized and there will be no reasons for struggle. For this to happen, it is crucial that the fullest realization of the juridical form is accompanied by the disappearance of the political form, which Kojève interpreted in terms of Carl Schmitt's friend-enemy distinction.[47] Kojève's end state would require nothing short of an empire in which there are no more warring parties or nations but solidaristic relations between "citizens" of the Universal Homogeneous State/Socialist Empire. It is not an accident that Kojève calls "Platonic" the notion of authority which rests on an unchanging and seemingly divine concept of justice.[48] Once the Socialist Empire is consolidated, there will be no reason for action and change.

Admittedly, Kojève does not detail the precise institutional parameters of his future-oriented account of private socialist international right in the Socialist Empire, other than insisting on the continuing relevance of exchange relations and the preservation of personal property rights and status differences between individuals.[49] Kojève's concluding discussion of this future juridical order merits comparison with Marx on the question of bourgeois right and its sublation (*Aufhebung*) under full communism. In Kojève's *Outline*, the transformation of bourgeois right into private socialist international right parallels the transformation of equivalence into equity. Equity is supposed to be more attentive to concrete differences between individuals, which are ignored and treated homogeneously under the bourgeois standard of equivalence. Although this dimension of Kojève's thinking is not fully developed, his account of equity remains at loggerheads with the underlying premises of the Universal *Homogeneous* State/Socialist Empire and differs considerably from Marx's description of full communism, where the "narrow horizon of bourgeois right" is superseded.[50] Homogenization remains a characteristic feature of bourgeois right and its standard of equivalence, elements of which are preserved in the first stage of communism, which Marx continues to associate with equal bourgeois right. Marx writes: "Right, by its very nature, can consist only in the application of an equal standard; but unequal individuals (and they would not be different individuals if they were not unequal) are measurable only by an equal standard insofar as they are brought under an equal point of view, are taken from one definite side only—for instance, in the present case, are regarded only as workers and nothing more is seen in them, everything else being ignored."[51] While Marx interpreted this juridical standard of equal bourgeois right as an advance in freedom, he continued to regard it as a defective standard because it ignored concrete differences in human abilities and needs, as Kojève's Socialist Empire would have to do. Could it be that Kojève's juridical standard of private socialist internationalist right, for all its virtues, remained "stigmatized by a bourgeois limitation"?[52] To ask this and other questions about Kojève and his relation to Marx is to acknowledge that Kojève, was, above all, a Kojèvian.

CONCLUSION

We have now arrived at the end of our critical comparison of Kojève and Marx, which provides a fitting occasion to revisit Allan Bloom's statement about Kojève being the most thoughtful of Marxists, who felt the need return to Hegel after he was confronted with the supposed thinness of Marx's philosophy. Bloom's statement has a rational kernel insofar as it encourages careful readers to discern Kojève's insights as an original thinker in his own right. However, it also betrays a visceral philosophical prejudice against Marx, which prevents Bloom from probing into the depths of Marx's thought and registering fundamental philosophical differences between Marx and Kojève. Although Kojève was influenced by Marx and shared elusive affinities with him, the two thinkers diverged substantively in three decisive respects. As we have seen, Kojève placed far greater emphasis than did Marx on Hegel's Master-Slave dialectic, particularly on the modality of desire and the accompanying struggle for recognition. Kojève and Marx also valued labour/work for different reasons and in varying degrees. Finally, Kojève and Marx diverged in their respective approaches to history and their preferred conceptions of the end state. Whereas Kojève theorized the end of history in the Universal Homogenous State/Socialist Empire and its juridical standard of private international socialist right, Marx wrote about the beginning of conscious human history under full communism, which would supersede the narrow horizon of bourgeois right. Therein lie their underlying philosophical differences.

NOTES

1. It should be noted that Hegel does not actually use the word *Sklave* (Slave) to describe this dialectic in the *Phenomenology of Spirit*, where it is rendered more precisely as *Herrschaft und Knechtschaft* (Lordship and Bondage). See G. W. F. Hegel, *Phenomenology of Spirit*, trans. A.V. Miller (Oxford: Oxford University Press, 1977), 111–119.

2. For the most recent interpretation of Kojève as offering a "Marxist" interpretation of Hegel, see Alan Brudner, *The Owl and the Rooster: Hegel's Transformative Political Science* (Cambridge: Cambridge University Press, 2017), 4.

3. Allan Bloom, "Editor's Introduction," in Alexandre Kojève, *Introduction to the Reading of Hegel: Lectures on the* Phenomenology of Spirit, ed. Allan Bloom, trans. James H. Nichols, Jr. (Ithaca: Cornell University Press, 1980), viii.

4. James H. Nichols, Jr., *Alexandre Kojève: Wisdom at the End of History* (Lanham: Rowman & Littlefield, 2007), 75.

5. Ibid.

6. Nichols, *Alexandre Kojève*, 82.

7. See Hannah Arendt, *The Human Condition* (Chicago: University of Chicago Press, 1958).

8. See Jean-Paul Sartre, *Being and Nothingness: An Essay on Phenomenological Ontology*, trans. Hazel E. Barnes (London: Philosophical Library,1956), 237; Jean Hyppolite, *Studies on Marx and Hegel*, trans. John O'Neill (New York: Basic Books, 1969), 29; Herbert Marcuse, *Reason and Revolution* (New York: Humanities Books, 1954), 115.

9. Kojève, *Introduction to the Reading of Hegel*, 159–60n6.

10. Ibid., 3.

11. Chris Arthur, "Hegel's Master-Slave Dialectic and a Myth of Marxology," *New Left Review*, 1st ser., no. 142 (November-December 1983): 71–72.

12. For a more comprehensive treatment of the role of labor in the thought of Hegel and Marx, see Chris Arthur, *Dialectics of Labour: Marx and His Relation to Hegel* (Oxford: Blackwell, 1986).

13. Karl Marx, "On James Mill," in *Karl Marx: Selected Writings*, ed. David McLellan (Oxford: Oxford University Press, 2000b), 124–33.

14. Karl Marx, *Grundrisse: Foundations of the Critique of Political Economy*, trans. Martin Nicolaus (Middlesex: Penguin, 1973), 463.

15. Kojève, *Introduction to the Reading of Hegel*, 7.

16. Leo Strauss, *On Tyranny: Corrected and Expanded Edition (Including the Strauss-Kojève Correspondence)*, ed. Victor Gourevitch and Michael S. Roth (Chicago: University of Chicago Press), 231–33.

17. Alexandre Kojève, *Outline of a Phenomenology of Right*, ed. Bryan-Paul Frost, trans. Bryan-Paul Frost and Robert Howse (Lanham: Rowman & Littlefield, 2000), 177.

18. See Karl Marx, "Economic and Philosophical Manuscripts of 1844," in *The Marx-Engels Reader*, ed. Robert Tucker (New York: Norton, 1978b), 116: "Man as an objective being is therefore a *suffering* being—and because he feels what he

suffers, a passionate being. Passion is the essential force of man energetically being on its object."

19. Marx, "Preface to A Contribution of a Critique of Political Economy," *Marx-Engels Reader*, 5.

20. Kojève, *Introduction to the Reading of Hegel*, 25.

21. Marx, "Critique of the Gotha Programme," *Marx-Engels Reader*, 531.

22. Kojève, *Introduction to the Reading of Hegel*, 159–60n6.

23. Ibid., 225.

24. Marx, "Economic and Philosophical Manuscripts of 1844," 80.

25. Ibid., 84. This is not to suggest that subsequent thinkers who were influenced by Hegel and Marx failed to interpret Marx's accounts of estranged labor and class struggle through the prism of the struggle for recognition; see Axel Honneth, *The Struggle for Recognition*, trans. Joel Anderson (Cambridge: Polity, 1995), and more recently, Domenico Losurdo, *Class Struggle*, trans. Gregory Elliott (New York: Palgrave Macmillan, 2016).

26. Marx, *Grundrisse*, 611.

27. Ibid.

28. Nichols, *Alexandre Kojève*, 84–85.

29. Marx, "Capital Volume Three," *Marx-Engels Reader*, 441 (my emphasis).

30. Ibid.

31. Kojève, *Introduction to the Reading of Hegel*, 20.

32. Marx, "On the Jewish Question," *Marx-Engels Reader*, 46.

33. Kojève, *Introduction to the Reading of Hegel*, 21.

34. In contrast to Kojève's reference to the Master-Slave dialectic, Marx regards as the "first contract" (Marx does not use the language of contract) the relation between the sexes. See Marx, "Economic and Philosophical Manuscripts of 1844," 83: "The direct, natural, and necessary relation of person to person is the relation of man to woman. [. . .] From this relationship one can therefore judge man's whole level of development. It follows from the character of this relationship how much man as a species being, as man, has come to be himself and to comprehend himself; the relation of man to woman is the most natural relation of human being to human being."

35. Karl Marx and Friedrich Engels, "The German Ideology," *The Marx-Engels Reader*, 150.

36. For an in-depth discussion of these topics in Marx, see Igor Shoikhedbrod, *Revisiting Marx's Critique of Liberalism* (New York: Palgrave Macmillan, 2019).

37. For an extended explication of Kojève's systematic legal and political theory, see Bryan-Paul Frost, "A Critical Introduction to Alexandre Kojève's *Esquisse d'une Phénoménologie du Droit*," *Review of Metaphysics* 53, no. 3 (1999): 595–640, as well as Frost's contribution in the present volume. For a helpful overview of Kojève's thought, which interprets his later writings as contributions to a systematic legal and political theory, see Nichols, *Alexandre Kojève*, 127.

38. Kojève, *Introduction to the Reading of Hegel*, 236–37.

39. Nichols, *Alexandre Kojève*, 95.

40. Marx elaborates his position on this matter in a critical rejoinder to Mikhailovsky. See Marx, "Letter to Mikhailovsky," in *Karl Marx: Selected Writings*,

ed. David McLellan (Oxford: Oxford University Press, 2000a), 618. "[Mikhailovsky] feels he absolutely must metamorphose my historical sketch of the genesis of capitalism in Western Europe into a historico-philosophic theory of the general path every people is fated to tread, whatever the historical circumstances in which it finds itself, in order that it may ultimately arrive at the form of economy which ensures, together with the greatest expansion of the productive powers of social labour, the most complete development of man. But I beg his pardon. (He is both honouring and shaming me too much.)"

41. Marx, "Preface to A Contribution of a Critique of Political Economy," *Marx-Engels Reader*, 5 (my emphasis).

42. Georg Lukács, *The Ontology of Social Being, Volume 2: Marx*, trans. David Fernbach (London: Merlin Press, 1978), 163.

43. Alexandre Kojève, *Outline of a Phenomenology of Right*, 94.

44. Ibid., 177.

45. Although Kojève does not reference Evgeny Pashukanis anywhere in his work, his understanding of the juridical form bears a striking resemblance to Pashukanis's "Commodity Exchange Theory of Law," with the notable difference that Kojève envisions the fullest realization of that form in the Universal Homogeneous State/Socialist Empire, while Pashukanis sees it withering away under full communism. See Evgeny Pashukanis, *Law and Marxism: A General Theory*, trans. Barbara Einhorn (London: Ink Links, 1978).

46. Kojève, *Outline of a Phenomenology of Right*, 94.

47. Ibid., 474.

48. Alexandre Kojève, *The Notion of Authority: A Brief Presentation*, ed. François Terré, trans. Hager Westlati (London: Verso, 2014), 21–22.

49. Kojève, *Outline of a Phenomenology of Right*, 475–79.

50. Marx, "Critique of the Gotha Programme," *Marx-Engels Reader*, 531.

51. Ibid., 530.

52. Ibid.

BIBLIOGRAPHY

Arendt, Hannah, *The Human Condition.* Chicago: University of Chicago Press, 1958.

Arthur, Chris. "Hegel's Master-Slave Dialectic and a Myth of Marxology," *New Left Review*, 1st ser., no. 142 (November–December 1983): 67–75.

Bloom, Allan. "Editor's Introduction," in Alexandre Kojève. *Introduction to the Reading of Hegel: Lectures on the* Phenomenology of Spirit, ed. Allan Bloom, trans. James H. Nichols, Jr. Ithaca: Cornell University Press, 1980.

Brudner, Alan. *The Owl and the Rooster: Hegel's Transformative Political Science.* Cambridge: Cambridge University Press, 2017.

Frost, Bryan-Paul "A Critical Introduction to Alexandre Kojève's *Esquisse d'une Phénoménologie du Droit*," *Review of Metaphysics* 53, no. 3 (1999): 595–640.

Hegel, G.W.F. *Phenomenology of Spirit*, trans. A.V. Miller. Oxford: Oxford University Press, 1977.

Honneth, Axel. *The Struggle for Recognition*, trans. Joel Anderson. Cambridge: Polity, 1995.

Hyppolite Jean. *Studies on Marx and Hegel*, trans. John O'Neill. New York: Basic Books, 1969.

Kojève, Alexandre. *Introduction to the Reading of Hegel: Lectures on the Phenomenology of Spirit*, ed. Allan Bloom, trans. James H. Nichols, Jr. Ithaca: Cornell University Press, 1980.

_____. *The Notion of Authority: A Brief Presentation*, ed. François Terré, trans. Hager Westlati. London: Verso, 2014.

_____. *Outline of a Phenomenology of Right*, ed. Brian-Paul Frost, trans. Bryan-Paul Frost and Robert Howse. Lanham: Rowman & Littlefield, 2000.

Losurdo, Domenico. *Class Struggle*, trans. Gregory Elliott. New York: Palgrave Macmillan, 2016.

Lukács, Georg. *The Ontology of Social Being, Volume 2: Marx*, trans. David Fernbach. London: Merlin Press, 1978.

Marx, Karl. "Critique of the Gotha Programme," in *The Marx-Engels Reader*, ed. Robert Tucker. New York: Norton, 1978a.

_____. "Economic and Philosophical Manuscripts of 1844," in *The Marx-Engels Reader*, ed. Robert Tucker. New York: Norton, 1978b.

_____. *Grundrisse: Foundations of the Critique of Political Economy*, trans. Martin Nicolaus. Middlesex: Penguin, 1973.

_____. "Letter to Mikhailovsky," in *Karl Marx: Selected Writings*, ed. David McLellan. Oxford: Oxford University Press, 2000a.

_____. "On James Mill," in *Karl Marx: Selected Writings*, ed. David McLellan. Oxford: Oxford University Press, 2000b.

_____. "Preface to A Contribution of a Critique of Political Economy," in *The Marx-Engels Reader*, ed. Robert Tucker. New York: Norton, 1978.

_____. "On the Jewish Question," in The Marx-Engels Reader, ed. Robert Tucker. New York: Norton, 1978.

Marx, Karl, and Friedrich Engels, "The German Ideology," in *The Marx-Engels Reader*, ed. Robert Tucker. New York: Norton, 1978.

Marcuse, Herbert. *Reason and Revolution*. New York: Humanities Books, 1954.

Nichols, Jr., James H. *Alexandre Kojève: Wisdom at the End of History*. Lanham, MD: Rowman & Littlefield, 2007.

Pashukanis, Evgeny. *Law and Marxism: A General Theory*, trans. Barbara Einhorn London: Ink Links, 1978.

Sartre, Jean-Paul. *Being and Nothingness: An Essay on Phenomenological Ontology*, trans. Hazel E. Barnes. London: Philosophical Library, 1956.

Shoikhedbrod, Igor. *Revisiting Marx's Critique of Liberalism: Rethinking Justice, Legality and Rights*. New York: Palgrave Macmillan, 2019.

Strauss, Leo. *On Tyranny: Corrected and Expanded Edition (Including the Strauss-Kojève Correspondence*, ed. Victor Gourevitch and Michael S. Roth. Chicago: University of Chicago Press.

Chapter Six

Alexandre Kojève and Carl Schmitt

Mythologies of Enmity

Massimo Palma

The story about Alexandre Kojevnikoff, better known as Kojève (1902–1968), who had come to Germany in 1967 and had just had a chat with radical leftist students in Berlin, is well known. As he met Jacob Taubes in a train station, Kojève told him that he was going to Plettenberg to meet Carl Schmitt (1888–1985). According to Kojève, the old jurist was the only thinker in Germany who deserved attention on his part.[1] Nonetheless, only recently scholars have started inquiring into Kojève's relationship with the German legal theorist. Although the presence of Carl Schmitt in his library is widely known,[2] certainly the publication of their few surviving letters came as a surprise to those who could not believe rumors about a strong relationship between the *soi-disant* French-Russian Marxist thinker and the Catholic jurist who had flirted with the Nazi Regime for years, and with antisemitism all his life.[3]

At the end of the nineties, the availability of their correspondence eventually allowed several dots to be connected.[4] A common atmosphere and language, not to mention common friendships or acquaintances, could be easily detected even before, but their quite different intellectual and ideological milieu had led scholars to undervalue their convergences from the Fifties onwards. Jacob Taubes, Raymond Aron, Iring Fetscher, and Leo Strauss are only some of the names the two shared along their biographical paths.

The correspondence between Kojève and Schmitt starts only in 1955, when Schmitt confessed his interest in Kojève's understanding of Hegel and asked him more about the quite esoteric formula of the "end of history" that

Kojève repeatedly uses in his Hegelian commentary. The correspondence, propitiated by legal scholar Roman Schnur, is cryptic, allusive, and largely avoids making direct references to past war experiences and mutual friends. Nevertheless, it offers a clear outline of the reciprocal influences.

Following the written conversation, Kojève and Schmitt met each other for the first time in 1957, when the jurist invited Kojève to Germany for a conference. Nevertheless, their paths might have crossed before. My hypothesis is that the "dangerous" encounter had happened more than twenty years earlier, at least on Kojève's side. In the early thirties, thanks to the mediation of Leo Strauss, Kojève may have had more than just hints about *The Concept of the "Political,"* the renowned essay Schmitt had written in 1927 and republished in 1932 (and with some national-socialist nuances also in 1933). Such a reading is very likely to have been decisive in the interpretation that Kojève gave in his famous seminar on Hegel's *Phenomenology of Spirit*, started in 1933. Kojève's repeated focus on struggle, rivalry, and the "real possibility" to kill the opposite self-conscience suggests an existentialist view on the struggle for recognition, but also an extensive "political" perspective on what he calls "anthropogenesis," that is, the beginning of mankind.

The debt eventually becomes explicit in two writings Kojève wrote during World War II. Both *The Notion of Authority* (1942) and, particularly, the *Outline of a Phenomenology of Right* (1943) explicitly tackle the "concept" of the "political." In the latter, Carl Schmitt is openly mentioned twice, though both times the mention curiously exhibits slight misspellings of his name or work. In the legal *Outline*, the phenomenon of the political as opposed to and intertwined with the juridical reaches its definition only through the distinction of friends and enemies. Thus, the whole text seems to be readable through Schmittian lenses. This familiarity with Schmitt's visions of politics prepares the path for the future exchange of letters and meetings.

My contribution intends to provide the reader with a reconstruction of Schmitt's traces in Kojève's thought. The two intellectuals, though apparently radically opposed in their ideologies (one a fierce conservative, and a Nazi-supporter, the other apparently dealing with a Marxist fame, though "right-wing"), are far from strangers in their philosophies, and they often seem to play a common game. They actually share a mythology—that of enmity—that deserves a new analysis. The present contribution is divided into three paragraphs, each one dealing with a single decade of a hard and quite ambiguous relationship. The conclusion will try to trace the point where the two ways diverge, reinterpreting some contents of the conference Kojève gave in the presence of Schmitt in 1957.

THE THIRTIES: A HIDDEN DEBT

If a letter by Schmitt allows us to date his knowledge of Kojève back to 1948, things seem to be quite different from Kojève's side. The language and the metaphors used in the Hegelian seminar that started in 1933 and ended in 1939 at the École Pratique des Hautes Études—eventually edited by Raymond Queneau in 1947 for Gallimard—suggest that Kojève may have already known Carl Schmitt's most famous essay, *The Concept of the Political*. Originally written in 1927, this text had been thoroughly discussed by Leo Strauss in 1932, when the German-Jew scholar reached Paris, where Kojève lived since the end of the twenties after his long German stay (Heidelberg and Berlin). The two started to meet each other and to share views on the history of philosophy. After a book on Spinoza in 1930, Leo Strauss was soon to become a distinguished Hobbes interpreter. In a footnote of his book on Hobbes in 1936, eventually published in English, he promised a four-handed reading of Hobbes *and* Hegel with Mr. Kojevnikoff.[5]

Curiously, Leo Strauss's Paris stay had been made possible by a Rockefeller grant sponsored by Carl Schmitt himself. During the Paris period—a short one indeed (Strauss soon fled to England[6])—Kojève helped Strauss to translate a short review of a Hobbesian study by Zbigniew Łubieński[7] into French, which eventually appeared in the journal directed by another renowned Russian émigré, Alexandre Koyré. The journal was *Recherches philosophiques*. Alexandre Koyré himself had no hesitation in assigning a seminar at the prestigious École Pratique des Hautes Études to his fellow citizen Kojève in 1933, though Kojève, thirty-one at the time, was not known as a Hegel-specialist nor, indeed, very well-known at all.

The seminar, notoriously attended by a bunch of soon-to-become *maîtres-à-penser* (Jacques Lacan, Georges Bataille, the aforementioned Queneau, Eric Weil, among others), lasted six years and was entirely based on an audacious reading of Hegel's master-slave struggle with existentialist traits. In a way, Kojève's intellectual job of interpreting Hegel based on some Schmittian and Straussian ideas whose political aftermath had not yet been revealed, looks like an efficacious importation of German concepts into a culture then dominated by other languages. Kojève's repeated mythologies—that is, literally circular discourses on storytelling—of the struggle for recognition helped to spread in democratic France warmongering mythologies of enmity by portraying "war" as the only "serious" situation in life and the only defining element of what "human" may mean.

If Heidegger's *Being and Time*, much more than Marx (whose *Economic and Philosophic Manuscripts* are cited in the epigraph of Kojève's 1947 book) has always been seen as the main source of the seminar's topics, a more hidden source could be Carl Schmitt, who could have come to influence Kojève through Strauss's mediation. Kojève's focuses on the main issue of the struggle for pure prestige between the two self-consciousnesses, where the slave feels deep anguish for his own bare life and the master understands what it means to desire another's desire, that is, the "autonomy," the "value," and "seriousness of existence."[8] This primal scene happens to be quite analogous to the terms that had been part of the Schmitt–Strauss hidden dialogue at the beginning of the thirties, since the very category of "*Ernstfall*," that is, "serious case" or "case of emergency," had been discussed by Strauss's review of Schmitt's essay.[9]

On Schmitt's side, only in the fifties and sixties will some aspects of the dialogue between the Catholic jurist and his younger Jewish critic Leo Strauss become written annotations, first in 1956 *Hamlet or Hekuba* and later in 1962 in some footnotes to *The Concept of the Political*. The hints at "play" and "seriousness" therein have slight Kojèvian overtones as well, as we shall later see.

Back in the thirties, the influence seems to go the other way round, from Schmitt to Kojève. It is the entire game played by the master and the servant in the *Phenomenology of the Spirit* (Kojève harshly translates *Knecht* with "*Esclave*," i.e., slave) that happens to be a bloody struggle where actual murder remains unthinkable, in a rather Schmittian way. It is actually Hegel himself, though, who states this: killing the other would mean to eliminate life as the necessary support for negativity—negativity being action (war and work) inasmuch as recognition is based on it. During this clash, where the struggle to death of the two never takes place in the end, but only menace and fear prevail, the conceptual figure of the friend–enemy emerges. It is the "concept of the political" in Schmittian terms.

The keys to the struggle for recognition—the key to the "autonomy" of consciousness—seem to be purely "political." Any self-consciousness desires to be desired. It wants the desire of the other: to be "recognized" as independent. Therefore, a first consciousness forces another one to fight and then, since the latter is afraid to die, the former forces it to recognize it as the master. What is in fact at stake is that a desire for "nothing" (pure prestige) felt by a subject becomes truly compelling for another. A sort of gift of negativity is the root for "extreme hostility," given that the self-consciousness of the rival that finally abandons the fight emerges precisely from the fear that he feels. The willingness to die, for its part, is the result of the desire to let an abstraction (value, or honor) be recognized. Such a willingness lays death as a "real possibility" in front of the other, either active (killing) or passive.

Notoriously, this very concept, "real possibility," has been profoundly discussed by Jacques Derrida in his 1995 volume on the *Politics of Friendship*, that faces Schmitt's ideas from the much-forgotten perspective of the first element—the friend—of the "concept,"[10] It is easy, following Derrida, to notice how this concept is widely used by Schmitt in his essay *The Concept of the Political*: "The friend, enemy, and combat concepts receive their real meaning precisely because they refer to the real possibility of physical killing. War follows from enmity. War is the existential negation of the enemy."[11] Such an expression can be found about five times in that essay, always referred to war, fighting, killing: in a word, enmity implies real ineffective chance of murder.[12]

Kojève therefore seems truly Schmittian as he says, "that fight reveals and realizes freedom only to the extent that it implies the Risk of life—that is, the real possibility of dying."[13] The "risk of life," itself a pure abstraction of the chance to die, is the emotional atmosphere created by war or enmity, the true opposition that needs to be maintained as such to create a political—that is, human—relationship. In several separate ways, later Kojèvian pupils will all take this as a point of departure for their own research in psychoanalysis, literature, anthropology, and philosophy. Speaking Carl Schmitt's—not only Heidegger's—language without knowing it.

THE FORTIES: JURIDICAL INTERACTIONS

The war started a few months after the completion of the seminar in April 1939. Kojève fought the *drôle de guerre*, and then joined the resistance, with quite a few adventures and thrills.[14] But certainly, he didn't stop writing. *The Notion of Authority* is an ambiguous treatise on a purely political phenomenon—a command that causes no resistance. Kojève wrote it in an occupied France, sealing it in Marseille in May 1942. It was a work on commission: apparently Henri Moysset (then a high hierarch in the Vichy government)[15] had asked for it. In this treatise, we read again that "generally speaking, the Authority of the Master presupposes the real possibility of war and bloody revolution."[16] The "Schmittian" automatism in Kojève's reading of the Hegelian master-slave scenario provides the foundation for one of the four typologies of authority the treatise addresses: the Master.

A relevant shift and complication of Kojève's debt with respect to Schmitt is only a year away. The political side of Kojève's "anthropology" gets enormous attention as he writes on law.[17] Indeed, the place where Kojève explicitly reveals Carl Schmitt as a source is his unwieldy unpublished volume on "right," the *Outline of a Phenomenology of Right*. The *Outline*—600 pages of quite long-winded expositions of the "legal" phenomenon from all its possible sides—was composed, it seems, in the summer of 1943.[18]

Carl Schmitt's presence in this work is discrete, but gigantic. Schmitt's "concept" is one of the two conditions Kojève deems necessary for a State to exist. A State is defined as a "society of friends," that is, as "brothers in arms" opposed to enemies, which is every nonmember. The second condition for a State is that in such a "friendly society," a group of governors is separate from those who are ruled, the "*gouvernés.*" When explaining the first condition and subsequently defining friendship and enmity ("Friend" and "enemy" mean: "*political* friend" and "*political* enemy"), Kojève takes for granted the reader's acquaintance with these two "specifically political categories" and refers to "Karl Schmidt, *Der Begriff des Politischen,*" slightly misspelling the name.[19] The "concept" of the political seems to be the first milestone for a State to exist in Kojève's phenomenology of right. The precondition for the State is actually the same as the one expressed at the very start of Schmitt's essay: "The concept of the State presupposes that of the political."[20]

Nonetheless, this is not the only appearance of distinctively Schmittian traces. Later in the *Outline*, when Kojève talks about the relationship between State and family and handles the slippery topic of "love" as the true human content of family and of familial right itself, Kojève quotes Schmitt's essay for the second time. This time it is the title that is slightly misspelled: "Now, as Carl Schmitt has plainly showed (*Über den Begriff des Politischen*), political enmity has nothing to do with Hate: there is hatred among Families, not among States."[21] This time, the reference is not that general. Kojève seems to quote that very place in chapter 2 of *The Concept of the Political* where Schmitt determines the enemy through negation and says: "He is also not the private adversary whom one hates."[22] Far more interestingly, later on in his essay Schmitt makes a further comment on young Hegel's *Scientific Ways to Treat Natural Law* and uses the difference between familial conflict and people's conflict to define a true concept of enmity as a "negated otherness." "This war is not a war of families against families, but between peoples, and hatred becomes thereby undifferentiated and freed from all particular personality."[23] Considering that in his *Outline* Kojève never quotes Hegelian works other than the *Phenomenology of the Spirit*, and particularly that the *Outline* lacks any reference to its "natural" ancestor, Hegel's *Elements of the Philosophy of Right*, it cannot be underestimated how Schmitt's reading of Hegel, and Jena's Hegel, much more than the "official" Hegel as a legal philosopher, may have influenced Kojève in defining the "political condition" of State itself.

But this is not the only point that presents Schmittian features. Also, the "exclusive group," the very core of the ties that bind law and politics in the *Outline*, has a distinctive Schmittian scent: "We shall call 'exclusive group' any group inside a State or a Society that can eliminate or simply exclude any other group, without causing thereby the end of Society or State. [. . .]

An 'exclusive group' will then be 'juridical' as soon as it can exclude any candidate to the role of C who could interpret it in a different way from any member of this group."[24]

In a work whose goal is to expose the very beginning of the phenomenon of the "Third,"[25] who reacts to an interaction between A and B that he or she considers a breach of law, the organization and systematization of law through different ages (aristocratic, bourgeois, and egalitarian citizenship) is given through the capacity of the political exclusive group to enforce law using its tool of domination. There is a time lag between politics and law, indeed. Such a *décalage* would only extinguish itself at the very end, that is, according to Kojève's thought-provoking intuition, with the universal and homogeneous State where citizens will mutually recognize each other. Meanwhile, the time lag gets to be filled thanks to the "force" of law in charge of making it efficient.

Experience shows that the juridical group is not identical in any time and place to the political group. In such a case, the government may establish by decree the law that is due to the governing group, and this law may disagree with those who are recognized by the juridical group. In this case, positive law may be said to be "unjust." It will therefore rest—generally speaking—on force, not on authority.[26]

The temporal dialectics between the two "exclusive groups" reflect the shift between the political and the legal spheres. It should be noted that the primacy of the political sphere is not easily recognizable from the very beginning of the *Outline*, where Kojève insists on the disinterested and neutral action of a "third" in an interaction between two persons. Nonetheless, as soon as Kojève explains his "second behaviourist definition" of right, the intervening "third" reveals his historic-political character. It is actually "supposed to be able to be anyone at all (inside an exclusive group of a given Society at a given epoch)."[27] The exclusivity of the group turns out to be, first of all, a political quality: the defining group is the one that enforces the law, notwithstanding resistance and opposition by local notables or magistrates that may appeal to other—natural, constitutional, consuetudinary—principles of lawmaking. According to Kojève, the idea and representation of justice is therefore concretely determined by the ruling class—even if the latter is often more neutrally defined as a "group." Thus, justice is implemented in legal initiatives despite any opposition by "juridical" authorities of any kind, that is, privileged subjects who exercise jurisprudence, but who are not immediately identical to the ruling governors.

In such a way, Kojève distinguishes between the two concepts of legitimacy and legality, a purely Schmittian dichotomy. The authority of the exclusive group lies in legitimacy, while the rhetorical and practical propaganda of the juridical group defines narratives of legitimate legality—be it traditional or divine, constitutional, or natural. In the end, the decision on law is entrusted to the exclusive political group at any time. The only legality, according to Kojève and Schmitt, is the political one: its legitimacy lies in the very intention to protect and spread (*propager*) the political institution (in the *Outline*, Kojève speaks of "entity").

THE FIFTIES: ESOTERIC DIALOGUE

Immediately after the war, Kojève started a new job as a bureaucrat at the Direction of External Economic Affairs and saw his courses on Hegel at the Sorbonne—the *Introduction to the Reading of Hegel*—in the thirties published as a book in 1947. Eventually, in May 1955 Alexandre Kojève writes to "Dear Professor," Carl Schmitt. In the meantime, the latter had had the chance to read his Hegelian commentary: Kojève wasn't unknown to him.

In the first letter, Kojève starts by thanking Carl Schmitt for having sent him his article titled *Nehmen, Teilen, Weiden* (*Produce, divide, graze*)—an article that he already knew, writes Kojève, since he had read it in its original version published in the journal *Gemeinschaft und Politik* in November 1953.[28]

That is the beginning of a five-year correspondence (1955 to 1960 is the period of the surviving letters between the two). The epistolary is a witty, tongue-in-cheek conversation. The two interlocutors seem to quite agree on everything, apart from the huge problem, on Schmitt's side, of the "end of history" as the "end of the political," something that Kojève had frequently repeated in his Hegelian commentary. As a reply to the German legal theorist's observations, Kojève refers to Schmitt's essay *Produce, divide, graze* and interprets it through the lens of his idea that "since Napoleon there is nothing more to 'take'" or that "Now I believe that Hegel was completely right and that history was already over after the historical Napoleon."[29] If such claims may appear provocative, what follows ("Hitler was only a 'new enlarged and improved edition' of Napoleon"[30]) must have had uncanny echoes even for his interlocutor.

Aside from these provocations, according to Kojève, in strictly Schmittian terms, this would mean—this already meant—a transition from "politics" to "police" and "administration." And this would happen in both Eastern and Western countries: Kojève, anticipating his famous added note in the *Introduction to the Reading of Hegel*,[31] considers the world exterior divisions as substantially overcome ("Molotov's cowboy hat is a symbol for the future").[32] With his peculiar Marxist eyes enhanced now by prophetic neoliberal lenses, Kojève sees a global society without a State as a forthcoming reality.

Schmitt will notably reassess his theory of several *Grossräume* (greater spaces) against Kojève's conclusions: international wider political spaces are "a plurality and, therefore, enable[s] meaningful enmity."[33] With respect to the possibility of a global, nonpolitical, empire-like unity, Schmitt opposes a further chance for "meaningful enmity" even to his loyal disciple Alexandre Kojève: "the 'taking' has not yet ended," adds Schmitt in his letter dated June 7, 1955.[34]

The dispute goes on and ends do not match. Significantly, Kojève treats Schmitt's concept of the political as essentially involving the question of "prestige" (in his own meaning, strongly indebted to Marcel Mauss),[35] and virtually puts an end to history as mankind falls short of reasons to fight for prestige, since enmity is over.

A further, innovative element is finally added when the two start talking about Shakespeare's *Hamlet*. Schmitt had just published a short essay called *Hamlet or Hekuba,*[36] where he identified tragedy and history, and determined *Hamlet* as a mere "play," a "playful" drama, though infested with ghosts, and "barbaric" in a sense that evades European and continental sovereignty. Kojève replies to Schmitt curiously thereon: rather than talking about the land-sea opposition that is at stake in Schmitt's comment, Kojève refers to the "tragedy of intellectuals." Thus, he fails to notice that his interlocutor's vision of England as a non-(continental) state could represent an anticipation of his own—Hegelian and Marxist—vision of a society without a State. England, using pirates to establish an empire overseas, matching commerce with profit, is the original of a type that seems to spread in the twentieth century. Kojève, as said, deviates the interlocutor's attention toward intellectuals: "'intellectuals' (and monks??) [. . .] live (or at least would like to live) in an autonomous ('immune') *Republique des Lettres*. And in this republic there are also tragedies."[37] Schmitt will not reply to that. Kojève, for his part, will not insist. From there on, the correspondence will focus on organizational issues concerning the conference.

At the beginning of 1957, they finally meet in person in Düsseldorf. It is January (16th). Invited by Schmitt to give a conference at the Rhein-Ruhr Klub before an audience of prominent industrial stakeholders of the area who find themselves together with Schmittian-imbued scholars, Kojève talks about "colonialism" in German. We do have the text of the conference, although the text's translation experienced some adventures. There are three different versions and two different titles (one of them being "Marx is God and Ford is his prophet," while a more serious one is "Colonialism in a European Perspective"). At the organizers' demand, the conference should avoid being too philosophical and deal with economic and political contemporary issues. Nevertheless, Kojève manages to steer his toward Schmitt's obsession with *Nomos*.[38] Starting from the very point they discussed in private, that of the "taking," Kojève overtly quotes his ambiguous pen friend.

> I just read, in one of the wittiest and most brilliant essays that I have ever read, that the ancient Greek *nomos* develops from three roots: from taking, from division and from grazing, i.e., from use or consuming. And that seems to me to be absolutely right. But the ancient Greeks did not know that the modem nomos also has a fourth, perhaps central, root, namely giving. This root of the socio-political and economic law of the modern Western world escaped the ancient Greeks: maybe because they were a small heathen people, and not a great Christian power? Who knows? One thing I know for certain. Namely, that what has just been said is absolutely no criticism of Professor Carl Schmitt. For his "division" implicitly includes my "giving": if everything has already been taken, one can naturally divide only if some give away what the others receive. I only wanted to point out that, from the etymological perspective, the verb "to give" perhaps sounds better than the verb "to take" even if it means practically the same thing! Thus, we say, for example, that we pay our taxes ourselves, and not that they are taken away from us![39]

The three roots of *nomos* are not enough. Therefore, Kojève proposes his version, a Maussian translation of the verb *nehmen*, that Schmitt had divided into three (take, divide, graze or consume). Adding a fourth sense to the word could pave the way for a future equalization between the North and the South of the globe: "the nomos of the modern Western world is, for me, undoubtedly what I have called, in an improvised and thoroughly bad way, 'giving colonialism.'"[40]

The image of a "giving colonialism" is certainly the core of Kojève's proposal and Schmitt takes it seriously into account. He decides to mention it twice. In 1958, a year after the conference, Schmitt republishes many of his dispersed essays in a collection called *Verfassungsrechtliche Aufsätze*. In the notes added to the text of a 1941 conference on *State as a Historical Concept linked to a Concrete Age*, Schmitt quotes, like Kojève did in their letters, article 4 of the Truman Doctrine: "We shall embark on a bold new program for making the benefits of our scientific advances and industrial progress available for the improvement and growth of underdeveloped areas." He notes how this has been the reason why Kojève has "seen a new Nomos of the Earth therein."[41]

The same goes for a second appendix added in his 1958 collection. This time Kojève appears on the very last page of *Nehmen/Teilen/Weiden*, where it all started. Schmitt sums up the content of Kojève's conference about a "giving capitalism," but objects: "no man can give without having taken before. Only a God that has created the world out of nothing can give without taking."[42]

Both added considerations briefly discuss the core of the private disagreement expressed in the correspondence. In Schmitt's perspective, the eccentric translation of *nehmen* as "give"—*geben*—in Kojève deserves a last epitaph reminding the reader that the act of "taking" is human, that is, political, and it is the very condition of any redistributing—"grazing"—policy. Politics, also known as history, is not over.

EPILOGUE. A CONFERENCE ON CAPITALISM

The 1957 conference must have displeased Schmitt considerably. After the two brilliant spirits met in person, the correspondence dies. The exchange of ideas, too. The two homages paid in 1958, mentioning Kojève in the reworking of past essays, are a public restatement of what Schmitt had already rebutted privately. If our hypothesis—a certain theoretical disappointment by Schmitt—is right, a last question might be: was Kojève's conference really so poor in Schmittian terms? Was it really exclusively concentrated on a "giving capitalism" that had prestigious evidence in the Marshall Plan, and both political and theoretical supporters all around the West?

A brief look at the main points of the conference may help us in providing an answer. A relevant element of its argumentation is the reading of Henry Ford as the perfect exegete of Marxist thought in the twentieth century. Ford, in Kojève's vision, is the one who made social revolution impossible through the redistribution of the income once detained by a small minority who never ceased to reinvest surplus value. Ford, Kojève explains, did a perfect favor to capitalism by reinterpreting it without the errors Marx discovered. Ford was a necessary correction of Marx's prognostic errors—the diagnosis being perfect.

After the first section of the conference, though, Kojève says why its title focuses on "colonialism" rather than "capitalism." "When this World is looked at as a whole, i.e., as it really is, it is not difficult to see that the Marxist definition of capitalism is very well suited to this world, and indeed with all the consequences which follow 'logically,' i.e., not only 'actually,' but also 'necessarily.'"[43] The way the West dominates the world reveals itself as typical of old-style capitalism, leading to class tensions, conflicts, "bloody" revolutions, since, outside Europe, there is a "gigantic proletariat."[44]

Thus, the political program Kojève proposes in 1957 can be easily summed up as a "reconstruction of colonialism": "colonialism will have to be reconstructed in a rational way, which is analogous to the way in which the capitalists before, around and after Ford reconstructed the old capitalism."[45] The more rational colonialism is the less probable revolutions are. The key is global redistribution, prophesizes Kojève. Through commercial agreements

on the import-export of raw materials—here it is the bureaucrat speaking—
the economic standard of living of underdeveloped, exporting-only countries
will be increased. This will allow them to earn more, spend more, and be
"better clients" in the global market conceived of as a global firm. A further
good deed would be to reinvest the colonial surplus value in the underdeveloped, colonized countries. Once more the high officer, the French civil
servant that Kojève was takes the floor: "France invests five to six times more
in its colonies and former colonies than these colonies and ex-colonies supply
in surplus value."[46]

Nonetheless, the Russo-French thinker points out in his conference a resistance to such good-sense, reasonable practices in making colonialism wear
new clothes. Said resistance Kojève sees coming from the United States,
which at the time radically opposed the commercial agreements on raw
materials. Since, for the US administrations, such redistribution measures ran
counter to the principle of free trade, Kojève considers that "the stronghold
of 'principled' colonialism is in Washington."[47]

If "all industrialized countries more or less unconsciously are colonial-
ist,"[48] Kojève goes on to say, a global Ford is needed. It is out of this urgent
need that Kojève reshapes Schmitt's semantic of the *nomos*. He talks of
a "giving colonialism" that still awaits a decent name, one that "gives the
backward countries more than it takes from them."[49] A sharing, giving colonialism should invest on the spot, not just giving away ready-made goods in
overproduction, as the United States do. It should "invest productively" in
underdeveloped countries.

In a crowded room filled with German industrials, in front of those who
had been enemies in an annihilating war only a dozen years before, looking
into the eyes of a brilliant intellectual who had also been a Nazi supporter,
Kojève does not feel the need to eliminate the very concept of capitalism nor
that of colonialism. He urges new Fordist policies. That is, a non-German,
post-Westphalian, noncontinental way to redistribution. National states
should now act like a rational private firm. They should raise the wages like
Henry Ford would do, and form a global consuming society, avoiding conflicts generated by harsh inequalities.

Such a society based on "reconstructed capitalism" would have no roots in
a territorial State. It would be *acephalous* and characterized by a worldwide
capacity to "spend." The Fordist-Marxist Russian French bureaucrat imag-
ines a commercial world of consumer people. Fair trade would be the cure
against the old-colonial disease that divides States into value-extracting and
"extracted" ones. A world-made society would function at its best.

In conclusion, the new colonialism put forward by Kojève seems like a
fully renewed version of the English way to what Schmitt, in his *Land and
Sea*, then in *Hamlet over Hekuba*, had called *Seanahme*. At the beginning of

the modern age, England had become postbarbaric by conquering the sea: using no continental form of State, it had fixed its world hegemony through the commercial deals it dumped on new territories overseas.

Which is probably a further, lateral answer to Schmitt's attempt to save "enmity," that is, the political, at any cost. The bureaucrat Alexandre Kojève, a continental philosopher in a continental administration, shows before a capitalist audience that the solution, for both colonialism and capitalism, is not to disappear, but to get out of the national State, and become society, spread into societal relationships across the borders.

Carl Schmitt may have scented this "anglophile" conclusion in Kojève's conference. This may be the reason why, in one of his two public observations on Kojève's proposal, Schmitt once more opposes, in a Neo-Kantian language, substance to function.

> In front of such a reality, one should not cede to any hyperhistorical idealism, nor should one make an ideological issue out of the State. It is different when, in perfect knowledge of the situation, we try to stop the voluntary or involuntary acceleration elements that lead to total, abyssal functionalization. We try to save those institutions, which could still bring historical substance and continuity.[50]

The State is something to be saved precisely as an element of continuity in the mythology of enmity. At the height of the mid-twentieth century, up to Kojève, the philosopher in action, the State is an obstacle to the grazing and to the giving. What counts, at the end of history, in a both universal and homogeneous Empire, is to give every person the right and opportunity to graze, to enjoy the result of increased productivity also in terms of a "savoir vivre," which is surely more "Mediterranean" and "European" than "Anglo-Saxon."[51]

In this proposal, the supposed Marxian inspiration in Kojève seems lost. Kojève never puts the commodity-form into question. Commodities, or rather their linkage through trade inside a global assembly line, are the answer. And the answer is not a merely tactical one. "How should one give? Now, I have neither time nor the desire to speak about Commodity Agreements," Kojève says.[52] Now, despite his unwillingness to expand on the current affairs he deals with in his post in the French Ministry of Economy, these are indeed the solution. Against any Schmittian nostalgia for the State-form, not land but more commerce and sea are needed. That is, more colonialism. And more capitalism, indeed. Funny enough, for a Marxist. And uncanny for Carl Schmitt, too.

The last word was Schmitt's. The last day of January 1957, a fortnight after the conference, a sad song by the "Old man of the Mosel" reached Alexandre Kojève.

> Humanity is now being integrated [. . .]
> the automatic becomes global
> the laity takes Veronal.

Poorly shaped verses with a clear content: in Schmitt's eyes, Kojève seemed now a traitor of the very concept of the political in favor of a purely economic version of societal life on a posthostile international scale. For the old theologian of politics, the exodus from the State-form toward "greater spaces" with no political action, the global quality of the economic machine and the mixture of "nations," has an incontrovertible lay nuance that leads to the very abyssal consequences he has tried to avoid throughout his life. While Kojève is at the eve of his 1959 trip to Japan that will lead him to write about post-history snobbism in the added note to his Hegel's commentary,[53] the old man of the Mosel prescribes barbitals to the lay individuals that live in a nonpolitical age.[54]

NOTES

1. Taubes 1987, 28.
2. Geroulanos 2011, note 2, recalls the presence of both *Romantisme politique*, trans. Pierre Linn (Valois, Paris, 1928) and *Der Begriff des Politischen*, in the collection Politische Wissenschaft, Heft 5: Probleme der Demokratie (Berlin, 1928) in Kojève's library.
3. The disturbing topic has been treated by Gross 2005, though Leo Strauss is hardly mentioned there (cf. 67, note 112). Anyone reading the diaries of the young Schmitt can find sufficient evidence of his "cultural" antisemitism (cf. Schmitt 1912–1915).
4. The epistolary has been first published in German (its original language), then in English in 2001, in Italy in 2003 (edited by Carlo Altini for *Filosofia Politica*), then recently (2017) in France (edited by Jean-François Kervégan for *Philosophie*). Rumors had been spread by statements such as that by Jacob Taubes, Ad Carl Schmitt. *Gegenstrebige Fügung* (Berlin, 1987), 24. For the first detailed analysis of the epistolary, cf. Tihanov 2002; Altini 2003; Vegetti 2005, 255–335, Howse 2017.
5. Cf. Strauss 1936, 58 note 1: "M. Alexandre Kojevnikoff and the writer intend to undertake a detailed investigation on the connection between Hegel and Hobbes."
6. On Strauss's English stay, see Smith 2009, 22–24.
7. Cf. Strauss 1932–1933. On the original text, full of messages by Strauss to Kojève, see the *Editorische Hinweise* in Strauss 2001, 779–780. For a first hint to Kojève as translator of the text (i.e., Lubienski 1932) see the first letter that has been saved, Strauss to Kojève, December 6, 1932, in Strauss 1954, 221.
8. Cf. Kojève 1939, 24.
9. Aside from Leo Strauss's essay, Meier 1988 provides the letters and a thorough reading of their relationship. It is quite important to note that, after his exchange with Kojève, Carl Schmitt will thoroughly discuss Strauss's critique, in an added note to

his essay in 1962 (see Schmitt 1927, German Edition, 111–112, not translated into English), where he also makes reference to the concept of *Spiel* in the recently published *Hamlet or Hekuba*. This problematic issue (politics, "seriousness," and play) reunites Strauss's, Kojève's, but also—something that we cannot discuss here—Walter Benjamin's critique of Schmitt's *Political Theology* (1922) in the *Origin of German Mourning Drama* (1928). Note that both Strauss and Kojève had met Benjamin at different times. For an overall view on this network of personal relationships, Müller 2003 gives a fascinating portrait of a generation where "les extrêmes se touchent."

10. Cf. Derrida 1994, 112 ff.

11. Cf. Schmitt 1927, Engl. trans. 33.

12. Cf. *ibid.*, pp. 28, 33 (twice), 45, 55, 64.

13. Kojève 1947, Engl. trans. 248.

14. See Filoni 2021, 193–229, for more details.

15. See *ibid.*, 202–222 for a thorough analysis of the complicated political and personal relationship between Kojève and Henri Moysset in wartime.

16. Kojève 1942, p. 102.

17. See on Kojève's debt also Filoni 2021, pp. 239–241.

18. There is very little literature explicitly commenting the *Outline*. In English, one should mainly refer to Frost 1999 and Nichols 2007, pp. 67–74. In French, for an actualizing view on the conception of Europe as political unity, see Pullano 2017.

19. Kojève 1943, 143–144.

20. Schmitt 1927, Eng. trans. 19

21. Kojève 1943, 497.

22. Schmitt 1927, Eng. trans. 28.

23. Hegel 1802, 499, cited in Schmitt 1927, Engl. trans. 63.

24. Kojève 1943, 90.

25. From a strictly phenomenological perspective, Kojève equates the "Third" to the person—any person—that acts as the impartial party inside the three-party relationship that lies at the core of the phenomenon of right.

26. Kojève 1943, § 24, 170–171.

27. *Ibid.*, 110.

28. Schmitt 1953.

29. Kojève-Schmitt 1955–1960; Engl. trans., 94 and 97.

30. *Ibid.*, 97.

31. Kojève 1947, Engl. trans. 159–162.

32. Kojève-Schmitt 1955–1960, Engl. trans. 104.

33. *Ibid.*, 102.

34. *Ibid.*

35. As for Kojève's debt to Mauss, see, among others, the fascinating essay by Ginzburg 2010, pp. 1314–1317.

36. Schmitt 1956.

37. Kojève-Schmitt 1955–1960, Engl. trans. 110.

38. Originally shaped in Schmitt's conception of a legal theory linked to "concrete order," back in the thirties, the concept of *Nomos* came to be the main character of Schmitt 1950, a work that tied international law to the specificity and concreteness of

any geopolitical area. *Nomos* is there, in the wake of Pindar (Engl. transl., 73) defined as "precisely the full immediacy of a legal power not mediated by laws; it is a constitutive historical event—an act of legitimacy." In Schmitt 1953, as seen, *Nomos* is analyzed in its threefold etymology as production, division and grazing.

39. Kojève 1957, Engl. trans. 123.
40. *Ibid.*
41. Schmitt 1958, p. 385. A first, abridged, version of the essay dates back to 1941 (Schmitt 1941), obviously not mentioning Kojève. The same is for Id. 1953: the mention of Kojève at pp. 503–504 is in a 1958 appendix.
42. Schmitt 1958, 504.
43. Kojève 1957, Eng. trans. 118.
44. *Ibid.*, 119.
45. *Ibid.*, 120.
46. *Ibid.*, 122.
47. *Ibid.*
48. *Ibid.*
49. *Ibid.*, 123.
50. Schmitt 1958, 385.
51. See Howse 2017, 46.
52. Kojève 1957, Engl. trans. 124.
53. Kojève 1947, Engl. trans. 161–162.
54. Kojève's reaction to the provocation is quite dismissive. In his reply, two weeks later, he writes, "thank you very much for the amusing poem. Although it seems that the good laity does not even need Veronal. I have recently experienced something completely remarkable in this field with so-called 'politicians'" (Kojève–Schmitt 1955–1960, Engl. trans., 114).

BIBLIOGRAPHY

Altini, Carlo. "Fino alla fine del mondo moderno. La crisi della politica nelle lettere di Carl Schmitt e Alexandre Kojève," in Id. (ed.), "Carteggio Alexandre Kojève–Carl Schmitt," *Filosofia politica*, 17.2 (2003): 209–222.

Derrida, Jacques. *Politiques de l'amitié*. Paris: Galilée, 1994; trans. *Politics of Friendship*. London: Verso, 2020.

Filoni, Marco. *L'azione politica del filosofo. La vita e il pensiero di Alexandre Kojève*. Torino: Bollati Boringhieri, 2021.

Frost, Bryan-Paul. "A Critical Introduction to Alexandre Kojève's '*Esquisse d'une Phénoménologie du Droit*.'" *The Review of Metaphysics* 52.3 (1999): 595–640.

Geroulanos, Stephanos. "Heterogeneities, Slave-Princes, and Marshall Plans. Schmitt's Reception in Hegel's France." *Modern Intellectual History* 8.3 (2010): 531–560. doi:10.1017/S1479244311000345.

Ginzburg, Carlo. "Lectures de Mauss," *Annales. Histoire, Sciences Sociales* 65.6 (2010): 1303–1320.

Gross, Raphael. *Carl Schmitt und die Juden: Eine deutsche Rechtslehre*. Second revised edition. Frankfurt a.M.: Suhrkamp, 2005.

Hegel, Georg Wilhelm Friedrich, *Über die wissenschaftlichen Behandlungsarten des Naturrechts* (1802), in *Sämtliche Werke. Jubiläumausgabe*, ed. by H. Glockner, Stuttgart Frommann, 26 voll.: vol. I (1927), now in Id., *Werke in 20 Bänden*. Frankfurt a.M.: Suhrkamp, 2011: vol. 2, *Jenaer Schriften. 1801–1807*: 434–532.

Howse, Robert. *L'Europe et le nouvel ordre du monde: leçons de confrontation de Kojève avec le* Nomos de la Terre *de Carl Schmitt*. Trans. Louis Morelle (originally in *Leiden Journal of International Law* 19 (2006): 1–11), in *Philosophie* 135 (2017): 41–53.

Kojève, Alexandre. "Autonomie et dépendance de la Conscience de soi. Maîtrise et servitude," *Mesures*, January 14.V (1939): 109–139. Trans. in Kojève, *Introduction to the Reading of Hegel*. Introduction by Allan Bloom, trans. James H. Nichols, Ithaca and London: Cornell University Press, 1969, 3–31.

———. *The Notion of Authority* (1942). Trans. Hager Weslati, ed. by François Terré, London: Verso, 2014.

———. *Outline of a Phenomenology of Right* (1943). Trans. Bryan-Paul Frost and Robert Howse, Rowman & Littlefield, Lanham, Md. 2000.

———. *Introduction à la lecture de Hegel*, ed. by Raymond Queneau. Paris: Gallimard, 1947. *Introduction to the Reading of Hegel*, Introduction by Allan Bloom, trans. James H. Nichols, Cornell University Press, Ithaca and London 1969.

———. "Colonialism from a European Perspective," (1957) *Interpretation*, 29.1 (2001), trans. Erik De Vries: 115–127.

Kojève–Schmitt. *Schmittiana. Beiträge zu Leben und Werk Carl Schmitts*, ed. Piet Tomissen. Berlin: Duncker&Humblot, 1998, vol. VI: 100–124; *Alexandre Kojeve-Carl Schmitt Correspondence*, in *Interpretation*, 29.1 (2001), trans. Erik De Vries: 91–115.

Łubieński, Zbigniew. *Die Grundlagen des ethischen-politischen Systems von Hobbes*. München: Reinhardt, 1932.

Meier, Heinrich. *Carl Schmitt, Leo Strauss und der Begriff Des Politischen: Zu einem Dialog unter Abwesenden*, Stuttgart: Metzler, 1988; *The Hidden Dialogue*, Trans. J. Harvey Lomax. Chicago: University of Chicago Press, 1995.

Müller, Jan-Werner. *A Dangerous Mind: Carl Schmitt in Post-War European Thought*. New Haven: Yale University Press, 2003.

Nichols Jr., James H. *Alexandre Kojève. Wisdom at the End of History*. Lanham: Rowman & Littlefield, 2007.

Pullano, Teresa. "Kojève et l'Europe come empire du droit," in *Philosophie* 135 (2017): 54–77.

Schmitt, Carl. *Tagebücher Oktober 1912 bis Februar 1915*, ed. Wolfgang Schuller with Gerda Giesler. Berlin: Akademie Verlag, 2010.

———. *Der Begriff des Politischen*, Leipzig: Duncker & Humblot, 1927; Engl. trans., *The Concept of the Political*, Translation, Introduction, and Notes by George Schwab, Chicago and London: The University of Chicago Press, 1996.

———. "Staat als konkreter, an eine geschichtliche Epoche gebundener Begriff," (1941), in *Verfassungsrechtliche Aufsätze aus den Jahren 1924–54*: 376–385.

138   *Massimo Palma*

————. *Der Nomos der Erde im Völkerrecht des Jus Publicum Europaeum*. Berlin: Duncker & Humblot 1950 (2nd ed., 1974); Engl. trans. *The Nomos of the Earth in the International Law of the Jus Publicum Europaeum*. Translated and Annotated by G. L. Ulmen. New York, Telos Press Publishing, 2003 (2017).

————. "Nehmen/Teilen/Weiden Ein Versuch, die Grundfragen jeder Sozial- und Wirtschaftsordnung vor Nomos her richtig zu stellen." *Gemeinschaft und Politik* 1.3 (1953): 18–27; then in *Verfassungsrechtliche Aufsätze aus den Jahren 1924–54*: 489–504.

————. *Hamlet oder Hekuba. Der Einbruch der Zeit in das Spiel*. Diederichs. Düsseldorff-Köln: Diederichs, 1956.

————. *Verfassungsrechtliche Aufsätze aus den Jahren 1924–54*. Berlin: Duncker & Humblot, 1958.

Smith, Stanley. "Leo Strauss. The Outlines of a Life," in Id. (ed.), *The Cambridge Companion to Leo Strauss*. Cambridge: Cambridge University Press, 2009: 13–40.

Strauss, Leo. *The Political Philosophy of Hobbes. Its Basis and Its Genesis*. Chicago: The University of Chicago Press, 1963 (Originally Oxford: Clarendon Press, 1936).

————. *"Einige Anmerkungen über die politische Wissenschaft des Hobbes. Anlässlich des Buches von Z. Lubieński, "Die Grundlagen des ethisch-politischen Systems von Hobbes"* (1932–1933), in *Hobbes' politische Wissenschaft und zugehörige Schriften—Briefe*: 243–261; French Trans., "Quelques remarques sur la science politique de Hobbes. A propos du livre récent de M. Łubieński," *Recherches philosophiques*, II (1933): 609–622.

————. *Hobbes' politische Wissenschaft und zugehörige Schriften—Briefe*, ed. by Heinrich and Wiebke Meier. Stuttgart: Metzler, 2001.

————. *On Tyranny. Including the Strauss-Kojève Correspondence* (1954), ed. by Victor Gourevitch and Michael. S. Roth. Chicago: The University of Chicago Press, 1991.

Taubes, Jacob. *Ad Carl Schmitt, Gegenstrebige Fügung*. Berlin: Merve, 1987.

Tihanov, Galin. "Regimes of Modernity at the Dawn of Globalisation: Carl Schmitt and Alexandre Kojève," in *Other Modernisms in an Age of Globalisation*, ed. D. Kadir and D. Löbbermann, Universitätsverlag C. Winter, Heidelberg, 2002: 75–93.

Vegetti, Matteo (2005). *Hegel e i confini dell'occidente. La* Fenomenologia *nelle interpretazioni di Heidegger, Marcuse, Löwith, Kojève, Schmitt*. Napoli: Bibliopolis, 2005.

PART II

Action/Revolution—End of History/Wisdom

The Concept toward Concretion

Chapter Seven

Wisdom, Self-Consciousness, and Empire

Alexei Rutkevich

Alexandre Kojève once told Iring Fetscher, the German political philosopher and translator of his work, that it was his own fate, woven into the fate of his mother country—meaning the October Revolution and his forced emigration from Russia—that prompted him to study Marx and Hegel: "He wanted to know how this could have happened, and why he as an individual was powerless in the face of events."[1] Every thinking historian understands that, like everyone else, they are entwined in a process that has its own dynamics and lugs individuals away regardless of their aspirations and goals. Fernand Braudel called this process "unconscious history," specifying that he meant the "social unconscious,"[2] but in this kind of historiography, even the most radical political revolutions take place on the shifting surface of "event history." Philosophy deals only with the brilliance of idea reflected in world history, as Hegel argued when concluding his lectures on the philosophy of history. Kojève interpreted history as something endowed with a hidden meaning and sought it, following the example of German philosophers such as Kant, Fichte, Hegel, in whose concepts, history had a beginning, a middle, and a final goal. Just as in Christianity, where the Incarnation of God is the point at which the movement toward completion begins, in this speculative philosophy of history there is a turning point. Kojève argued that Hegel discovered this turning point in the French Revolution that brought Bonaparte to power; *anima mundi* was visibly revealed in the streets of Jena in October 1806. The storms of our modernity date back to 1789, the archetype of all subsequent revolutions. Witnesses of this archetype, like Joseph de Maistre, had already noticed that the revolution controlled its activists more than they controlled it, people being mere tools of a process that took place through them. In Kojève's reading of Hegel's "Phenomenology of Mind," it was this original revolution and the Napoleonic First Empire emerging from it that appeared to be the central event of world history. However, what Kojève was interested in was neither the revolution as such, nor the history of thought: the revolution leads to the Empire, the history of philosophy leads to Wisdom. If Herbert Marcuse, who, similarly, interpreted Hegel using Heidegger's ontology, titled his book written about the same time *Reason and Revolution*, Kojève's doctrine of "the end of history" could be titled *Wisdom and Empire*.

Hegel's philosophy gives rise to divergent interpretations; in his *Phenomenology of Mind* we can find the origins of Marxism and Kierkegaard's existentialism (it is enough to compare the section "Pleasure and Necessity" with the Danish thinker's *Either/Or*), Dilthey's *Lebensphilosophie* (cf. the beginning of chapter IV, "The Truth of Self-Certainty") and his theory of *Wirkungsuzammenhang*, Cassirer's "Philosophy of Symbolic Forms," and even Dewey and Mead's pragmatism. All these and many other doctrines can be presented as theses "canceled" in the course of the development of mind, for the Hegelian system is such that it incorporates its possible refutations as well. "The Phenomenology of Mind" is written in complex language. Numerous attempts have been made, beginning with K. Fischer, to retell it in a more or less comprehensible way and to clarify some of its unclarities. This is not at all what Alexandre Kojève was doing in his course of lectures delivered between 1933 and 1939, although formally it was a commentary on this work by Hegel. From the very beginning of Kojève's interpretation, we encounter reservations and indications that Hegel contradicts himself in *Logic* and in *The Philosophy of Nature*. Moreover, after stating that Hegel's phenomenology is "as 'existential' as Heidegger's phenomenology," Kojève goes on to say that "Whatever Hegel himself thinks about it, 'Phenomenology . . . ' is a piece of philosophical anthropology."[3] For anyone who has read either *The Phenomenology of Mind* or the later *Philosophy of Mind* with its section on "Anthropology," it is clear that Kojève's was not historical and philosophical research, that is, he was not trying to find out things as accurately as possible *as they really were*. What he was doing was presenting his own teaching in Hegelian terms. In doing so he made Hegel not even the predecessor of Marx, Nietzsche, or Heidegger, but rather the author of their ideas. There are numerous other links between Kojève's course of lectures and the Russian and German intellectual scenes, but Kojève delivered it to French students, who—with a few exceptions such as Raymond Aron—did not have a command of German nor the faintest idea of Hegel or various versions of neo-Hegelianism. Though they had heard something about Marx and Nietzsche, they knew nothing about either Husserl or Heidegger. It was a time when Alexandre Koyré was just beginning his work on the popularization of German thought through the journal *Recherches philosophiques*, a work in which Kojève also took part by contributing several reviews of German philosophers' works. In France, Hegelian studies would only begin with Jean Hippolyte, at the time one of his students at the École Pratique des Hautes Études. Lacking experts, Kojève was taken at his word by future masters like Bataille and Lacan without questioning the accuracy of his interpretation.

This is why there is no point in reproaching him for distorting the original, as French Hegelologists sometimes did, saying Kojève had mistakenly translated *Knecht* as *esclave* instead of *valet*. In this specific case Kojève was absolutely right, since he understood that the chapter on the "Master and Slave" was undoubtedly written under the influence of Hobbes's *Leviathan*,[4] and his German was much better than that of his accusers. We are dealing with Kojève's own doctrine but disguised as an interpretation of *The Phenomenology of Mind* and presented in Hegelian idiom.[5] It has a different starting point, different motivations, a different trajectory and, therefore, a different ending, which is Wisdom: it is not a "System of Science" (the subtitle of *The Phenomenology of Mind*) but *Sophia* that stands at the end of his intellectual journey.

It is well known how Kojève views the question of Wisdom in his lectures of 1938–1939: there are two criteria for its realization, namely "the achievement of a universal and homogeneous State in which the Wise one lives, and the *circularity* of his Knowledge."[6] There is no point in retelling these lectures here, nor in repeating the arguments regarding "circular discourse" in the manuscript "Le Concept, le Temps et le Discours" written by Kojève between 1952 and 1956. The point is that this work is preceded by a work written in his native Russian in 1940–1941, in which he attempted to set out his doctrine systematically. It is this Russian text that will be discussed below.

SOPHIA AND PHILO-SOPHY

A large manuscript (almost a thousand pages) was discovered in Georges Bataille's papers; it was not immediately clear to whom it belonged. Bataille worked at the National Library in the 1930s and '40s. In a letter to another employee of the library, J. Bruno, dated August 23, 1945, he wrote about two manuscripts he had saved during the German occupation: one belonged to Walter Benjamin (a version of his famous text, *On the Philosophy of History*), the other to Kojève. While Benjamin's manuscript was quickly found and published, the trace of Kojève's manuscript was lost. Although Kojève and Bataille continued to communicate after the war—indeed, Bataille published several articles by Kojève in his journal *Critique*—neither of the two ever mentioned that manuscript.

When it became known that Kojève was its author, the problem of deciphering the manuscript arose. Kojève's handwriting was such that only his life companion, Nina Ivanova, could read his writings with relative fluidity. At my request, she taught first N. A. Rutkevich, then O. V. Golova to read Kojève's handwriting, and they began deciphering the manuscript. For a variety of reasons, this work was interrupted, and after the death of Nina Ivanova it is unlikely to be resumed in the near future. As of today, we have at our disposal approximately 150 pages of the text, of which two-thirds have been fully transcribed,[7] while the remaining fifty contain many gaps and unclarities.

Before turning to the content of the manuscript, it is worth saying a few words about the circumstances in which it was written.[8] Judging by the dates inscribed in the manuscript, Kojève began working on it in late October 1940 and completed it on June 8, 1941, in a German-occupied Paris. This work was preceded by a brief period of military service. Kojève became a French citizen in early 1938[9] and was therefore mobilized in September 1939. In May 1940, with German troops breaking through the front, his unit was moved to the outskirts of Paris. Kojève, like all other residents of the French capital, was given forty-eight hours to visit home. When he returned to his unit's location, it was no longer there: it had been rushed into combat. A couple of days later, the French army was gone. So Kojève had no choice but to return home and take off his uniform. What happened next is well known: on June 14, German troops entered Paris, and a month later Marshal Pétain became head of the French state.

Kojève lived in his small apartment on the outskirts of Paris, where he wrote almost a thousand pages in six months. Nina Ivanova told me that in May 1941, he and Léon Poliakov, who would later become a historian of anti-Semitism, visited the Soviet embassy and that Kojève took a manuscript there.[10] Most likely it was a typoscript of some part of the text he was working on at the time, but this is only a hypothesis. It might have been some other text, or it might not have been there at all, as the only evidence is the story told by Nina Ivanova, who spoke about this "fact" as a presumable one. When I asked her whether Kojève was typing any text at that time, or whether he gave something on to the typist, she answered the former question in the negative and the latter with great doubt. In any case, most of the papers were burned on June 22, 1941, before the evacuation of the embassy, making it impossible for us to find out what exactly Kojève had brought there. The speculations of today's "postmodern" writers who claim that it was some kind of "letter to Stalin" testify only to their adherence to the anything-goes principle and their typical speculation *à la baisse*. Kojève gave the completed manuscript to Bataille before leaving Paris. He went south to the unoccupied zone of France, where he joined the Resistance forces in 1942.

Of all the texts Kojève produced, this manuscript represents the first attempt at a coherent presentation of his own philosophy. The manuscript of 1940–1941 thus occupies a place between the course of lectures he delivered and the numerous works he wrote in French. However, it is only one-third of the lengthy introduction that has been deciphered so far, while the two parts of the book's main body remain entirely inaccessible to us, as do the numerous footnotes referring to the deciphered pages: they are either at the end of the undeciphered manuscript or lost altogether, and Kojève was in the habit of transferring to the footnotes his reflections in which he compared philosophical theses with contemporary social reality.[11] Thus, all we have now is a part of the introduction, the outline of which survived. It looks as follows:

"Sophia, Philo-Sophy and Phenomenology
I. Perfect knowledge or 'wisdom' (sophia) and philosophy as the pursuit of perfect knowledge.
§1. The ideal of 'wisdom' as the ideal of consciousness.
A) 'Wisdom' as full self-awareness.
B) 'Wisdom' as revolutionary-socialist 'consciousness.'
C) 'Wisdom' as moral perfection.
§2. Perfect knowledge as 'wisdom,' i.e., as the completion of consciousness.
A) 'Wisdom' as completed self-awareness.
B) 'Wisdom' as complete or 'absolute' knowledge.
(The idea of a philosophical system).
§3. Philosophy as the pursuit of completed consciousness, i.e., as the path to perfect knowledge.
A) Philosophy as incomplete or imperfect knowledge, i.e., as deficient or fragmentary knowledge.
B) Philosophy as the ability to ask questions.
II. Phenomenology as a dialectical introduction to philosophy.
§1. The goal, the theme, and the subject matter of phenomenology.
A) The goal of phenomenology.
B) The theme of phenomenology.
§2. The method of phenomenology.
A) Phenomenological description and the real dialectic.
- An excursus on dialectics.
B) Phenomenological 'deduction a posteriori.'
C) The circularity of phenomenology.
§3. The structure of phenomenology.
A) The place of phenomenology in the System.
B) The three constituent parts of phenomenology.

C) The structural features of phenomenology.
Vanves. February 22, 1941"[12]

In terms of content, this introduction overlaps with one of the appendices to Kojève's course of lectures of the 1930s, namely the first of the three, "The Dialectic of the Real and the Phenomenological Method." Given that much of the 1940–1941 manuscript has not yet been deciphered, it is impossible to say how he developed his interpretation of phenomenology previously presented in French. Judging by the titles, the basic thoughts remained the same: Hegelian phenomenology is converging with the phenomenology of Husserl and, in particular, Heidegger. Kojève writes about the structure of *The Phenomenology of Mind* both in his *Introduction to the Reading of Hegel* and in this manuscript. We can assume that the Russian text is similar in its content to the French, but there may be differences between the two as well. As for the basically deciphered first chapter of "Sophia," there is no French text similar to it. Indeed, similar reflections are scattered throughout *Introduction to the Reading of Hegel*; he wrote about Wisdom (as the final goal of philosophizing) afterward as well.

The transcribed part of the manuscript deals primarily with the history of philosophy, describing the way philosophical problems were posed in the past, and tracing the path of thought from Plato and Aristotle to Descartes, and from him to Hegel. Another important topic is the relationship between theistic and atheistic philosophical thought. Philosophy begins with the maxim, "Know thyself." Knowledge of the world is impossible without self-knowledge and self-awareness. Kojève proceeds from the Cartesian "cogito ergo sum" to the Hegelian "concrete concept." The polemic with Descartes is related not only to the fact that Cartesianism relies on the onto-logical proof of the existence of God, but also to a different understanding of philosophy as a science. Hegel's words that the only true form in which truth can exist is its scientific system and that the goal of his *Phenomenology* . . . is to bring philosophy closer to the form of science should not be interpreted in the spirit of positivism or neo-Kantianism. Philosophy is not some special kind of science, engaged in the search for a method and a justification of other sciences and for a theory of cognition. In this, Kojève's thoughts overlap with those of Heidegger, who stressed the difference between *The Phenomenology of Mind* and the scientistic tendencies of modern philosophy.[13] The critique of empiricism in the manuscript overlaps with three dozen pages of a book on Pierre Bayle's *Dictionnaire* Kojève started writing in 1937[14]: both are about skepticism, criticism, and positivism. Basically, this criticism goes back to Hegel's *Encyclopedia* (Three Attitudes of Thought to Objectivity, §§37–60).

The sciences are preoccupied with abstractions, with abstract objects singled out of context.

Philosophy, on the contrary, is concerned with concrete things and in the sense that it does not separate the thing cognized from the cognition of this thing [. . .], philosophy is not the fantastic theory of cognition (gnoseology) which had such success in the nineteenth century, studying the cognition of things while abstracting from the things themselves and thus being an allegedly particular science. Philosophy studies a concrete thing as a whole, now the thing cognized, now the cognition plus the thing that is cognized, now the thing plus its cognition. And the full knowledge of a given whole concrete thing is perfect knowledge or all-knowledge.[15]

Having attained a scientific system as its goal, Hegel wrote, philosophy will give up its name of *love of knowledge* to become *actual knowledge*. To become wisdom, philosophy must move from Descartes's geometrical reason to a dialectical or historical reason. The dialectic developed by Socrates and Plato as a way of posing and solving philosophical questions (discussed in the partially deciphered chapter "Philosophy as the Ability to Pose Questions") has been forgotten in later doctrines.

Kojève considers Spinoza's *Ethics* with its axiomatics as an example of a metaphysical system. With respect to the world of (really and ideally) existing things, a complete system of axioms is quite conceivable. Only there is no possibility of establishing it independently of experience, that is, there is never any guarantee that the system found is really full and comprehensive. But with respect to the human and historical world, such a system is not even conceivable for the reason that there are no definitions or axioms of the mathematical type that pertain to man. "Indeed, since Man is historical, since he changes his qualities, there are no once and for all given definitions that would establish (fix) the properties of man, and there are no eternal laws (axioms) that would once and for all define his interaction with the natural world and other worlds." If a philosophical system is to be comprehensive, and Man cannot fit in Spinoza's geometrical system, then it is necessary to find a special, absolutely nonmathematical type of system. This type of philosophical system was found by Hegel: it is a historical and dialectical system. It has two features: First, Hegel dispenses with the false notion of philosophical axioms or self-evident truths that are allegedly independent of experience. Each provision of the system, taken individually, is in no way obvious, and sometimes even simply implausible. Only the system as a whole is true and obvious, because as a whole it corresponds or should correspond to the real natural or historical world. And its individual provisions are true only because they are inextricably linked to the whole. Therefore, if the system as a whole is true, then all of its constituent provisions are also true, for it necessarily presupposes all of them together and each of them separately. An individual provision is true only because without it a true system cannot exist. Thus, the system as a whole and it alone guarantees the truth of all its constituent parts. "Second, Hegel's system guarantees (or should guarantee) its exhaustiveness. The system as a whole shows not only that all its constituent provisions are true, that is, they are genuine knowledge, but also that all true provisions in general lie within the system and are thus valid all-knowledge."[16]

This is achieved by what Hegel called the circularity of his system. Kojève refers to the Hegelian triad (thesis—antithesis—synthesis) and argues that it is possible to complete the movement of concepts: if, advancing in this way, we ever discover that the next synthesis we arrive at is nothing other than that first thesis, which served as the outcome of the entire dialectical process, then we will know that we cannot go any further, that we have exhausted all logical possibilities. Indeed, to go further would mean to go again the way we have just gone, and so on to infinity. Assuming that all concepts are logically connected to each other and constitute a unified system, finding their expression in one coherent speech, the conclusion is inevitable: "The closed dialectical circle contains all concepts and thus all the knowledge the speaking Man can have."[17] If, once begun, reasoned speech in which all meaningful questions have been posed and all rational answers to them have been obtained, returns to its starting point, it can be said that it has exhausted itself. Outside of this coherent speech there is and can be no other. Everything that can be said (both true and false) has already been said in it. Thus, what is expressed by this speech is, therefore, the notion of all-knowledge. And it is true knowledge, because there is and can be no objection to it, there can be no doubt in it, since objections or doubts must be shown by speech-logical means, which are already entirely exhausted by this universal speech. One should not think that the system is all-encompassing because it is circular. On the contrary, it is circular only because it is all-encompassing. The circularity of the system only reveals to us its universality, rather than creating it. In other words, human speech already includes everything that can be expressed in speech so that it can be organized into a circular (dialectical) system. Speech must already reflect by itself and in itself all (real and ideal) existence.

> And to this end, in turn, all that can exist must actually exist (in the present or in the past). In other words, there must be an end to world history in knowledge that takes place outside the new and outside the new possibilities of human existence. Comprehensive circular systems are possible only at the "end of time."[18]

This means a stoppage of history: humanity will reach a final state someday, the movement will cease because all possibilities will have been exhausted. History will pass from the real world to the history books. It is then and only then that it will be possible both to exhaust all the possibilities of knowledge and to give the comprehensive system of knowledge a circular form. The fact of the emergence of such circular, and thus universal comprehensive knowledge, shows us that the real historical process of human development is finished and that Man has reached his perfection. But this development is finished not because this knowledge appeared, but on the contrary: this knowledge could appear only because the real development is finished.

Kojève repeats time and again that only full and concrete knowledge of concrete things or people is necessarily universal or perfect knowledge, and that decisively everything that is possible to know is included in the circular system of comprehensive knowledge. It must include knowledge not only of nature but of all history, including all theses that could be conceived: "It must include not only all truths, but also all fallacies, that is, all the theses that have been advanced by mankind during the course of its history."[19] The origin of such a view is clearly Hegel's history of philosophy, showing that none of the great teachings of the past are obsolete, unlike the fickle scientific theories. But in Kojève, this view extends to any statements that claim to be true: all of them are included in the final synthesis. The system as a whole is true; it includes all of humanity's errors made along the path of history. The comprehensive character of knowledge can be established only when knowledge is brought into a circular system, and this system must be dialectical and historical. But it can be dialectical and historical only at the end of time, when the real process of humanity's historical development is completed.[20]

What Kojève says in this manuscript clearly diverges from what he said in his lectures, where he argued more than once that history ended with Napoleon's deeds and Hegel's thought. In the manuscript he says Hegel correctly defined the tasks of philosophy and its final goal, but he was mistaken when he thought that he had already achieved perfect knowledge. The *end of times* has not yet come and will not come anytime soon, and therefore philosophy knows that it is not yet and cannot be the perfect knowledge; "We do not and cannot now have final 'knowledge' of Man and his true, socio-political world, simply because both this Man and his world themselves are not yet final."[21] If nature can be viewed largely beyond time, and therefore even an incomplete knowledge of it can still be true, in the case of history we are dealing with shifting opinions, not with knowledge. Historical changes are so important, so essential, that knowledge of the eternal qualities of Man will yield nothing for knowledge of particular persons, and there is no partial, knowledge of men that is perfectly (absolutely) true. Even knowing fully all that people were before, one cannot, for example, say that those are eternal qualities of Man and that knowledge of them is true (though partial) knowledge. Man can still change so radically that what would have been clear concerning men up to that point would cease to be so. And this means that only concrete knowledge of Man is possible, that is, knowledge of the real existing mankind and its history, but not abstract knowledge of Man in

general. This also applies to self-knowledge: "To know fully what my concrete human self means, I must know its historical past from the first Man
on Earth to this minute in which questions about him are being answered."[22]
Philosophy which seeks to know Man must pursue concrete knowledge and
thus all-knowledge or "wisdom," since all concrete knowledge is comprehensive. But it is only with the completion of history that philosophy will reach
this goal. The manuscript proclaims communist society to be the completion
of history, the way to which is paved by revolution.

ALLGEMEINES BEWUSSTSEIN AS
REVOLUTIONARY CONSCIOUSNESS

Kojève delivered his lectures between 1933 and 1939 to French intellectuals
who had little knowledge of German philosophy but had a fairly good grasp of
French history, as the Lycée at that time offered a relatively satisfactory general education in the humanities, and certainly its graduates knew the events
of 1789–1793 and the Napoleonic Empire in detail, for the Third Republic
was ideologically grounded in the greatness of the Revolution. Kojève's
audience was not at all surprised by him mentioning the pair "Robespierre–
Napoleon" along with the pair "Napoleon–Hegel." Back at school, they used
to sing *"Le chant du depart,"* the Bonaparte Empire's anthem from 1804 until
1814, which they knew was approved by Robespierre, who was even the one
to give the song its title. This "Song of Departure" says that the French bring
freedoms to other nations and threaten despotic kings, and its refrain repeats
time and again that a Frenchman must live for the republic and die for it ("Un
Français doit vivre pour elle, pour elle un Français doit mourir"). Taking this
into consideration, Kojève's words about the readiness of the rebellious Slave
to fight and die overthrowing the Master and about the mortal risk incurred
by the one who is a Citizen, a toiler and a soldier at the same time, were
perceived against the backdrop of examples from French history. The difference between the empire that emerged as a result of the revolution and all
the monarchies that had preceded it was also indisputable for this audience.

However, if history did not end with one revolution, if there are still
many transformations ahead, the view of both the French events of the late
eighteenth century and the Russian Revolution of 1917 cannot but change.
Kojève turns to the Russian experience: he recalls the revolutionary rhetoric
of the civil war times (e.g., "conscious proletarian," "conscious woman")
and speaks of a single ideal of consciousness that is the same for the philosopher and for the toiler. To be sure, this kind of thesis had been proclaimed
for an entire century before him, and not necessarily by Marxists.[23] The

development of philosophical thought, social progress, and revolutionary struggle are inextricably linked.

In the chapter on "Wisdom as Revolutionary Socialist Consciousness" in Kojève's manuscript, references to communist theory are incorporated in a logic alien to the Marxists of the time:[24] a discourse on revolutionary consciousness is followed by the section of "Universal Self-Consciousness" from Hegel's *The Philosophy of Mind* (§436) retold in simple language. In Hegel, the transition away from lordship and slavery takes place through the elevation of individual consciousnesses "to the consciousness of their *real universality*—the inherent *freedom of them all*—and thereby to the visualization of a *certain identity of them with each other*. The Master confronting the Slave was not yet truly free, for he did not see himself with full clarity in the other. Only through the emancipation of the slave does the master therefore also become free." It is true that for Hegel this state of universal freedom is still a "violent separation of mind into various selves," impenetrable and opposing monads. But at this stage there has already been the formation of what is the *moral substance* of family, state, love for fatherland, "and also courage when the latter is expressed in readiness to sacrifice one's life for the common cause."[25] In Hegel, the transition from self-consciousness to mind takes place at this stage. It is these ideas that Kojève interprets when saying that *revolutionary consciousness* and the corresponding transformation of society are the prerequisites of wisdom. We may say that Kojève—following Hegel—defends the republican understanding of wisdom as opposed to the liberal one (*negative freedom* in Isaiah Berlin's terms).

His reasoning in the paragraph on "Wisdom as Moral Perfection"[26] is also ideologized. Since Socrates and Plato, genuine philosophy relates to the life of the polis, the state, and society. The Stoic sage's flight from reality, the adherence to church authority, and bourgeois individualism are rejected by Kojève in favor of the philosopher's openness to societal problems and of his joining the efforts of revolutionary struggle. It is indicative that Kojève does not mention at all here the inevitability of terror which he so often recalls when speaking of revolution.

While Kojève did acknowledge the global significance of both the French and the Russian Revolutions, this did not prevent him from taking a far from enthusiastic look at revolution and revolutionaries. Of course, for him History is "permanent Revolution, because it progresses by means of *negations* of what is socially given"[27]; therefore, behind the real revolution there is always some philosophical idea of the future society. However, it is not philosophers who make revolutions, but *men of action*, in association with whom Kojève recalls Nietzsche's *blond beasts*: these people change the world and change themselves, but they do so out of excess animal power, restlessness, and non-conformism. "And experience shows, for example, that people who made Revolutions proved unable to hold on to power precisely because they remained (or are thought to have remained) the same as they were before the Revolution, namely, non-conformists [. . .]. According to Hegel's definition, such *blond beasts* are swine just like the inert and passive animals, the conformists."[28] From the point of view not of the will to power but of values, Kojève argues, there is no difference between such representatives of the *animal kingdom.* The world of values belongs to mind (or spirit, which is the same in Hegel).

The struggle between revolutionaries and counterrevolutionaries acquires this spiritual dimension when one's values are contrasted with others. In his essay on the phenomenology of right, Kojève writes about the *tragedy of revolution:* the human struggle is tragic when two truths, two ideas of justice, uncompromisingly collide. But for the philosopher, these tragedies repeating themselves in history are a subject of contemplation and reflection. He is obliged to leave his personal preferences aside. Raymond Aron, who was a friend of Kojève's and often met with him in the second half of the 1930s, wrote that although Kojève called himself a "Stalinist," he actually was a White *emigré* as far as his worldview was concerned: "In private, he did not at all deny that Russia repainted in red was ruled by swine, that the Russian language was being debased, that culture was in decline. On the contrary, he occasionally spoke about this as something obvious, which only complete idiots could ignore."[29] To him, the figures of Napoleon or Stalin were interesting and significant not in themselves, but only as symbols expressing the Gestalt of Empire.

THE EMPIRE

As an orientalist by training, Kojève was well aware that the term "empire" is widely used by historians for such states as Rome and Byzantium, but also for China from the time of Qin Shi Huang on, for ancient Assyria and for early modern Turkey and so on, but he did not care about that. He cared even less about European nations' colonies and all that is associated with imperialism in the twentieth century. What he calls an empire is a "universal and homogeneous State" that completes history and is the condition for achieving "all-knowledge." Philosophy can reach its goal, that is, turn into wisdom, only when special sociopolitical historical conditions are provided in the world. Therefore, the pursuit of wisdom in the broad sense, along with philosophy in the narrow sense, that is, along with the ideological development of theoretical knowledge, must also include the "effective" development of the historical conditions of its existence. Thus, History, taken as a whole, consists of two parallel processes of a real and effective sociopolitical process leading to the establishment of an ideal and conscious sociopolitical order throughout the world, and of an ideal-cognitive process corresponding to the former one and dependent on it. The latter also includes philosophy, as an expression of self-consciousness for humanity itself, which the former process "realizes." Therefore, the completion of history is simultaneously the completion of these two processes; hence the achievement of the social and political ideal is simultaneously the achievement of the cognitive and philosophical ideal, that is, the achievement of "wisdom." Thus, one cannot consciously aspire to wisdom, that is, be a philosopher, without simultaneously aspiring to the sociopolitical ideal, just as one cannot quite consciously aspire to this ideal without aspiring to wisdom, that is, without being to some extent a philosopher.

Kojève ignores all the terminology of historical materialism (mode of production, formation, base and superstructure, etc.). Marxism is praised, but at the same time it is not seen as a true doctrine because it belongs to today's time, far from the end of history.

> We must assume that humanity in its historical development "judges" the state in the same way that the state judges its citizens and the theories they put forward. Only a theory that will be recognized by humanity "at the end of time" and by that final (absolute, ideal) state which will exist alone, forever, and unchanging, can be considered finally (absolutely) true. In other words, we come again to the conviction that the absolute knowledge of Man can only be the all-knowledge verified by the all-encompassing state, i.e., by a communist society.[30]

In other words, Kojève did not recognize Marxism-Leninism-Stalinism of his time as the finally true theory. The completeness of self-knowledge and self-consciousness is also possible only with the completion of history. Today's ideologue of the proletariat does not possess such completeness. Moreover, revolutionary ideology, which changes the sociopolitical order and acts as the antithesis to the pre-revolutionary ideology, is "canceled" in synthesis: the observation of historical dialectics shows that the revolutionary idea is never wholly incorporated into postrevolutionary ideology. The people who made the revolution are usually almost as hostile to its final result as the supporters of the former sociopolitical order, precisely because the new state does not accept entirely what it does not consider finally true. In fact, what a revolution results in, it is never a choice between a prerevolutionary "thesis" and a revolutionary "antithesis" but a certain "synthesis" in which the "thesis" and the "antithesis" neutralize each other as it were, entering into a "chemical compound" to form a new body sociopolitic. "Pure" revolutionaries may see this as a "betrayal" of the revolutionary idea. "The philosopher, however, shall consider only those aspects of it that are preserved in this synthesis to be true knowledge. What perishes in the process of revolution he will regard as 'revolutionary ideology,' i.e., an *opinion*, revolutionary but already false, just as that pre-revolutionary opinion opposite to it, which, too, perishes in the process of the revolutionary struggle." Nor is the resulting synthesis final, since it generates new social contradictions, a new political struggle, and thus a new revolutionary "antithesis."

Kojève's view of modernity is defined by his historiosophical scheme: History, which began with the "struggle for recognition" and with the emergence of lordship and slavery, comes to an end. It is only in this manuscript that this scheme is identified with the prophecies of the "Manifesto of the Communist Party."[31] Two years later, in *Outline of a Phenomenology of Right* the kind of society which is the goal of history is described in a way that diverges from communist dogma[32]; suffice it to say that private property still exists in this society, and so do employment relations and surplus value (i.e., all the things communists termed the exploitation of Man by man). Here Kojève develops the optimistic socialist view of a universal and homogeneous state and its citizens outlined in the manuscript of 1940–1941: "Far from being beasts, nihilists or even playful snobs, the inhabitants of the final order will be citizens, workers and members of families, with reciprocal rights and duties appropriate to these human roles, whose distinctively human needs are met through the recognition in work and love in the family."[33] In a footnote to the 1959 edition of his *Introduction to the Reading of Hegel*, Kojève wrote that the communist revolutions in Russia and China, the accession of Togoland to independence, and the self–determination of the Papuans were but an extension in space of the universal revolutionary force actualized in France ("Robespierrian Bonapartism") to backward nations, while this universal movement toward a "universal homogenous state" was headed by the United States; the USSR and the People's Republic of China, Kojève went on to argue, aspired to the same goals but were still poor; in other words, "the Americans give the appearance of rich Sino–Soviets," whereas "the Russians and the Chinese are only Americans who are still poor but are rapidly proceeding to get richer."[34] Around 1949, Kojève's view of this movement toward the *end of history* becomes pessimistic, for it is a movement toward the Nietzschean *last man* realm, indeed, even a return to the animal realm, whereas previously he had rather shared the utopian projects of all European leftists (not only Marxists). For him, communist revolutions were a direct continuation of bourgeois ones, all being part of a single movement toward a universal and homogeneous state.

Now, it is obvious to anyone who has read Hegel that Kojève's interpretation has as little in common with the original regarding the philosophy of history as in any other respect. Even if one doesn't consider Hegel a "Prussian reactionary," as liberals from Rudolph Haym to Karl Popper did (they would be surprised to learn that Stalin held the same opinion of Hegel), one cannot write him off as an unqualified admirer of Napoleon, for it was with great joy that he said, concluding his lectures on the philosophy of history, that the fiction of an Empire has utterly vanished, and welcomed its breaking up into sovereign states. His *Philosophy of Right* clearly indicates that it is not Napoleon's empire that ends history. Kojève's interpretation of individual stages of historical formation differs greatly from Hegel's, too. While Hegel's chapter VI of *Phenomenology* outlines complex dialectical transitions between *Gestalten*, Kojève is essentially speaking about one and the same character, the bourgeois Intellectual. While Hegel extols Protestantism, Kojève sees the Catholic Church as the precursor of the universal and homogeneous state.[35] Indeed, the entire history of Christianity is presented differently in Hegel than in his interpreter's work, beginning with the *Unhappy Consciousness*, which Kojève sees through the prism of Nietzsche's double world ideas. Obviously, Hegel did not identify scientific cognition with the labor of the slave, nor did he attribute stoicism and skepticism to "Slave Consciousness." To see just how far away from Hegel Kojève moves in his interpretation of the history of thought, it is enough to compare the first volume of Hegel's *History of Philosophy* with Kojève's three-volume *Attempt at a Reasoned History of Pagan Philosophy*.

The main difference between the two thinkers, however, is that Hegel was heir to the optimistic philosophy of the Enlightenment, with history declared to be the realization of reason and freedom, whereas in Kojève's dualistic ontology Man is nothing, which nullifies, dialectically canceling what exists and creating that which does not yet exist. It is dissatisfaction that holds this nothing in being. This is why, while history lasts, it is the history of struggle and labor.[36] It would seem that Kojève asserts a thought close to the ideas of young Hegelians in general (and partly to those of Marxists as well): "The Man who is completely satisfied with his existence and thus completes the historical evolution of mankind is the Citizen of the universal and homogeneous State, that is, according to Hegel, the toiler-soldier of the revolutionary and Napoleonic armies. War (for recognition) therefore completes History and leads Man to his perfection (=satisfaction)."[37] But, by saying this, he sets the main themes of the French atheistic existentialism, which, as Stefanos Geroulanos rightly pointed out, is not humanist, for the anthropotheism it proclaims denies both god and the image of man that prevailed in European humanism, and then man himself. Throughout history, "nothingness annihilates," while self-consciousness strives for recognition but never achieves it, and therefore it cannot become "something" or does so in an inauthentic way. At the end of the path, with the attainment of universal recognition, this nonbeing passes into being and disappears.

Given that Kojève's philosophical trajectory began with an interest in Buddhism, one might say that his interpretation of self-consciousness reminds of the Yogachara *"concept of store-consciousness (Ālaya-vijñāna)"*: the story ends not with the stilled ocean of the *Laṅkāvatāra Sūtra*, not with the network of consciousnesses reflected in each other—the crystals of the *Avataṃsaka Sūtra*—but with "negation of negation" that transforms being-in-the-world simply into a kind of stilled being. People who love to talk today of technological singularity or Yuval Noah Harari's admirers who are fond of imagining such a singularity as inhabited by impassioned science fiction cyborgs should be reminded that, since the late 1940s, Kojève spoke of the time of the kingdom of "the last Man" turned animal, the time of *homo ludens* aesthetically playing with pure forms. The difference between him and all previous humanism is also clearly visible in the way Kojève describes the humanists as intellectuals of the *Republique des Lettres*, poor bourgeois yearning to become rich, a "spiritual bestiary."[38] Liberal humanism, according to him, is the ideology of *Slaves without Master*, but the transition from the realm of necessity to the realm of freedom proclaimed by Socialists turns out to be an illusion and only prepares the transition to the realm of Nietzsche's *last man*.

In *Outline of a Phenomenology of Right*, Kojève wrote that all history, which began with the anthropogenic desire for recognition, contains only the possibility of Man, Man in act appears only with complete satisfaction (*Befriedigung*) through the action generated by this desire,[39] and this is feasible only at the end of history with the disappearance of he who toiled, fought, and died in battle. If it is true that, by arguing that only in the perspective of its own death a finite being discovers Being, Kojève follows Heidegger's thought, is no less true that, in contrast to the German thinker, for him, "Notion is Time," and therefore Being is open to dialectical conceptual comprehension. Hegel's "canceling" (*Aufheben)* refers to finite being, "and therefore History itself must be essentially finite; the collective Man (humanity) must die, just as the human individual dies; universal History must have a certain *end.*"[40] This end comes with absolute Knowledge, a Book written by the Sage. This absolute Knowledge is the last moment of time, after it there is no future. If even some events are still taking place in the human world, this is no longer history, because nothing new is born either in social life or in philosophy; instead, there is only a whirligig of doctrines that have already been "canceled" in the history of thought. Even the saying that with much wisdom comes much sorrow is too optimistic in the case of Kojève's teachings: Wisdom attained is murderous for thought, and therefore, rather than increasing sorrow, knowledge "cancels" it along with the thinker himself.

NOTES

1. Iring Fetscher, *Vorwort des Herausgebers zur deutschen Ausgabe* // *Alexandre Kojève, Hegel* (F.a.M., Suhrkamp, 1975), 7.

2. Fernand Braudel, *Ecrits sur l'histoire* (Paris: Flammarion, 1969), 62–63.

3. Alexandre Kojève, *Introduction à la lecture de Hegel* (Paris: Gallimard, 1947), 39.

4. Shortly after meeting Kojève, Leo Strauss pointed out that it was Kojève who discovered this influence. Cf. Leo Strauss, *The Political Philosophy of Hobbes: Its Basis and Its Genesis* (Oxford: Clarendon Press, 1936). Hobbes did not distinguish between Slave and Bondsman: for him, both are *servus*.

5. Kojève indirectly admitted this in his correspondence with Trần Đức Thảo.

6. Kojève, *Introduction* . . . , 289.

7. This part of the manuscript was published in A. Kojeve, *Sofiya, filo-sofiya i fenomenologiya [Sophia, Philo-Sophy, and Phenomenology]* (Moscow: Praksis, 2021).

8. See Marco Filoni, *Le philosophe du dimanche. La vie et la pensee d'Alexandre Kojève* (Paris: Gallimard, 2008), 253–256, for details.

9. Although he did not change his last name, remaining Kojevnikoff officially, the nickname Kojève given to him by his students at the École Pratique des Hautes Études took hold. Soon he would sign his French texts "A. Kojève."

10. This visit was likely the reason that Kojève ended up on the so-called "Mitrokhin list,"—he was listed as a Soviet intelligence agent. This is a possibility that cannot be ruled out completely: in addition to the fact that Kojève was an adventurer by nature and had sympathies for the Soviet Union at the time, he could have given consent to cooperate at that time because of his mother who remained in Moscow. However, it is just as likely that he was put on this list without being asked for consent. The totally implausible version put forward by the French counterintelligence says he was recruited in 1953 and became a liaison person of Charles Hernu (the future defense minister of France and a friend of Mitterrand). Constantin Melnik, a well-informed member of the French intelligence community, who supervised all these services under De Gaulle (and, by the way, strongly disliked Hernu, who hampered his career), described this version as "absolute nonsense" put forth by someone who was just settling scores with Hernu. Suffice it to say that after Hernu was accused of cooperation with the communist bloc (Bulgarian and Romanian intelligence), there were publications in the media saying that he was a CIA agent since the late '40s! Just as we have every reason to discard the version according to which Kojève was a "liaison man," his being an agent is unlikely if only for the lack of motive: in those years he was already completely disappointed by the "Communist experiment," and money meant almost nothing to him.

11. This is manifest in the *Introduction to the Reading of Hegel* as well as in subsequent manuscripts. Kojève preserved this habit later in life, too: in his three-volume history of ancient ("pagan") philosophy, footnotes make up about a quarter of the text.

12. A. Kojève, *Sophia* . . . , 23–24.

13. Cf. Martin Heidegger, *Hegels Phaenomenologie des Geistes* // M. Heidegger, Gesamtausgabe, Bd.32, Vittorio Klostermann, F.a.M.

14. Cf. Alexandre Kojève, *Identité et Realité dans le "Dictionnaire" de Pierre Bayle* (Paris: Gallimard, 2010), 40–75.

15. Unpublished part of the manuscript, 78

16. Unpublished . . . , 86–87.

17. A.Kojève, *Sophia* . . . , 148.

18. A.Kojève, *Sophia* . . . , 149–150.

19. Ibid., 152.

20. Ibid., 155.

21. Unpublished . . . , 152.

22. A. Kojève, *Sophia* . . . , 133.

23. Suffice it to recall Saint-Simon and his followers. Auguste Comte, who emerged from this school, devoted a third of *The Spirit of Positive Philosophy* to a discussion of the "conditions of the triumph of the positive school," the main condition being "the union of proletarians and philosophers."

24. Kojève was hardly familiar with György Lukács's early work, *History and Class Consciousness*, which was also considered "revisionist" (including by Lukács himself, who was in Moscow at the time).

25. G.W.F. Hegel, *Enzyclopädie der Philosophischen Wissenschaften im Grundrisse Dritter Teil. Die Philosophie des Geistes* (Berlin: Dunker und Humblot), 1845, 284.

26. Unpublished, 27–38.

27. A.Kojève, *Introduction* . . . , 404.

28. Ibid., 402.

29. Raymond Aron, *Mémoires. 50 ans des réflexion politique* (Paris: Julliard, 1983), 131.

30. Unpublished . . . , 131.

31. In fact, Kojève was not a Marxist in any strict sense of the word either before or afterward. Stefanos Geroulanos writes extensively on this subject (Cf. Stefanos Geroulanos, *An Atheism That Is Not Humanist Emerges in French Thought* [Stanford: Stanford University Press, 2010], 167–172). He only became a Marxist in the opinion of the French leftists in the postwar decades when they conflated Hegel and Marx with Nietzsche and Heidegger: Kojève had a considerable influence on these "synthesizers."

32. The French term *fin de l'histoire* can be translated as both "the end of history" and "the goal of history."

33. R. Howse and B.-P. Frost, *Introductory Essay. The Plausibility of the Universal and Homogenous State//Alexandre Kojève, Outline of a Phenomenology of Right* (New York, Oxford: Rowman & Littlefield, 2000), 3.

34. Alexandre Kojève, *Introduction à la lecture de Hegel*, 436–7.

35. Moreover, in a letter to Leo Strauss (12.11.1936) he compared the struggle between communism and fascism of that time with the struggle between Catholics and Protestants in the sixteenth and seventeenth centuries. He himself sympathized with the "Reds" and not the "Browns," but the historical analogy had to do with the

fact that Protestantism was associated with "bourgeois" individualism, while the Catholic Church, in Kojève's opinion, was preparing the Empire on earth. One can also think of the high praise for Catholicism in his sketch of the "Latin Empire." Cf. Alexandre Kojève, *L'Empire Latine. Esquisse d'une doctrine de la politique fran-çaise, La Regle de jeu* 1, no, 1 (1990).

36. A.Kojève, *Introduction*, 474–5.

37. Ibid., 563.

38. Kojève also considered the community of French writers who pretended to be philosophers such a "bestiary." They either reproduced old theses without reference or threw out sets of "fashionable ideas" composed for the sake of fame. If one "original" book is superseded by another, say, when "L'être et le neant" gives way to "Les mots et le choses," this does not add to knowledge, he argued.

39. Alexandre Kojève, *Esquisse d'une phénoménologie du droit* (Paris: Gallimard, 1981), 237.

40. Alexandre Kojève, *Introduction à la lecture de Hegel* (Paris: Gallimard, 1947), 380.

BIBLIOGRAPHY

Aron, Raymond, Aron. *Mémoires. 50 ans des réflexion politique*. Paris: Julliard, 1983.

Braudel, Fernand. *Ecrits sur l'histoire*. Paris: Flammarion, 1969, p. 62–63.

Filoni, Marco. *Le philosophe du dimanche. La vie et la pensee d'Alexandre Kojève*. Paris: Gallimard, 2008.

Geroulanos, Stefanos. *An Atheism That Is Not Humanist Emerges in French Thought*. Stanford: Stanford University Press, 2010.

Hegel, Georg Friedrich Willhelm. *Encyclopaedie der filosophischen Wissenschaften im Grundrisse. Dritter Teil. Die Philosophie des Geistes*. Berlin: Dunker und Humblot, 1845.

Heidegger, Martin. *Hegels Phaenomenologie des Geistes* // M. Heidegger, Gesamtausgabe, Bd.32, Vittorio Klostermann, F.a.M., 1997.

Kojève, Alexandre. *Introduction à la lecture de Hegel*. Paris: Gallimard, 1947, p. 39.

———. *Esquisse d'une phénoménologie du droit*. Paris: Gallimard, 1981.

———. *L'Empire Latine. Esquisse d'une doctrine de la politique française* // La Regle de jeu 1, no. 1(1990).

———. *Sofiya, filo-sofiya i fenomenologiya* [Sophia, Philo-Sophy, and Phenomenology]. Moscow: Praksis, 2021.

———. *Identité et Realité dans le "Dictionnaire" de Pierre Bayle*. Paris: Gallimard, 2010.

———. *Hegel*, F.a.M., Suhrkamp, 1975.

Strauss, Leo. *The Political Philosophy of Hobbes: Its Basis and Its Genesis*. Oxford: Clarendon Press, 1936.

———. *De la tyrannie. Suivi de Correspondance avec Alexandre Kojève (1932–1965)*. Paris: Galimard, 1997.

Chapter Eight

Tyranny or Wisdom?

A Reading of the Strauss–Kojève Debate

José Daniel Parra

INTRODUCTION

Although they find themselves in profound disagreement about the sources and ends of political life, Leo Strauss and Alexandre Kojève seem to agree that the philosopher would be capable of assuming political rule. The crucial problem is whether he would want to or not. Kojève considers this an "exceedingly complex, and even insoluble question." The issue for him is time. Human life being essentially finite, rational decisions would have to be prioritized, making an approximation to political choice apparently a matter of human necessity. What is philosophically speaking the best way of life given our human finitude? The philosopher, according to Kojève, will devote his time to the quest for wisdom, which is his guiding objective. This would lead him to renounce the life of action, making him ultimately an epicurean philosopher. Kojève associates this situation with transpolitical "divine revelation" and with Platonic "intellectual intuition," both of which in his materialistic account produce isolation, quietism, and disinterest in the fortunes of other human beings.

This chapter discusses Kojève's argument in favor of Hegelian historicity, which, he believes, would be the way to overcome philosophical quietism. His argument unfolds in response to Strauss's detailed commentary of Xenophon's *Hiero*.[1] In Strauss's estimation, Xenophon's dialogue may be a close point of contact between ancient philosophy and modern political science. Xenophon's teaching might not be too far from Machiavelli's. While

Strauss considers the direction of the modern project to be potentially tyrannical, for Kojève the intervention of thought in the practical shaping of historical time is eventually fated to manifest in the Universal and Homogeneous
State (UHS) effected by the *all-too-human* desire for recognition.

TYRANNY AND WISDOM

Kojève begins his response to Leo Strauss expressing that the relevance of
Xenophon's *Hiero* is not only to understand the philosophical intent of the
author, but to grasp the significance of the dialogue for contemporary world
affairs. The dialogue depicts a seemingly discontented tyrant in conversation
with a wise foreigner who offers him political advice. Kojève notes that it
is Strauss's intent to read the text between the lines, to grasp its tacit hints
and allusions (135). Strauss infers that the dialogue describes the potential
advantages and disadvantages of exercising tyrannical rule. Kojève suspects
that Strauss's study goes "well beyond Xenophon's authentic and perhaps
unknown thought" (136).

Strauss presents himself not as a wise man in possession of ultimate
knowledge, but as a philosophical *reader* in quest for wisdom. At the outset,
it seems to Kojève that Strauss does not say explicitly what his thoughts are
regarding the problem of tyranny, or about the potential relation between the
tyrant and the wise man. Kojève gathers that although Strauss leaves it at
signaling problems, he also raises them with a view to their solution (136).
Kojève's essay seeks to address some of the challenges obliquely indicated
by Strauss, beginning with the problem of tyranny.

The first aspect that is noteworthy to Kojève is that it is not Hiero
the tyrant who seeks advice from Simonides, but the other way around:
Simonides offers his advice "spontaneously."[2] Hiero, at a moment of leisure,
listens to Simonides, without offering an explicit response. Kojève interprets
Hiero's silence as an apparent acquiescence regarding Simonides's wisdom.
Hiero, however, does not give an indication of whether he will implement
Simonides's recommendations. Kojève finds Hiero's reticence naturally
"shocking." Kojève claims that, had we been in Hiero's position, we would
have "drop[ped] everything" to receive such comprehensive advice. Kojève
depicts the spontaneous reaction of dropping everything as a "natural
impulse" and contrasts it with an exercise in political reflection. The tyrant is
not in a position to let go of everything: the tyrant "always has some 'current
business' which is impossible to drop without first completing it" (137). Such
current business may take a long time to fulfil, perhaps centuries. At any rate
it may take longer than the tyrant's own lifetime.

To exercise power the tyrant has to take unpopular measures. From Simonides's perspective, however, it may be possible for the tyrant to remain in power without resorting to violence, relying on sustainably popular procedures. Kojève suggests that Simonides is behaving toward Hiero not like a wise man but more like an *intellectual*, juxtaposing a discursive ideal with a concrete situation that in his view could be reasonably reformed.[3]

In Kojève's practically minded reckoning, what is problematic about discursive ideals is how they may be brought about in the here and now, so that concrete reality can be progressively reformed. He ironically points out that after all Strauss may be right mentioning that Simonides, the wise man, is also a poet. The sophist-poet Simonides presents a "vision, a dream, a utopia" to which Hiero in turn reacts like a "liberal statesman."[4] The visionary poet Simonides does not explain the mechanics, the *effectual truth* of how to implement his political reforms. Hence "like a good liberal" Hiero remains silent: "he does nothing, decides noting, and allows Simonides to speak and to depart in peace" (138). Strauss's Xenophon hints that Simonides's advice to Hiero may be utopian. Simonides's enlightened as well as popular advice appears in the ancient dialogue to be an unrealizable ideal.

The interpretative concern at this initial juncture for Kojève is whether in certain cases renouncing tyranny would mean giving up the exercise of government altogether. Such renunciation of government may as well mean surrendering the prospects for political reform within a given set of historical conditions. Still, is Simonides's advice necessarily utopian? For Kojève what might have appeared utopian to Xenophon, in the contemporary world has become an actual reality: a historical development manifested in the active role of the modern state in the fields of commerce, agriculture, industry. Also, in the turning of mercenaries into a national army and a police force, and the use of the tyrant's personal fortune for public works in the common interest. It seems that the tyrant can gain his subjects' affection by progressively enfranchising them as fellow citizens.

Xenophon knew only of tyrannies exercised in the interest of an established ruling class: dynastic tyrannies based on personal or family intrigues and ambitions. Although Xenophon did not experience ideological and revolutionary regimes for the improvement of social, economic, and political conditions, Kojève polemically contends that Strauss should know better. Kojève disagrees with Strauss's skepticism because, in his view, such utopian visions have become progressively actualized through the modern state. According to Kojève, the "heart of the matter," the efficient cause of history, the motivational mechanism that turns the modern state into an actual regime and not a utopian speculation is the *desire for recognition* (139). In his view, this is also analogously expressed in the dialogue: Simonides explains to Hiero that the pursuit of honor is the key motivation of men. Kojève's essay proposes to explain the dynamics of honor or the desire for recognition as it develops in the direction of immanent human emancipation.

MASTER AND SLAVE DIALECTIC: THE EFFICIENT CAUSE OF HISTORY?

Kojève infers that Simonides begins his dialogue with Hiero taking a pagan and aristocratic perspective: the "master" in the Hegelian dialectic of recognition. He contrasts this stance with its counter-side: the "slave" that Kojève characterizes historically as the "Judeo-Christian" or "bourgeois" man. Apparently, Simonides unpacks the perspective of the master, driven by honor, in a "radical manner" (140). The pursuit of honor distinguishes such "real man," the *aner*: the man willing to risk his life for the sake of recognition.

In Kojève's interpretation, the pursuit of glory is manifest in the honor-seeking masters and appears to be missing in the "servile natures." There seems to be a distinction between the ruling masters who live for worldly glory, and the servile slaves (*anthropoi*). While the master struggles for recognition the slave accepts to labor for the master's interests, to preserve his life. Kojève adds that this anthropological view of the human condition is indeed shocking for a bourgeois person, who as such is an heir of the Judeo-Christian legacy. In contrast to the pagan view, in the secularized version of the Judeo-Christian dispensation what has come to be valued is a person who works hard for the joy of carrying out a project, "transforming an 'idea' or even 'ideal' into a reality shaped by his own *efforts*" (140).

This logic of potentially transformative hard work may also account for the public life of a monarch, a tyrant, or a bourgeois statesman in so far as they exercise political rule rather than "sink into a life of pleasure" (141). In the Judeo-Christian world human beings have been habituated to renounce earthly vainglory.[5] In order to avoid the problem of decadence, the mentality of the idle aristocrat has been progressively made obsolescent by the bourgeois work ethic. For Kojève, the desire to be honored is inherent in the human situation: in the case of the tyrant or statesman, this translates into an attitude of *struggle* for political power. Tragically, the tyrant does not desire another to do the job of ruling, even when somebody else could do it equally well or even better than himself.

In Kojève's reckoning, Hiero appears to follow Simonides's instruction attentively. However, upon closer inspection, it becomes evident that he does not accept Simonides's "justification" for tyranny. Although honor seems the highest pagan end, the tyrant never reaches that goal (142). Why? Because the tyrant "rules by terror" and intimidation, hence, cannot trust that the honors he is bestowed are indeed authentic. Services by compulsion are "acts of slavery" which as such do not give satisfaction to the master.

Kojève describes Hiero's situation as "the tragedy of the master" in Hegel's *Phenomenology of Spirit* (chapter IV, section A). The master "struggles to the death" for the sake of recognition of his human dignity. If the opponent is also a master, he will also fight till the end in an *either/or* struggle. In this power-dynamic submission is interpreted as slavery. But also, if the vanquished party recognizes the victor, such recognition would be "worthless" to the winner. The master cannot win recognition by a vanquished unequal party: a slave who, as Kojève brutally puts it at this juncture, "is not truly a human being" (142).

Kojève distinguishes the feelings of love, affection, and happiness, from the hard realities of the politics of recognition. It is satisfaction and *neither love nor happiness* which is expected from the desire for recognition. Kojève asserts that tyrants aim for recognition above anything else. In his reading, what Hiero expects from Simonides's advice would be how to gain the willing obedience of his subjects. Hiero is concerned with whether his authority will be recognized. The tyrant therefore appears to exercise virtue instrumentally: for the sake of recognition or to impose his authority safely. Kojève concedes that, as a wiseman, Simonides seems to grant this perspective only for *pedagogical* motives. His aim would be the incremental *therapeutic* education of a tyrannical despot away from narcissism toward the common interest by means of the hardnosed dynamics of the dialectic of recognition. In Kojève's account, genuine authority entails to be recognized without inspiring deadly fear in the other. Ultimately, authority also seems interchangeable in his opinion with the problem of the horizontal recognition of human value (143).

FROM THE POLITICS OF RECOGNITION TO THE UNIVERSAL HOMOGENEOUS STATE

For Kojève, Hiero's psychological problem, given that he has to resort to force, is his unsettled lack of recognition. Hiero, therefore, experiences insecurity as well as a chronic lack of ego satisfaction. A political ruler, however, always has recourse to something beyond force: that is, political authority. Such authority is the basis of stable political power. The recognition of authority, for Kojève, implies obedience without manipulation or undue constraint (144). Kojève asserts that the meaning of tyranny in a "morally neutral" sense would be the imposition of authority, without compromise, of a minority not recognized by the majority. This may occur through the imposition of force or terror: instilling in the majority the fear of violent death to get their social compliance. The political actor is moved by his desire for recognition; ultimately such desire—the *desire for desire*—is driven by *pleonexia* and as such it is apparently limitless. Its scope has an expansive reach, and full satisfaction is expected to come if its domain encompasses the whole of humankind (145).

The desire for recognition will also lead the political ruler to decrease the number of people who merely offer slavish obedience. The means for this project of emancipation will be social and economic policies driven by that self-interested objective. Paradoxically though, the tyrant sees anyone's resistance as evidence of their "human worth." Such resistance, domestic and foreign, drives him toward conquest for the sake of recognition. This dynamic of conquest in the name of emancipation leads to the construction of a state that is not only universal, but also, in Kojève's infelicitous and anti-pluralistic expression *homogenous* (146). Kojève contends that the modern tyrant/ Hegelian statesman will not be satisfied till the realm of recognition of his authority be both universal and classless or homogeneous. It is his lack of satisfaction in this front that leads the tyrant to listen to the wise advisor. In order to gain a hearing, the advisor has to avoid sounding impractical or utopian. The "ideal" of the UHS is postulated on the basis of the tyrant's desire for immanent or worldly glory: becoming recognized by all (147).

Presumably, the expectation of this historical ambition would prepare the tyrant to listen to the realistic or concrete advice of the wise man. Kojève wonders though, whether the wise man would want to leave the realm of speculative utopia or general abstraction to become a political advisor/indirect actor. Does the wise man desire to *go down to the cave* to advise the political *thumotic* ruler in concrete policy terms he would understand and accept?

Kojève feels the need at this point to introduce a distinction between the wise man and the philosopher. In Kojève's account, the philosopher lacks wisdom or full self-consciousness or "omniscience." From his materialistic interpretation of Hegel, such full self-consciousness is time-bound or is produced in the context of a given historical epoch (143). For Kojève historical wisdom is an actual possibility.

Kojève reiterates that Hiero's lack of satisfaction derives from his latent need to exercise force upon his subjects. Apparently, Hiero exaggerates his discontent with tyranny to discourage the political envy of potential rivals. On the other hand, "pure terror," the sheer exploitation of the subjects' fear of death, would presuppose ruling by mere physical force, which Kojève grants is not possible, at least not in a political sense. Political rule always entails something other than sheer force. The head of state always has recourse to political authority (144). He owes his political power to the recognition of his authority. The same logic applies to a minority ruling a majority. Their authority would be despotic unless it were based on some sort of shared compromise. Hiero's problem seems to be that he is recognized *by some* but not universally. Again, in this account of the human condition a disposition of resistance is interpreted as signal of human worth. Technically speaking, the modern tyrant's satisfaction would only come from complete recognition when the state becomes *global*, including the whole of humankind (145).

This implies a logic in which the distinction between foreign and domestic spheres of influence apparently ceases to be definitive. The generic slave reacts in such a way that he would do anything to save his life. The dialectic of recognition drives the tyrant to enfranchise the former slaves and to develop the general material conditions that make universal emancipation possible. In Kojève's account, this constitutes not merely a subjective but an objective measure of emancipatory historical "justification" (146). The immanent project of the UHS assumes that the tyrant is driven by the desire for worldly glory to enfranchise the slaves who progressively become the skilled workers and technicians who craft the modern state. The question for Kojève is not about the tyrant's motive, but whether the wise man will muster concrete, measurable, policy-driven advice instead of remaining in the realm of speculative, abstract, utopian generality and nonintervention.

EPICUREAN PHILOSOPHY OR
HEGELIAN HISTORICITY

Kojève acknowledges that Strauss and Xenophon seem to proceed with the figure of the philosopher dedicated to the pursuit of trans-political wisdom. The wise man, in Kojève's own Hegelian reckoning, can come to full self-consciousness of a given historical epoch. He adds that both the philosopher and the wiseman have the status of "initiates" in the art or science of dialectics (148). Hence a key question regarding the philosopher: can he reasonably desire political participation by way of giving concrete advice to the tyrant? Kojève presents a stark dichotomy between the life of the wise advisor becoming politically engaged for the sake of human emancipation, and the "epicurean" or "solipsistic" philosopher who perennially stays apart from the melee.

More specifically, Kojève wonders about the advantages of the philosopher over the "uninitiate" in the art of governing. He expands upon a series of traits that may define philosophical initiation: (1). Expertise in the art of dialectic (which he understands as the capacity for discussion and argumentation). (2). Freedom from prejudice, as a result of the application of the dialectical art. This freedom from prejudice allows him to not have a distorted sense of reality; as such, he is less dependent on the conventionalism of a given context.

(3). An appreciation for the reality of the concrete, or the grasp of "general ideas" that may allow him to give a panoramic and precise account of the part-in-the-whole. Kojève distinguishes this form of reasoning from cogitation in terms of abstract or isolated particulars. Strauss had signaled Hiero's awareness and distrust of Simonides's dialectical skill. Kojève finds this assessment correct: once a government structure is in place, the activity of ruling is mostly discursive: a master of discourse may well become a master of an established government structure (148).

Thus, the philosopher would be better suited to rule than the "uninitiate" because dialectics would allow him to be free from prejudices and to have an ability to "see" the concrete in his thinking (149). This is especially key in the case of structural reforms or in times of profound transformation, when it is no longer possible to rely on on-going and established conventions. In regular times it is apparently not harmful to not have philosophers in power. However, in times of structural reform, which for Kojève is synonymous with revolutionary action, it is key that philosophers be in a politically relevant position to set in motion the overcoming of embedded prejudices and contradictions.

Although there are times of preservation and times where change is objectively feasible, the key reference for Kojève in the midst of the density of reality, is to focus on the concrete. The "uninitiate" man of action tends to grasp the concrete in terms of abstractions: isolating parts by means of a specialization of some sort. He tends to confuse the concrete with the abstract or isolated *particular*. The philosopher, on the other hand, can make the distinction between the abstracted or isolated particular and the concrete within a larger whole. The philosopher can see general patterns in singular cases: he can see therefore their source, function, general composition, and overarching purpose.

For Kojève this implies that the philosopher, at some level in the manner of a Tocquevillian statesman, can see *further* in space and time (150). Kojève reiterates that in his view (and in that of Strauss, Xenophon, and Xenophon's Hiero), the philosopher is indeed capable of assuming political rule, specifically in the role of political advisor. The central concern here is the grounds for the philosopher to make such burdensome commitment. As we noted previously, Kojève suspects that this may be an "exceedingly complex and even insoluble" problem. The problem lies in the limitations of human time. In Kojève's Heideggerian reckoning, human temporality and finitude provide a set of possibilities where human beings experience freedom by means of exercising their choice. The philosopher would have to choose between the quest for wisdom or engaging in political activity in the role of advisor. Again, why would the philosopher cease his quest for wisdom for a lower or less desirable goal? Giving up political activity would be the conclusion of what Kojève calls epicurean or apolitical philosophy. The epicurean philosopher leaves public life choosing instead a retired or isolated life of theoretical contemplation.

Kojève adds that there are two types of epicurean philosopher: (a). The pagan or aristocratic epicurean who is economically self-sufficient and dedicates his life to tend his "garden" (151). This kind of philosopher will, for the most part, be left alone or be tolerated in so far as he remains purely theoretical or non-political in his thinking. (b). The Christian or bourgeois epicurean, who enters market relations out of economic necessity. Such thinker would choose to make a living through academic writing or teaching: replacing the serenity of the epicurean garden for participation in the *Republic of Letters*.[6]

Kojève notes that it is difficult for epicurean philosophers, either of the classical or modern sort, to stay completely away from public affairs. Hence political rulers are always suspicious of them.

At this point of the text Kojève contrasts the epicurean way of living with his grasp of Hegelian historicity. He speculates that to uphold the epicurean *lathe biosas* one would have to acknowledge the eternal immutability of Being. As such, the philosopher could intuit the truth or the revelation of the ontological realm everywhere and always, giving him a source to acknowledge and restfully integrate his serene contemplation.[7] In such scenario, it would be perfectly understandable that the philosopher be retired from public life, a life of appearances, and opt for the epicurean garden. Or, in case of not being aristocratically self-sufficient, he may opt for the Republic of Letters where struggles for existence and economic competition are sought peacefully, by way of reasoned argument and storytelling.

This view of the wise man, self-sufficiently detached from the fortunes of other men, seems to be the philosophical preference of both Strauss and Xenophon. A preference aligned with the classical Platonic-Aristotelian view of the eternal stillness of Being that Kojève also defines as a "*theistic* conception of Truth" (152). Kojève, however, critically disregards this form of life as revealing the choice of an "*egotistical* philosopher." From this we may infer that Kojève, in Strauss's terms, does not distinguish between Athens and Jerusalem.[8] Unlike Strauss, he does not make a distinction between Platonic-Aristotelian metaphysics and religious revelation. In contrast to this view, he seems to endorse an "atheistic" or materialistic reading of Hegel. In such interpretation Being is taken to be *temporal* or identical with Becoming. Being therefore *becomes*, creating or revealing itself anthropomorphically in the course of history. Kojève synthesizes this historicist and nonrelativist conception with the equation: "Being = Truth = Man = History" (152). Kojève believes historical truth objectively unfolds in the becoming of time. Being becomes historically: Being reveals itself in time, making discourse of objectively apparent phenomena a form of temporal "wisdom." Being becomes historical wisdom through human involvement, not in the solitude of the epicurean garden, nor in the small society of the Republic of Letters, but as the comprehensive reckoning of historical active political engagement.

Kojève therefore disagrees with the "epicurean" solution to the problem of the philosophic way of life. To put it somewhat differently: the epicurean conception assimilates "subjective certainty" (*Gewissheit*) with "objective truth" (*Wahrheit*) (153). This would allow the solitary philosopher to acknowledge his own feeling or the "intellectual intuition" of truth as sufficient self-evidence. Kojève interprets Plato, Descartes, and Husserl as essentially in agreement with this inner-oriented understanding. In Kojève's interpretation, the classical Straussian view of philosophical separation is based on "egoism" or pagan pride. In his challenge to Strauss's position, Kojève also brings up the problem of madness (when a mad person is alone in taking his own subjective knowledge as self-evident), or the phenomenon of "false prophets" and the problem of how to recognize them based on an inner criterion of truth. One way to step out of the problem of madness (albeit without necessarily entering the pursuit of truth), is by way of sharing our thoughts with others and finding that we can discuss them with shared interest and a sense of exploration even if they turn out to be ultimately wrong. The solitary epicurean philosopher lacks that possibility of extrinsic validation.[9]

Strangely enough, Kojève also finds "Socratic origins" in his interpretation of epicurean philosophy. He adds that the epicurean philosopher need not merely be a *solitary walker*, but may also have like-minded friends, whom he pejoratively refers to as "the elect" (154). It is the open discussion with such friends, either in the garden or in the Republic of Letters, which may offer a safeguard against solipsistic madness. He adds that it is not uncommon for someone who ceases to be part of a closed "philosophical" group to suffer ostracism and be sent away to a mental asylum.

However, this may be, Kojève's point at this juncture is that philosophical "gardens" are by design exclusive. Although the Republic of Letters may be more open, still, it also tends to be restrictive for the "uninitiated." Kojève finds Strauss consistent with the classical distinction between the few and the many. The Straussian philosopher, in Kojève's characterization, is satisfied with the approval of a select minority: their communication will have the quality of an oral teaching full of hints and ironical tacit allusions. Here Kojève is referring to Strauss's discovery of esoteric writing in response to the problem of historicism, or Strauss's hypothesis regarding why philosophers seem to be of a different mind across the ages. In Kojève's view, however, an esoteric teaching reveals an "aristocratic *prejudice*" which he associates with an imperialistic ethos. In his estimation, the notion of an intellectual elite is a dangerous proposition for a philosopher to entertain. The danger consists in the dreadful problem of sectarianism or the "cloistered mind."

Although the different sects seem to prevent the problem of asocial madness, their exclusivity makes them liable to the proud fostering of prejudices. Kojève, though, reformulates a distinction between philosophy and wisdom: in so far as philosophy partakes in subjective truths, it is also liable to remain attached to prejudices of some sort. But the philosopher would seek to overcome such prejudices. Closed groups tend to accept foundational doctrines that have a propensity to consolidate prejudices over time. The philosopher finds the cloistered group too narrow, and that would direct him to the open world of the marketplace: the way of Socrates (155).

Kojève's Hegelian portrait of Socratic philosophy takes critical distance from the prejudices of aristocrats and of the sophisticated *literati*. Such Hegelian interpretation of human life postulates that reality is not created once and for all: the human condition creates itself in the course of time. Under this state of affairs, the contemplatives would tend to be left behind by the course of events. Truths are historical, and what was true at one point may become a prejudice down the road. Such are the dangers Kojève finds in the cloistered life: close mindedness and missing out the train of history. Both potentially leading to the possibility of remaining anchored in truths that may become prejudices in the course of time.

EROS AND THE EXPECTATIONS OF RECOGNITION

Kojève analyzes now Strauss's distinction between the psychological motivations of Hiero the tyrant and Simonides the philosopher. While Hiero aspires to be "loved" by all human beings (*anthropoi*), Simonides may be satisfied with the qualitative appreciation of a few friends. The incentive for Hiero to become a public servant and benefactor lies in his desire for the recognition of the people at large: to be loved by many and potentially by all. On the other hand, according to Kojève, the sense of appreciation sought by Simonides follows without any effort beyond the manifestation of his own perfection. Hiero's patronage may be widely distributed despite the imperfection of the tyrant. The question at this juncture would be whether such public services, in their imperfection of origin, are ultimately truly beneficial.

In Kojève's rendering of Strauss's philosophical anthropology, the need for love and the desire for admiration or appreciation are different. It is the desire for admiration that leads in the direction for self-perfection. The need for love apparently is not driven by perfectionism, and as such it is not necessarily a philosophical desire.

Kojève takes the desire for recognition to be the incentive behind the actions of the tyrant or statesman. Like Machiavelli and Hegel, he merges the distinction between "is and ought." Kojève also has a private conception of love: love is the purview of the family and of intimate relationships. In the public realm it is political recognition which the public actor is after. Hence, he follows the Hegelian development from household or family life to civil society and eventually to public service (156).

The love Simonides manifests would be related not to his actions, but to his being. Kojève, however, appears skeptical of deifying Simonides, and interprets his character as seeking the political recognition of his perfection or wisdom: hence he seeks to gain the tyrant's ear. Unexpectedly, we learn from the text that Kojève's conception of love is also mystical or suprarational: the love of perfect being "*without* reason." But this love would probably be beyond desire and action. All action is the negation of imperfection. Hiero, the imperfect tyrant, wants to be recognized for his actions. Simonides, in Hiero's view, also partakes in the logic of the desire for recognition. The tyrant and the philosopher want to deserve their recognition: to have their being and becoming coincide publicly or historically. The self-conscious tyrant is also driven by the desire for perfection, even if for the mercenary motive of self-protection.

The question in Kojève's view at this point of the argument is whether the desire for recognition is universal, or, as Strauss seems to claim, can be divided into political recognition for the many and intellectual recognition for the few. Kojève offers a *precis* regarding the problem of political recognition: it is a matter of democratic politics as such. Apparently, only democratic leaders are dependent on public opinion. Tyrants seem to be able to stay in power in so far as they have the support of an inner circle and of a praetorian guard. Kojève stresses that the support of an inner circle and of "competent judges" is not necessarily incompatible with the support of a majority (157). The Kojèvian philosopher does not necessarily disregard the flattering approval of the many. The key point is that the philosopher should beware of disregarding the approval of the well-informed for the sake of popular acclaim, or of meeting *demagogically* the demands of the most unruly parts of the population.

In sum, Kojève seems to approve of a circular logic of recognition: full satisfaction comes from the recognition of those a man deems worthy of recognizing him. This logic is expansionary: the number of those worthy of offering recognition should enlarge progressively as much as possible. This is a shared pedagogical task of philosophers and statesmen that is in principle unlimited. Political education and education in modern philosophy can become universalized. Strauss's view on higher learning might be no more than a premodern prejudice as far as Kojève is concerned. He also finds worrisome that in the closed circle of the epicurean garden or in intellectual cloisters there is a narcissistic tendency to deem worthy only those who offer reciprocal approval.

Kojève finds a point of contact in the desire for recognition in both the classical sophist and in the Hegelian statesman. He concludes that in that matter, there is no difference between the "philosopher" and the tyrant. That may be the reason why both Strauss and Xenophon seem skeptical of Simonides's motivations. Simonides is not Socrates, but whereas their distinction for Kojève is one of degree, the difference for Strauss is one of kind.

Strauss and Xenophon would therefore approve of the figure of the philosopher independent of public opinion. Kojève would not disagree, but only if the philosopher "attained the Truth by some direct personal vision of Being, or by an individual revelation proceeding from a transcendent God" (158). At this point in the text, he seems to grant that if Strauss's contention that perennial philosophy and divine revelation are possible, then the philosopher may contemplate the possibility of self-knowledge independent of public opinion. But he wonders: if philosophical reason or biblical faith are genuine possibilities, what would be the incentive of the philosopher to communicate his knowledge given the likelihood that he will not be understood?

Differently put: if expressing his knowledge depended on reasons that his interlocutors would not understand, then the philosopher may as well remain silent. But this solipsistic possibility might have pathological consequences, or at any rate it would be fundamentally anti-Socratic. The figure of Socrates participates in public discourse, cross-examining the opinions of his fellow citizens. As a lover of wisdom, maybe he would find that his evolution toward knowledge and virtue is a sort of progress. This progress will give him a sense of self-satisfaction, and if his interlocutors are free from envy, they will also get to admire his shared advancement in understanding. This experiment would give him a sort of pleasure that Kojève associates with "pure joy" and "disinterested satisfaction" (159).

Kojève acknowledges that at times some men have ascetically renounced bodily pleasures for the pursuit of truth and the practice of virtue (wisdom being the combination of knowledge and virtue). He proposes, however, that the exercise of virtue and the pursuit of truth come together in *sui generis* pleasures. He finds intractable the problem of distilling whether a man pursues truth and virtue out of duty or out of the pleasure of self-satisfaction (160). Christianity offers a corrective for arrogant self-admiration or vainglory: if the divine is completely *other* (although articulated in the unfathomable mystery of its own incarnation), then envy ceases to be a problem regarding God for the Christian man.

Besides the Christian solution to the problem of human envy, Kojève turns back to Socrates. Socrates is interested in the opinions of others in so far as they allow him to partake in self-examination. Kojève seems to be interested to probe whether Socrates is immune to human vanity: does Socratic self-knowledge rely on the recognition of others? Kojève seems to ignore the platonic notion of *divine mania* and proposes that unless Socrates relied on the recognition or admiration of others for his own self-satisfaction then he would have to be mad. Socrates, however, does not pursue wisdom merely for the recognition of others. It is possible to pursue virtue without witnesses, "simply out of fear of falling short in one's own eyes" (161). But why fear and not *eros*? Socratic dialogue requires recognition by at least one interlocutor to be pursued.

Kojève remarks that the pursuit of truth may occur introspectively in so far as theism of some sort is possible. In his atheistic hypothesis, however, God is replaced by Society, the State, and History. It is sociopolitical history which makes validation possible in his immanent framework. Anything beyond this context is a speculative opinion outside the purview of historical validation, which as such may remain intractable and uncertain. In other words, Kojève seems to *begin* with an intersubjective criterion of truth. On this basis he concludes that the field of objective validation requires extrinsic criteria, which in the absence of a transcendent referent, becomes immanent and thus can be potentially measured by concrete and objective standards. In this immanent framework, the state becomes a "pedagogical institution" whereby the philosopher and the tyrant potentially meet in the making of history (162).

PHILOSOPHY AND THE END OF HISTORY

Pedagogical practice will incline the Kojèvian philosopher to influence state policy. He does this, in part, to create the conditions for philosophy, to educate disciples, whose company are for Kojève what prevents the philosopher from descending into madness. Finding disciples would be an objective criterion of the power of his teaching, at least in terms of its resonance with the historical times.

Beyond inner subjectivity, philosophy becomes pedagogical development. The philosopher becomes an educator. If the philosopher does not want to be enclosed in prejudice he will want to openly share and refine his teaching. This will put him in a position of public participation, which for Kojève translates into political activity: to influence state policy to make his philosophical teaching actually effective.[10] This, for Kojève, is the meaning of political philosophy: the coming together of thought and action by way of philosophical influence on the structural transformation of state policy. He comes back again, however, to the problem of human temporality and finitude: the pursuit of wisdom is a permanent exercise, and government activity "*takes all of a man's time*" (163). This scenario of two full-time occupations produces a dilemma. So, philosophers have found a compromise: the philosopher will be involved in limited, specific tasks of government. Philosophers will not attempt to govern the entire state apparatus but will give rulers specific advice. This compromise, however, is fraught with difficulties, beginning with the lack of effect of their advice (164). The influence of practical philosophical writing is ineffectual at least in the short term. In an exercise of self-reflection, Kojève finds that the philosopher is in a poor position to offer criticism to the political ruler. He is also in a hurry: his contribution to political reform is systemic but is uninterested in the minutiae of policy implementation. Fast changes, moreover, are more feasible from concentrated power (tyranny) than from democratic procedures.

The philosopher is as such apparently lacking in political patience. Kojève mentions Alcibiades in this context of the fraught relationship between disciples of philosophers and the problem of bringing about political reform.[11] At any rate, for Kojève it is enlightened tyrants who are more likely to listen to the philosopher's advice. If the tyrant does not follow philosophical advice, it may be because of his skepticism regarding utopian propositions. The tyrant needs to act in the present, having direct know-how with regards to concrete policy formulation and implementation. To be heard, the philosopher would have to address the issues of the day. This would require of him to be fully up to date on policy matters: but this is precisely what the philosopher cannot not do while remaining a philosopher (165).

Thus, the philosopher's advice is necessarily general, untimely, and ineffectual. If one adds factors of conscience and reflection, the philosopher will not be able to give straightforward advice on time. He will also have a "guilty conscience" for not devoting his time to philosophical pursuits (166). Kojève defines this scenario as the conflict of the thinker faced with the problem of human action: the tragedy of Faust or of Hamlet. The embodied contradiction of two principles, thought and action, that cannot be synthesized. A problem with no solution. The philosopher therefore gives up political action.

But how does the philosopher "justify" such decision with sufficient reasons? Qua philosopher, he acknowledges that he lacks wisdom, and therefore his life ought to continue to be devoted to its wholehearted pursuit through philosophical dialectics or meditation (Kojève here assimilates Plato's Socrates and Descartes). Dialogue or discussion are the means to test philosophical meditations. This discussion seems to find no end. Kojève responds with the modernist formula of "knowing as making" to find objective measures to solve this philosophical aporia: the "method of *historical verification*" (167).

Dialectic therefore ceases to be dialogical or Socratic and becomes the historical negation or overcoming of timely contradictions. False or disorderly notions—between man and society, or man and man, or man and nature—can be overcome by way of historical dialectics. What is historically preserved is therefore what is "true" (168). The mechanism of overcoming takes the shape of *work* for the negation of nature, and *struggle* for the negation of human prejudice. This process of negation unfolds until its end point, the Universal Homogeneous State, the completion of human time: the end of history. A point where negating action is no longer desirable or even possible. History as such virtually puts an end to seemingly endless philosophical controversies.

In this state of affairs, what is then the philosopher's reasonable response to the problem of government? Human temporality and finitude put man in a position to choose. A circumstance that would not apply to an eternal God with endless possibilities.

In Kojève's reading of Hegel, history and historical progress have meaning, and can find its completion or fulfilment in "Absolute Knowledge" or coherent, circular, and non-contradictory discourse (*Logos*). This seems to mean that historical knowledge could be equated with 'eternity' in the sense of the "totality of historical or human time" (169). The man gathering such historical and circular knowledge would apparently be a wise man on earth.[12]

In relation to the man of action, Kojève mentions the likes of Alcibiades, Alexander the Great, Caesar, and Napoleon: all driven to instantiate the universal, to go beyond the limits of the particular city-state.[13] Kojève provocatively speculates the hypothesis that *Socrates* may be at the source of this universal vision applied in the political world: the idea of empire or the universal state as a new political unit. A new, rational, free, multicultural whole (170).

Kojève's Socrates is therefore also an educator of young ambitious tyrants. An educator of princes, like Machiavelli. Thus, Kojève conceives a possible thread of pedagogical continuity between Socrates, Xenophon, Machiavelli, and Hegel.[14] Perhaps like Heidegger, he seems to be making the sweeping claim that "Socratic-Platonic" philosophy has a political goal of ruling particular ways of political life through general forms or empires of global and meritocratic citizenship. Moving as well from biological particularities (peoples or castes) to the universality and human equality of the *logos* in the shape of one consolidated worldview. Kojève references not only Aristotle's student, Alexander the Great, with this political aim but goes back to the Egyptian figure of the pharaoh Ikhnaton to signal the pre-Greek sources of this transnational and transethnic type of political project (171).[15] This idea in Kojève's mind can take the shape of unity under a single God (as in the Egyptian, Hebrew, Christian, or Islamic models), or it can be philosophical and anthropological in nature based on a shared rational and for Kojève *immanent* "essence." The theistic view comprehends a fundamental universal equality under a single God that may become secularized and actualized in the UHS once the drama of history is over.

Kojève provocatively contends that besides its theistic versions, the notion of a universal state can be traced back to Socratic-Platonic philosophy. In the modern epoch, however, the most salient attribute of the project of the universal state is its "homogeneity" or bringing about the "classless society" (172). The universal state, in its synthesis of distinctions, does away with races and rigid social classes, in a way analogous of how Paulinian Christianity did away with closed particular distinctions.

Thus, universal religious "'homogeneity" gives way to the political goal of a secular classless state. Such goal in Kojève's mind is the negation of religious Christianity. The aim of modern philosophy, in his materialistic conception, has been to secularize Christian belief in the shape of rational, immanently transformative, potentially coherent discourse.

How does philosophical speculation find its instantiation in concrete practice? How can it be mediated or bridged? This is the role of the engaged "intellectual." As we have seen, in Kojève's Hegelian conception, the evolution of philosophy mirrors the evolution of history. Philosophy for Kojève means immanent reflection of a given historical epoch. Apparently, such consciousness of a given time gives the philosopher sufficient critical distance to take a stance with regards to his time. If the philosopher finds a certain distance between the "ideal" and the "real" or given material conditions, he will find incentive to bridge that gap by means of historical negation: he will struggle with other human beings, or will work and thus transform the natural elements, in order to reform social and political reality. This process aims at reaching more integrated levels of coherence or noncontradiction toward the "revelation of a new historical reality" eventually aiming at "absolute knowledge or Wisdom" (174). Such historical wisdom is attainable in Kojève's Hegelian estimation. In his mind that is what makes historical progress a matter of human possibility.

Kojève's thought-provoking and irreverent closing question asks whether the compendium of historical wisdom called the Bible, which has been used for the last 2,000 years, will be replaced by a new Book of Wisdom that may eventually encapsulate the truth of our new upcoming era (175). Before that textual crystallization takes place, history, the implementation of wisdom by way of action, or the reasonable relation between the tyrant and the philosopher on the plane of practice has to find closure. If the distance between theory and practice is too large, then philosophical advice will appear impracticable or utopian to the statesman. The intellectuals fill in the gaps between comprehensive theory and concrete decision-making. It is their persuasive capacity for giving concrete advice on the matters and affairs of the day— their "reasonableness"—that gives intellectuals a political hearing.

Perhaps it would be unreasonable for the tyrant to disregard the pursuit of theory based on its apparent immediate impracticability. Analogously, it may be unreasonable for the philosopher to disregard the statesman/tyrant for his inability to bring about a philosophical vision directly in a given political context. Kojève advocates for mutual patience in this regard. The final judgment, from his perspective on philosophical speculation, intellectual adaptation, and practical tyrannical statecraft, comes from History. Historical success or achievement is the ultimate source of all-too-human validation. Kojève therefore stands opposite to the perennial philosophy of Strauss and the Arendtian evocation of the politics of Cato.

NOTES

1. References by page number in the text are from Alexandre Kojève "Tyranny and Wisdom" in Leo Strauss, *On Tyranny*. Including the Strauss–Kojève Correspondence (Chicago: University of Chicago Press, 2000): 135–76. Kojève's essay is a critical response to Strauss's exegesis of Xenophon's classical dialogue *Hiero*. Some of the relevant commentaries and studies I have consulted include Stanley Rosen, *Hermeneutics as Politics* (New Haven: Yale University Press, 1987), chapter 3; George Grant, *Technology and Empire* (Toronto: Anansi, 1969), chapter 4; Steven Smith, *Reading Leo Strauss* (Chicago: University of Chicago Press, 2007), chapter 6. Tom Darby, *The Feast: Meditations on Time* (Toronto: University of Toronto Press, 1982). Waller Newell, *Tyranny: A New Interpretation* (Cambridge: Cambridge University Press, 2013). Michael Roth, "A Problem of Recognition: Alexandre Kojève and the End of History," *History and Theory* 24, no. 3 (October 1985): 293–306. Robert Pippin, "Being, Time, and Politics: The Strauss–Kojève Debate." *History and Theory* 32, no. 2 (May 1993): 138–61. Tim Burns and Bryan-Paul Frost, eds. *Philosophy, History, and Tyranny: Reexamining the Debate between Leo Strauss and Alexandre Kojève* (Albany: SUNY Press, 2016).
2. Contrast with Niccolò Machiavelli, *The Prince*. Leo de Alvarez Trans. (Waveland: Prospect Heights, 1989), chapter XXIII, on how unlikely it is that rulers be open to receive spontaneous advice.
3. For Strauss the founding of modernity is specifically related to Machiavelli's focus on the "effectual truth of the thing" as opposed to the "imagined republics" of classical thought. *Prince*, chapter XV.
4. Grant, *Technology and Empire*, 89, takes the universal state as the ethical "ideal" of contemporary political liberalism. Cf. Rosen, *Hermeneutics as Politics*, 138.
5. Thomas Hobbes, *Leviathan* (Indianapolis: Hackett, 1994), chapter. XV. For Strauss, Hobbes continues the trajectory set by Machiavelli, taming the prince, as it were.
6. Contrast with Hannah Arendt, *Lectures on Kant's Political Philosophy*. Ronald Beiner ed. (Chicago: University of Chicago Press, 1989), 33–40.
7. Cf. Kojève's letter to Strauss (October 29, 1953), where he grants that "if there is something like 'human nature,' then you are surely right in everything." *On Tyranny*, 261.

8. See Leo Strauss "Progress or Return?" in *The Rebirth of Classical Political Rationalism* (Chicago: University of Chicago Press, 1989), 227–70.

9. Cf. Horst Hutter, *Shaping the Future: Nietzsche's New Regime of the Soul and Its Ascetic Practices* (Lanham, MD: Lexington, 2006), 75–107.

10. Hans-Georg Gadamer, *Truth and Method* (New York: Continuum, 1975), 267 ff. Contrast with Leo Strauss, *What Is Political Philosophy? And Other Studies* (Chicago: University of Chicago Press, 1988), 9–55.

11. Cf. José Daniel Parra, "Political Psychology in Plato's Alcibiades I," *Praxis Filosófica* 31 (Julio–Diciembre, 2010): 25–44.

12. Darby, *The Feast*, 187.

13. *Ibid.*, 158–69.

14. For Strauss's critique, see *On Tyranny*, 24–25; 236–39. Cf. also Waller Newell, "How Original Is Machiavelli?: A Consideration of Skinner's Interpretation of Virtue and Fortune," *Political Theory* 15, no. 4 (Nov., 1987): 612–34.

15. Cf. Plato *Timaeus* 22 b–c.

BIBLIOGRAPHY

Arendt, Hannah. *Lectures on Kant's Political Philosophy*. Edited and with an edited essay by Ronald Beiner. Chicago: University of Chicago Press, 1989.

Burns, Tim, and Bryan-Paul Frost, eds. *Philosophy, History, and Tyranny: Reexamining the Debate between Leo Strauss and Alexandre Kojève*. Albany: SUNY Press, 2016.

Darby, Tom. *The Feast: Meditations on Time*. Toronto: University of Toronto Press, 1982.

Gadamer, Hans-Georg. *Truth and Method*. New York: Continuum, 1975.

Grant, George. *Technology and Empire*. Toronto: Anansi, 1969.

Hobbes, Thomas. *Leviathan*. Indianapolis: Hackett, 1994.

Hutter, Horst. *Shaping the Future: Nietzsche's New Regime of the Soul and its Ascetic Practices*. Lanham, MD: Lexington, 2006.

Kojève, Alexandre. "Tyranny and Wisdom" in Leo Strauss *On Tyranny*. Including the Strauss–Kojève Correspondence. Chicago: University of Chicago Press, 2000.

Machiavelli, Niccolò. *The Prince*. Trans. Leo de Alvarez. Waveland: Prospect Heights, 1989.

Newell, Waller. "How Original Is Machiavelli?: A Consideration of Skinner's Interpretation of Virtue and Fortune." *Political Theory* 15, no. 4 (Nov., 1987): 612–34.

———. *Tyranny: A New Interpretation*. Cambridge: Cambridge University Press, 2013.

Parra, J. D. "Political Psychology in Plato's Alcibiades I." *Praxis Filosófica* 31 (Julio-Diciembre 2010): 25–44.

Plato. *Timaeus*. Trans. Donald J. Zeyl, in John M. Cooper ed. *Complete Works of Plato*. Indianapolis: Hackett, 1990.

Pippin, Robert. "Being, Time, and Politics: The Strauss-Kojève Debate." *History and Theory*, 32, no. 2 (May 1993): 138–61.

Rosen, Stanley. *Hermeneutics as Politics*. New Haven: Yale University Press, 1987.
Roth, Michael. "A Problem of Recognition: Alexandre Kojève and the End of History." *History and Theory* 24, no. 3 (October 1985): 293–306.
Smith, Steven. *Reading Leo Strauss.* Chicago: University of Chicago Press, 2007.
Strauss, Leo. *The Rebirth of Classical Political Rationalism*. Chicago: University of Chicago Press, 1989.
———. *What Is Political Philosophy? And Other Studies*. Chicago: University of Chicago Press, 1988.

PART III

Three Concrete Kojèvean Outcomes and Their Likelihood

Authority, the Mirror Stage, and Global Trade

Chapter Nine

Authority and Legitimacy in Alexandre Kojève's *The Notion of Authority*

Bryan-Paul Frost

It is hard to imagine a worse time for sustained philosophical reflection *and* productivity than occupied France during World War II—especially if one was actively working for the Resistance and was nearly executed by the Nazis.[1] But for Alexandre Kojève, these years were in fact some of his most productive *and* reflective. In 1942, Kojève completed *La notion de l'autorité*; in 1943, he finished a massive, 600-page tome titled *Esquisse d'une phénoménologie du droit*; and in 1945, he produced a fascinating policy paper, *L'Empire Latin*, about the possible future course of Europe (and especially France) in the postwar world of the superpowers.[2] And if this was not enough, Kojève was also planning to complete detailed discussions of the family, the state, and the character of work.[3]

The Notion of Authority has received almost no scholarly attention, perhaps because it was so recently published and translated among Kojève's posthumous writings.[4] It must be admitted as well that *Notion* is not as complete as many of his other works: while the phenomenological analysis of authority occupies the majority of the book and is quite robust, the sections on ontology are cursory and insufficient by Kojève's own admission (the metaphysical analysis falls somewhere in-between, but with a rich discussion of the relation of Authority to Time).[5] Nevertheless, *Notion* clearly influenced his later writings. To cite one of many examples, in his famous exchange with Leo Strauss in *On Tyranny*, Kojève discusses the concept of authority in an important and prominent place; but in a new critical edition of Kojève's *complete* response to Strauss—parts that were never published previously—it is revealed that Kojève made even more extensive use of his analysis in *Notion*, grounding many of his arguments and claims in this hitherto apparently unknown text.[6] Moreover, *Notion* also helps to resolve certain puzzles in Kojève's thought (e.g., how Masters, who seek recognition from others in a struggle to the death, could ever form a cohesive political order) as well as to reveal new ones (e.g., an eminently traditional or even conservation strain in his thinking—and this from a radical, Leftist, Hegelian-Marxist). With these observations in mind, the purpose of this essay is twofold: in the first place, to limn the most significant philosophical and political themes and implications of his argument as a whole; and in the second place, to situate these themes and implications in critical places in his corpus more generally. What we hope to demonstrate (or at least to make plausible) is that the argument and conclusions of *Notion* deserve no less attention than his famous discussion of Hegel's Master-Slave dialectic: indeed, one might argue that *Notion* is even more foundational than the latter, given that the authority of the Master is one of only four archetypes, and it does not seem privileged over the other three in any strict sense.

THE ARGUMENT OF *NOTION*: WHAT IS AUTHORITY?

Kojève announces in the "Preliminary Remarks," in a seemingly cavalier and even preposterous fashion, that the idea of authority has been very "little studied" by political philosophers.[7] But what Kojève means by this is that there has not been an exhaustive and thorough study of authority—an attempt to disclose and to unravel its very essence. On the one hand, previous philosophers have privileged one kind of authority over another, without seeing or acknowledging its various manifestations; and on the other hand, a comprehensive analysis based on phenomenology, metaphysics, and ontology has not been completed. Indeed, Kojève asserts that without a proper understanding of authority, there cannot be any full and complete analysis of political power, the structure of the state, or even of the state in and of itself. In respect to the first point, Kojève immediately indicates that there are four kinds of authority, three of which are associated with a particular philosopher, and one of which is associated with a school of philosophy. These four types of authority are the theological or scholastic theory, where authority belongs to God; the Platonic theory of justice; the Aristotelian theory of wisdom or anticipatory prudence; and Hegel's Master-Slave dialectic. In respect to the second point, Kojève suggests (as indicated in the table of contents and the division of the book as a whole) that the phenomenological analysis will have political applications; the metaphysical moral or ethical; and the ontological psychological ones. Kojève most fully develops only the phenomenological and metaphysical aspects of his theory, admitting that his analysis and deductions are therefore only provisional at best. At all events, authority comes first in his interwar writings as it must be understood before the state, right, the family, and work (even though Kojève was able to discuss all four of these concepts to a greater or lesser extent throughout his prewar writings).

The phenomenological analysis begins with a general definition of authority. Kojève offers several formulations of the character of authority, all of which are in contrast to the use of force. Authority is a social relation between at least two individuals, with the authoritative agent being a "*free* and *conscious*" person: an "*authoritarian* act is distinguished from all other acts by the fact that it does not encounter *opposition* from the person or persons toward whom it is directed. This in turn presupposes both the *possibility* of opposing it and the *conscious* and *voluntary* renunciation of realizing this possibility." In other words, the authoritarian act or actor can change the "outward human given without suffering a repercussion from this action, i.e., without himself changing as a result of his action," or again, that authority "is the possibility of acting without making compromises."[8] The necessary use of—or even the threat of the use of—force to compel one to do something, therefore, displays a failure of or imperfection in that authority. One's mere will is sufficient if it is authoritative—even having to persuade someone to do something displays a lack of authority. We might say that there is a majesty—or even an uncompromising purity—in the concept of authority in its relation to force, whether verbal or physical. Even the hint of the need of or recourse to the use of force renders that so-called authority partial, conditional, defective, or wholly absent.

Kojève helps to clarify authority by contrasting it with right (*droit*), God, and love, the former of which is perhaps the most instructive. Whereas authority admits the "*possibility*" of opposition and force (but it is never "*actualized*"), "Right implies and presupposes force while being something different from it (there is no Right without Court of Law, no Court without Police that can carry out the decisions of the Court by force)." Thus, having the right to something may require the forceful and even violent intervention of the state, judge, and/or police in order to actualize or to vindicate that right, even when one has the authority to exercise that right; authority, by contrast, means that "one needs to *do nothing* in order to exert [that] Authority." Right may or may not have authority in the eyes of the person over and against whom one exercises that right: if right has recognized authority, force will not be needed; if not, force will be needed but without at all destroying the character of right. As for love, according to Kojève, a lover "*spontaneously*" does what his/her beloved desires (there is no need to order or to command their will). Divine authority differs from human authority in that it is "absolutely *impossible*" (by definition) to react against God or the divine (i.e., an omniscient, omnipresent, and omnipotent Being): reaction against human authority, while possible, is self-consciously and voluntarily renounced. Of course, as Kojève indicates, it is easy to see how human authority is often confused with or cloaked in terms of love and religion, while being essentially distinct from both.[9] Human authority, therefore, is always recognized by others, potentially perishable, and inherently risky.

Kojève then proceeds to describe the four "simple, pure or elementary" types of authority. Each of these phenomenological descriptions can be thought of as Weberian archetypes of sorts—analytical constructs which bring out in relief certain defining characteristics of the (historical) phenomena in question. Let us briefly state them in chronological order.[10]

1. The Platonic theory is the authority of the Judge (Type J). Variants include the authority of an arbitrator, supervisor, and moderator, as well as that of the confessor, the just, and the honest man.
2. The Aristotelian theory is the authority of the Leader (Type L). Variants include the superior over a subordinate (in multiple spheres of life, e.g., employer, scholar, technician, and so on), teacher over student, and revealingly, the soothsayer and prophet over their followers and flock.
3. The Scholastic theory is the authority of the Father (Type F). Variants include the elderly over the young (i.e., age differences), tradition, and the dead over the living (e.g., the power of a will and testament).
4. The Hegelian theory is the authority of the Master over the Slave (Type M). Variants include the noble over the serf, soldier over civilian, man over woman, and the victor over the vanquished.

Each of these "pure" types of authority can stand alone, or they can be combined with one, two, or three others in a variety of combinations, depending upon which type of authority is preeminent or most prominent, and those which are of secondary or tertiary importance, or absent altogether (e.g., JL or LJ, FML or LMF, JLFM or MFLJ, and so on). Trusting to Kojève's math, there are a possible sixty-four variations of authority in theory: four pure types, twelve doubles, twenty-four triples, and twenty-four quadruples. Whether all of these combinations exist in fact (or have existed historically) is a question Kojève leaves aside for a more comprehensive analysis. What he stresses here, however, are the following two implications: on the one hand, each type of authority has a "natural tendency" to appropriate or to claim all of the other types of authority in order to become a "total Authority"; and on the other hand, it is possible to have one type of authority without any of the others, and without that original authority necessarily being cancelled out (e.g., a Leader can be considered a bad Judge, but this does not necessarily eliminate his authority as a Leader, but rather only weakens, erodes, and perhaps annuls it over time—and vice versa with all the other permutations). In other words, there is both *"absolute"* and *"relative"* authority.[11]

Kojève then discusses each pure type in detail, distinguishing each from the others in an attempt to demonstrate its singular uniqueness—that is, to show that no philosopher or school had a complete or thorough understanding of authority. Not surprisingly, Kojève begins with Hegel's theory, which he claims is the most developed of them all.[12] Kojève offers a short synopsis of Hegel's Master-Slave dialectic, referring readers to his seminal article in *Mesures* for a more complete elaboration.[13] What is essential to emphasize here is that the Master's authority over the Slave is not based on force (as this would annul his authority) but rather on the risk of his (the Master's) life for the sake of recognition in a struggle to the death for a "non-biological" or "non-animal" end—namely, confirmation of his "human reality or dignity" through victoriously enduring the struggle for prestige and recognition. The Slave, therefore, voluntarily and self-consciously submits to the Master's authority and is now subjected to his will, having subordinated or renounced his (potentially) human desire for autonomy and respect to his animal and biological desire for mere life. Kojève offers a poignant contemporary reference to solidify his explanation of the genuine authority of the Master over the Slave (or the victor over the vanquished). "Compare the German slogan *'im Felde unbesiegt'* [undefeated in battle], which destroyed the emergent Authority of the victors of 1918; the latter, having not had their victory 'recognized,' had no Authority; they thus had to call on force—with the known result that followed."[14]

In the course of Kojève's explanation of Hegel's theory of authority, he repeatedly remarks that, contrary to what Hegel may have thought or believed, it is not in any way a complete or general theory of the phenomenon. Kojève concludes his discussion by noting that Hegel's theory

> does not account for the Authority of the *Leader*. A Master does not have Authority only in relation to the Slave (qua Master, in the narrow sense); he can also have (in his capacity as Leader) an Authority in relation to other Masters. But Hegel's theory does not account for the existence of an Authority of the *Leader* among men who are socially *equal*. And it applies even less to facts pertaining to the Authority of the *Father* or the *Judge*, where the element of Struggle and Risk of life is totally lacking.[15]

This is one of Kojève's most poignant criticisms of Hegel in all of his writings: for those who might argue that Kojève was little more than a mere interpreter (or commentator) of Hegel's texts, this passage would seem to belie that claim.[16] There can be no doubt that Kojève was deeply indebted to Hegel and considered him a towering philosopher—but Kojève was in no way wedded to or completely dependent upon him. To put it bluntly, Kojève was a genuine and independent thinker in his own rank, and regardless of how much he respected Hegel, he was always ready to strike out on his own and to pursue the truth wherever it lay. Indeed, we could argue that Kojève was the founder of a new political philosophy or understanding (or at least might have considered himself as such), and that, while building upon the foundations laid by thinkers of the past, may have surpassed them in depth and magnitude in certain fundamental respects.

As important as the preceding remarks are in clarifying Kojève's relationship to Hegel, what is perhaps more revealing is how the discussion of the authority of the Master, coupled with the ensuing descriptions of the other forms of authority (Leader, Judge, and Father), help to resolve a critical ambiguity or even impasse in Kojève's political thought as a whole: how is it possible that genuine Masters—who prefer death to slavish recognition of the superiority of another—can create and peacefully coexist together in a political community? In other words, how does Kojève account for the origins of political life given his account of the struggle for recognition? Kojève is acutely aware of this dilemma and stresses its seriousness when he writes that "In truth, Hegel does not explain how a Master can be recognized by another Master. In other words, he does not explain the genesis of the State. And this is the most important gap in his phenomenology."[17] What *Notion* allows us to see for the first time, in its most complete form, is how Kojève initially answered this challenge.

What the four-fold typology of authority demonstrates, in broad outline, is that "Masterful" authority is not the only authority "Masters" respect. Masters also respect the authority of the Father, the Judge, and the Leader (in and to various degrees), and that this respect allows them to coexist in relative harmony in a stable political order. Although Kojève does not specifically refer to this, one might think of the *Iliad* (after all, the Master-Slave dialectic is closely associated with classical antiquity): while Achilles is clearly understood as the greatest warrior (Master?), he acknowledges (sometimes) and even submits to a number of other individuals and to their respective authorities and judgments, from Agamemnon (Leader?) to Priam (Father?) and to Nestor (Judge?). Kojève's understanding of the dynamics of the Master-Slave dialectic are much more capacious than previously thought. Masters can respect and even obey other Masters in capacities other than the authority of the Master.

In the *Esquisse* Kojève further elaborates, and makes more refined and supple, how Masters might create a political community, and thus a hierarchical political order, among Masters themselves. Kojève first describes some of the ideas that could arise in a Master's mind after he successfully risked his life in the struggle for recognition. Because the Master is now a self-conscious being, and because he has overcome his animal nature, he can consider his human self not only as a subject but as a "subject of right." What Kojève has in mind here is that the Master will want to be thought of and treated in a particular way. The Master is no longer an animal but a self-conscious human being, and he will demand that his humanity be respected when he interacts with others. What is more, the Master can distinguish between his previous condition as an animal and his present one as a dignified human being: in other words, he can distinguish between what he once *was* and what he *is* or *ought to be*. By assigning a positive value to the fact that he has conquered his own fear of violent death, the Master can come to believe that it is his and everyone else's *duty* to realize their humanity through the negation of their animal nature. The Master will hold in utter contempt those who fail to do their duty, and he will look upon and treat them as unworthy of any rights and respect.[18]

Kojève then goes on to describe a situation in which a Master witnesses two other individuals engaged in a struggle for recognition. The spectator knows from his own experience that the combatants have freely consented to risk their lives (otherwise one of them would flee), and he can see that the conditions of the struggle are equal for both of them (i.e., neither combatant has any sort of advantage over the other and either one of them could become a future Master or Slave). Because both adversaries have voluntarily agreed to fight, and because the struggle is engaged under "*the same*" or "*equal*" conditions, the spectator will want to treat the victor of the struggle in the same way as he wants to be treated, namely as an equal in his interactions with other Masters. In other words, if it is a person's duty to risk his life, and if the conditions of the struggle are "strictly symmetrical" for both of them, the spectator will detach the concept of *equality* from the struggle itself, and he will want to apply that concept to his interactions with those individuals who, like himself, are worthy to be considered subjects of right. Kojève argues that the spectator will want to realize what he calls the idea of the justice of equality "*everywhere*" and "*every time*" he sees persons emerging victorious from the fight for pure prestige.[19]

Finally, Kojève asks us to imagine a situation in which several individuals are engaged in a struggle with several others. As each of the combatants is simultaneously a participant in the struggle as well as a spectator of the struggles of others, those who win the fight and enslave the others will consider themselves as equals; and as compatriots or fellow citizens they will want to apply the idea of the justice of equality in their interactions with one another. From Kojève's comments here and elsewhere, it would appear that the desire for recognition can just as easily be satisfied in collective as in individual struggles, whether engaged or witnessed: Masters can realize their humanity together as brothers-in-arms, without ever feeling compelled to challenge one another in a fight to the death.[20] Of course, Masters do not recognize one another as unique individuals but only in their universal aspect of human existence. The fight for pure prestige is the same for everyone who engages in it, and there is no reason why any one Master should have fewer or greater rights and duties than any other. From the Master's point of view, what counts most is to emerge victorious from the struggle for recognition, and one can do so either by engaging in a one-on-one struggle with another individual or by joining a group of Masters in order to do battle with another such group. It is now possible to see how a Leader (or even a tyrant) could arise among a group of Masters and subsume their particular wills under his own. If Masters want to apply the idea of the justice of equality to their interactions with one another, they will sooner or later need to articulate specific rules that will govern their conduct. The Leader would be that rare individual who successfully concretizes his incipient understanding of justice into a code of law—the one who is somehow able to put into words how all the Masters want to be treated as fellow citizens. It would seem that once a Master is recognized as a Master by at least one other individual (be it another Master or his Slave), he is just as interested in applying an idea of justice to his interactions with others as he is in fighting for the sake of recognition. In true Hegelian fashion, Kojève shows how the desire for recognition—a desire which initially drives individuals into mortal conflict—generates from within itself a new desire (or authority) which brings them together as fraternal compatriots. Kojève emphasis here in the *Esquisse* is on the resultant idea of justice and right (the authority of the Judge) that originates between and is created among Masters, but that is certainly because it is the principle theme of the book—but the authority of the Leader and even the Father are not far behind. In sum, despite all the teasing references to authority in the *Esquisse*, one would be hard pressed to conceptualize and to articulate Kojève's full and complete conceptual framework without *Notion*.[21]

In turning to the two classical notions of authority (Plato and Aristotle), let us note the following high points. Aristotle's theory of Leadership seems most closely allied to Hegel's theory of Mastery; but here the crucial difference is that the Leader can anticipate or see a project or goal in the future—an event horizon that others are willing to follow but cannot discern themselves. It is the Leader's prudence, foresight, and anticipatory capacity that allows him to guide a band of Masters and eventually to become their sovereign, king, or dictator (without ever relinquishing their status as "equal" Masters). The ability to see farther into the future also characterizes teachers over students, superiors over subordinates, and soothsayers and prophets over the uniniti-ate.[22] In respect to Plato's theory of the Judge, we seem to have here a clear break from the previous two types of authority, if only because struggle, risk, and leadership are completely lacking, and because the authority of the Judge tends to reject the legitimacy of all other kinds of authority: Justice seems to be—or claims to be—a *sui generis* authority. But Kojève claims that this is false: the authority of the Judge requires the assistance of the state (for both defining laws and enforcing them). Nevertheless, the character and qualities of a Judge—"impartiality," "objectivity," and "disinterestedness"—carry an authority that is outside the strict provenance of Mastery and Leadership, and the authority of a Judge can compete with or even subvert the other two (although all three are able to overlap and to coexist together).[23] It is worth noting that in respect to the authority of the Leader and the Judge, Kojève brings up the classical examples of Xenophon in the *Anabasis* and Deioces in Herodotus—the former having a spontaneous origin as Leader among the Ten Thousand Greeks and the latter a cleverly designed plot (according to Herodotus) to become Judge over all the Medes in order to ascend to absolute political power based on his justice.[24] One eagerly wishes to know how Kojève would have applied his authoritative schema to other classical legends, from Themistocles to Pericles, Cleon to Brasidas, or Alcibiades to Nicias.

The scholastic theory of the Father is perhaps the most arresting and contains (as we will see) some of the most far-reaching and perplexing implications. Unlike the authority of the Judge, which tends to claim an exclusive authority outside of—or transcending and thus superseding—the authority of Masters and Leaders, the authority of the Father tends to engulf or to integrate all other forms of authority under its own auspices or rubric. Simply put, the authority of the Father (according to the scholastics) is the authority of God, and every legitimate authority has a divine essence. God is the Master or lord over his host; God is the Leader of his people and has knowledge of their destiny; and God is Judge of all man, dispensing perfect "divine" justice. In sum, God is the creator—the cause over the effect—and all effects must acknowledge the authority of their cause lest they deny themselves in the process. But the scholastics missed the forest for the trees: Plato, Aristotle, and Hegel have accounted for the Judge, the Leader, and the Master, and what is needed is an account of tradition, of age, of generation, of heredity, of inheritance. "The theological theory must therefore account for what we have called the Authority of the Father, and for that which the three other theories cannot explain." One need not have recourse to God to explain the authority of the Father. "We can therefore classify this theory along with the other three, while stripping it of its *theo*-logical character." The divine right of kings or hereditary monarchy, for example, has a fully secular explanation, namely the hereditary transmission of authority from father to son. The scholastics understood the independent status of the authority of the Father and all that it entailed, but mistakenly attributed that characteristic to God (our Father in heaven and thus the ultimate creator and cause). Interestingly, at the end of his descriptive analysis, Kojève claims that the purest form of this authority might be that which "an Author (in the broadest sense of the word) has over his Work [*Œuvre*]," whether it be literary, artistic, or philosophic, or that of a founder, political or otherwise.[25]

FROM PRINCIPLES TO APPLICATIONS: ELECTIONS, MAJORITY RULE, AND TIME

Kojève continues his phenomenological description of authority with a discussion of how it is generated and transmitted. In terms of its genesis, authority is either spontaneous or conditioned. The spontaneous creation of authority can (seemingly) occur in all four cases: the Master overcomes his fear of death in a struggle for recognition; the Leader proposes a future-oriented project accepted by others; and the Judge demonstrates his authority through impartial and disinterested decisions. In the case of the Father, however, it is hard to understand this authority as spontaneous or active since every individual has this ability (i.e., to be a father) in principle. Once again, the authority of the Father is a bit unique and even problematic: the authority of the Father is therefore best understood not as spontaneous but as transmitted.[26]

In terms of conditioned authority, Kojève also suggests that it is more correctly conceived of as a case of transmission—how authority is passed from one person (or entity) to another. To illustrate his point, Kojève draws upon social contract theory, where the authority of a ruler is purportedly conditioned upon the agreement of those over whom he rules.

> According to the "social contract" thesis, for example, the "first" (political) Authority has its origin in a (collective) decision—that is to say, an act, not that of the person who will exercise Authority, but of those who will be subject to it. Authority is, therefore, *conditioned* here by something *other* than itself, by acts *other* than those of the person who will embody it. And the same applies when the man who has to embody Authority is randomly chosen [in the sense of drawing lots] or designated by something which has nothing to do with his own acts ("merits") or his "personality" in general (the case of the Dalai Lama, for example).

Kojève demurs:

> But we can ask ourselves if there is truly, in such cases, a *genesis* of Authority. It seems, on the contrary, that we are dealing with the *transmission* of Authority,

the emergence of the new Authority being conditioned by the preliminary existence of another *Authority*.[27]

Kojève therefore concludes that "every genuine *genesis* of Authority is necessarily *spontaneous*" and that the "so-called *conditioned* 'geneses' . . . are nothing other than cases of *transmission*."[28] In drawing out the full implication of this claim, Kojève contends that an election does not *confer* authority on the person elected but rather only *confirms* or makes *manifest* the authority the elected has already achieved or earned (whether as Master, Leader, Judge, or Father). In other words, the elected has spontaneously earned his or her authority beforehand, which the election simply affirms or makes manifest: the loser of an election never had authority to begin with, and the election simply made that manifest. One wonders, on Kojève's own terms, why elections are needed at all—or if there is the proverbial chicken-egg problem here: which comes first, the election (which makes manifest the already recognized authority of the elected) or the authority (which seems to make superfluous the election as the elected already possessed that hitherto authority to begin with)? Perhaps elections are needed only as a sort of crowning achievement or ultimate manifestation of the preexisting but as yet unrecognized authority of the elected—but an authority that is not conditioned in, by, and through the election itself but was generated spontaneously or transmitted.[29]

In turning to the transmission of authority more fully, Kojève claims that there are three kinds of such authorial transmissions: heredity, nomination, and election. Although the heredity transmission of authority is possible in all four cases, it would seem most appropriate with the Father (the son—but not the daughter—inheriting through tradition the virtues of the father and the family as a whole), and least appropriate with the Judge (there is no guarantee that the son will be as just as the father): the Master and the Leader would seem to fall somewhere in between. But overall, Kojève has little belief in this idea: it is fundamentally a "primitive" and even "magical" way of thinking, a residue of the divine that mistakenly believes virtues can be passed on from one person(s) to another (nominally their male offspring or their designated heir apparent). As for nomination and election, Kojève distinguishes them as follows:

[T]here is transmission of Authority by *nomination* when the candidate for Authority is designated by the person (or persons) who already possess an *Authority*, and one *of the same type* (a Leader nominated by a Leader, for example); there is transmission by *election* when the candidate is designated by persons or a person who either have *no* Authority or have an Authority *of another type* (a Judge nominated by a Leader, for example).

This last point is critical. If the electors do not have authority, or if they do not have the same type of authority as the elected, then Kojève avers that "[s]trictly speaking, election does not differ in essence from drawing lots. . . . Therefore, direct *universal* suffrage—and referendum—do not differ from drawing lots." It would seem that the only viable type of transmissible authority is that by nomination (especially of a current Leader to a future Leader). But even here, Kojève once again reminds us and reemphasizes that by "its very essence, Authority implies a *spontaneous* generation. Any form of transmission of Authority always diminishes it more or less."[30] It would seem that new Leaders (and others) must strike out on their own in order to maintain or to create their full complement of authority.

Kojève's remarks here are part of a much larger discussion about majority (or minority) rule, and why the majority (or the minority) is not a type of authority per se. Now Kojève admits here in *Notion* that the majority (or the minority) can possess one of the aforementioned types of authority—but they cannot have genuine authority simply based on the fact that they are merely part of a whole.[31] In other words, for a majority (or a minority) to have authority they must have a *qualitative* value and not merely a *quantitative* one. The majority's public opinion qua number has no more validity than the minority's elitism qua snobbery: as philosophers from Aristotle to Hobbes have concurred, such a claim by the majority would be based on force alone.[32] Majority (and minority) rule has no authority as such—only the illusion of one. Kojève is of course aware that the majority need not employ force in order to rule and to get its way: the mere threat or possibility of the use of force is enough. But again, the threat or possible use of force is not authority, and thus a regime "based *purely* and *solely* on a majority is a regime founded on force only." He continues:

> In short, the fact of being in a majority or a minority can never by itself engender an Authority; the Authority of the Majority or the Minority is either illusory (simple force), or it belongs to one of the types mentioned above or to their "combinations" (this Authority could, as a matter of fact, belong to the Minority as much as to the Majority).

As Kojève wryly concludes: "If a boxing champion tells me to leave a café, I do it without 'reacting,' but certainly not because he has any Authority in my eyes."[33]

Kojève's discussion of majority (and minority) rule takes place within a discussion of Jean-Jacques Rousseau (perhaps the only sustained discussion of Rousseau in Kojève's corpus as a whole).[34] Kojève admits (with Rousseau) that the general will and the majority are not at all necessarily the same, and that the former can be directly opposed to the latter: the general will is the authority of the whole over the part(s) and not a part (majority) over a part (minority). As such, Kojève argues that the general will is akin to a living organism (where the parts are subject to the whole), and thus will have the characteristics of *"heredity"* and *"harmony"* (i.e., *"permanence"*).[35] Translated into authoritarian language, the general will displays the authorities of the Father and Judge (but not that of Leader or Master). Kojève also makes the incisive comment that when the general will lost its divine character (which it had acquired or appropriated in pagan times and during the Middle Ages, whether through the pronouncements and interpretations of the Delphic Oracle or the Church and the Papacy), it was then assumed and acknowledged that the majority expressed the will of the whole. In the twentieth century, there was an attempt to replace that divine character with a different "support," as for example the "'Proletariat' of Lenin-Stalin, the '*Impero*' of Mussolini, the *Volk* of Hitler, and so on."[36] In sum, while the general will is an indisputable fact, it is not a *sui generis* authority and can be subsumed under two of the authorities Kojève has previously described.

The above remarks on majority rule, in general, and the general will, in particular, help to explain—or at least to clarify—one of Kojève's most bold and perhaps contentious claims in his debate with Leo Strauss in *On Tyranny*. In discussing the fundamental character or nature of tyranny, Kojève writes:

> In fact, there is tyranny (in the morally neutral sense of the term), when a fraction of the citizens (it matters little whether it be a majority or a minority) imposes on all the other citizens its own ideas and actions, ideas and actions that are guided by an authority which this fraction recognizes spontaneously, but which it has not succeeded in getting the others to recognize; and where this fraction imposes it on those others without "coming to terms" with them, without trying to reach some "compromise" with them, and without taking account of their ideas and desires (determined by another authority, which those others recognize spontaneously). Clearly this fraction can do so only by "force" or "terror," ultimately by manipulating the others' fear of the violent death it can inflict upon them. In this situation the others may therefore be said to be "enslaved," since they in fact behave like slaves ready to do anything to save their lives. And it is this situation that some of our contemporaries label *tyranny* in the pejorative sense of the term.[37]

According to the above argument—and this buttressed by similar arguments in *Notion* and the *Esquisse* (see esp. part 1, chapter 2)—regimes lacking at least one type of authority must be considered tyrannical, whether past or present. Kojève would seem to rip the veil off of the character or nature of majority rule if it is shorn of any genuine authoritarian basis: what we might say or believe about the grandeur or nobility of democracy properly so-called is simply a hoax and is bogus. Of course, these claims make us wonder whether any regime—past or present—has lived up to Kojève's standards, or whether all have been tyrannies to a greater or lesser extent, not differing in kind but only in degree. Without saying so directly in *Notion*, it would appear that only Kojève's universal and homogeneous state could somehow integrate one or more forms of authority, or supersede them altogether in some fashion: only a universal and homogeneous state can achieve a true, and therefore truly just and rational, homogeneous cosmopolitanism, where all individuals can be full members of the only whole that matters—as free and equal citizens of the whole earth.

Kojève concludes his phenomenological analyses with a brief discussion of metaphysics, and in particular how each type of authority relates to time. As authority is a human, social, and historical phenomenon, it must have a temporal structure in all *four* of its phenomenological manifestations—past, present, future, and eternity—and it is this connection or correlation to time that establishes the foundational ground that there are four types of authority and four types only.[38] Each type of authority in its temporal relation is readily recognizable on Kojève's own terms.

1. The Past is the Scholastic theory of the Father (Type F), where heredity, history, tradition, seniority, and, thus, venerability, predominate.
2. The Present is the Hegelian theory of the Master (Type M), where we wish to be up-to-date, contemporary, fashionable, and never behind-the-times (or, as Kojève later explains, in the risk of life for the sake of recognition in a present action).
3. The Future is the Aristotelian theory of the Leader (Type L), where revolution, anticipatory projects, the young, and tomorrow, are preeminent.
4. Eternity is the Platonic theory of the Judge (Type J), where so-called eternal principles of justice and right are applied to all and for all time.

For those familiar with Kojève's thought, it is hardly surprising that he privileges the future (and thus the Leader) above the other three modes: "Authority par excellence is that of the (political, religious, and so on) 'revolutionary' Leader, having a *universal* 'project' (Stalin)."[39] Otherwise, the most intriguing type of authority in respect to temporality is the Judge (and not the Father) in that the Judge's authority rests upon eternity (i.e., to eternal principles of justice and right) and not time: strictly speaking, eternity is not temporal but a negation of time, and is thus in a dialectical relationship with time. The uniqueness of the authority of the Judge consists in the fact that it does not readily lend itself (as discussed earlier) to transmission as the other three types often do (especially hereditary transmission), and that it is an authority that can set itself against the other three in a way that those other three cannot (i.e., principles of justice exist outside of time, and they can be used to judge the authority and wills or decisions of the other three types at all times and places). But it must be emphasized (perhaps unbeknownst to the Judge) that justice and right also have their own dialectical transformations and integrations over time, as are most fully articulated in the *Esquisse*: the justice of equality (of Masters) dialectically interacts with the justice of equivalence (of Slaves) to achieve the justice of equity in the universal and homogeneous state (of the Citizen). Whether these claims concerning temporality ultimately demonstrate that his authoritative scheme is complete and coherent is left to the reader to decide; but from a Hegelian-Marxist historicist perspective like Kojève's, it is rather illuminating, impressive, and even convincing.[40]

MONTESQUIEU REDUX: A NEW UNDERSTANDING OF THE SEPARATION OF POWERS

Kojève concludes *Notion* with a series of "Deductions," both political, moral, and psychological. The latter two are very incomplete, and consist only in stating that the political implications need to be supplemented with an understanding of how these pertain to "the individual-citizen and the State in their mutual relations" (moral consequences) and "the individual-citizen in himself" (psychological consequences).[41] What is most consequential and arresting is Kojève's new interpretation of the separation of powers doctrine (political consequences), his apparently longest extended discussion of this theme in his work as a whole.[42]

We are all familiar with the separation of powers doctrine from Montesquieu and elsewhere: legislative, executive, and judicial. But what Kojève asserts is a need to understand how this separation occurred and how it relates to the four forms of authority previously discussed. Kojève argues that for "medieval theory . . . *every* Authority came from divine Authority." As such, divine authority attempted to integrated or to incorporate all four types of authority unto itself, and then to transmit that fourfold authority (through nomination or heredity) in a complete fashion to the civil servant of God. The only problem with this solution, however, was that there were actually two (recognized) civil servants of God, the one religious (the Pope) and the other political (the Emperor or national King); and to make matters worse, both were understood to be universal in their application and principle, thus making it impossible to separate a religious from a political sphere. Absolutism attempted to solve this problem (in the same way that medieval theory did) by giving the Monarch all authority and power (at least in theory); but this solution proved equally unsatisfactory (and probably for the same reasons as the medieval solution). To solve both of these problems, a new constitutional theory arose which gave three independent powers independent pillars of support, effectively removing the divine civil servant from power or authority but also dividing up the political power of a single Monarch. The authority of the Master is now the executive; the legislative the Leader; and the judiciary the Judge.[43] What is missing in this new scheme, however, is the authority of the Father: this authority has more or less been "amputated" ("unconsciously" for sure) from modern politics, and "one is tempted to say that political Authority decays or *falls apart* ('splits up') precisely because of this *amputation*."[44] It would seem that the tension or problem of the separation of church and state in politics had been solved, as had the problem of absolutism and medievalism—but at what cost?

At the cost of "permanent revolution"! In one of the most remarkable passages in *Notion*, Kojève more or less states that it is Montesquieu (and perhaps James Madison as well) who are the true revolutionaries, and not necessarily Marx (or Hegel) themselves. Once the bourgeoisie have repudiated their past as common or low, and thus rejected the authority of the Father, they will become revolutionary.

> [The Bourgeois] thus unconsciously negates the bourgeois value, that is to say, his bourgeois *past*, which *in his own* eyes is nothing more than the past of a "commoner." It is only then that he becomes "constitutional," that is to say, that he stands for the separation of Powers, which from then on are for him only *three*: and by so doing he becomes, or is, revolutionary.

Kojève continues:

> Political Authority amputated of its "Father" limb necessarily becomes, therefore, in so far as it remains *political*, primarily an Authority of the Leader. . . . It is thus that the "constitutional" theory, in and by its "bourgeois" revolutionary *realization*, necessarily terminates in the "Dictatorship" of a Napoleon or a Hitler. But since the Present, deprived of a past, must necessarily imply the Future so that it can be human, or even political, the Leader-Dictator must always represent a *"revolutionary* project" in the process of being implemented. Thus, the logical culmination of the "constitutional" theory of a Montesquieu is the theory of the "permanent revolution" of a Trotsky.[45]

In short, a separation of powers based on the Leader (legislative) and Master (executive) types will inevitably have one type of authority envelope the other or to be combined with it. This will leave the authority of the Judge without any existential support, and it will descend into nothing more than "class justice" à la Marx and to the undermining of authority in general.[46] For Kojève, therefore, the proper division of powers is between the authority of the Father, a combined Leader-Master type, and that of the Judge. This alone will provide governmental stability, power, and authority.[47] Kojève thus makes the eminently *conservative* argument that when authority as represented in the Father drops out of the political equation, a regime will be subject to constant revolutionary change and dictatorship (whether it be a Napoleon or a Hitler—or a Stalin or a Mussolini [?]). In essence, political stability (i.e., genuinely balanced constitutionalism) requires some element of Fatherly or paternal authority, and therefore of the past and tradition, to be respected—perhaps along the lines of the ancient Roman Senate or Censors as Kojève frequently mentions. (One is immediately led to wonder whether the French Fifth Republic's Senate or Britain's House of Lords might be a more modern manifestation of what Kojève had in mind.)

At all events, one can certainly raise the question of how any of this can be manifested in the modern world given that Kojève has said that the hereditary transmission of Fatherly authority is little more than primitive magic and is bound to disappear over time.[48] Is permanent revolution all that we have left?

Kojève spends the remaining pages fleshing out the implications of these ideas, as well as suggesting possibilities of how a proper division of powers could be constituted. For example, he speculates whether the authority of the Father could be grafted onto the other three types of authorities through families rather than individuals, and then buttressed or enhanced through inheritance and the education of children (only seemingly to reject it).[49] Or again, he suggests how the separation of powers originated in the authority of the Judge (with its claims to Eternity) setting itself against the temporal claims of the Leader (Future) and the Master (Present), with the Magna Carta being an early example of this (the authority of the Father and the Past perhaps having been diminished at this point or eliminated altogether).[50] Or yet again, he argues that the authority of the Leader separated from that of the Master (the Future bereft of the Present) would be nothing more than a utopia as it would lack all possible realization in the here and now, while the Master separated from the Leader (the Present bereft of the Future) would degenerate into an administrative police state without any goal or direction other than force.[51] And finally, Kojève even articulates a new understanding of the division of regimes, rejecting (more or less) Aristotle's six-fold classification scheme in the *Politics* and adopting a more simplified system along the lines of Machiavelli (one versus many, the latter whether a majority or minority).[52] But one puzzle remains throughout these final discussions: how does all of this conform with his stated view in the *Esquisse* and elsewhere that at the end of history, all of these distinctions will tend to vanish in a generally harmonious, peaceful, and equitable universal and homogeneous state? Kojève is not unaware of this, and before discussing the distinction of regimes based on authority, he makes this candid remark (the only one of its kind in *Notion*).

As he looks at the relationship between Master and Leader in a proper division of powers, and claims that they cannot really be separated, he clarifies:

> [T]here is here no political hindrance, because we can show that with political progress the Authority of the Master must give way to that of the Leader—that is to say, it will "degenerate." It even seems that it must completely disappear in the "ideal" State of the future. Generally speaking, the Authority of the Master presupposes the *real* possibility of war and bloody revolution, and it thus presupposes its own disappearance along with them.[53]

At the end of history, in the universal and homogeneous state, it would seem that all of Kojève's careful analysis might no longer be useful or applicable. If what he says above is true, then how could the authority of the Leader be made manifest or transmitted in the present shorn from the authority of the Master? Indeed, one might ask whether the authority of the Leader would also disappear or be made superfluous altogether (let alone the Father) since the "ideal" state by definition would no longer need improvement or seek a new goal since it is the full and complete realization of human self-consciousness and thus the end and perfection of our historical self-development (in general agreement with Hegel and Marx). Perhaps it is to answer these and other questions that Kojève turned next to the *Esquisse* in order to articulate most fully the principles of justice and right that will obtain at the end of history. One is of course left to wonder if the only operational authority at the end of history is the eternal justice of the Judge (but with the interesting and essential caveat, as identified before, that right does not lose its character as right with the use of force, while authority does).[54]

TWO APPENDICES, TWO QUESTIONS

The Notion of Authority concludes with two brief appendices, both of which are concrete applications of his theoretical analysis to current events in May 1942. The first concerns the authority Marshal Philippe Pétain obtained and exercised before, during, and after the fall of France in 1940.[55] Kojève argues that he possessed all four: As the "Victor of Verdun," he was a Master; as the one who put down the army mutinies of 1917, he was a Leader with foresight; because of his disinterested, impartial, and objective character, he was a Judge; and because of his quintessential French lifestyle and avuncular demeanor, he was also a Father and embodiment of the Past. Pétain had a total political authority that was spontaneously generated (Kojève remarks that what the precise order of the four types is would require a more meticulous investigation, e.g., FLMJ, LMFJ, or MLJF, and so on). As of the time of

Kojève's writing, some of the Marshal's authority was waning: because of his age, his authority as Master was being transferred to his nominated successor, "the Admiral" François Darlan (who was assassinated in December 1942); as for the Marshal's authority as Leader, this was migrating to Pierre Laval (who was executed in October 1945).

Kojève's admittedly brief analysis is full of insights and possibilities, showing us how his authoritarian typology is both fruitful and promising— but for those of us in the post–World War II era, a question that immediately comes to mind is how Kojève would have described the authority of a General Charles de Gaulle! On the one hand, de Gaulle resigned and seemed to renounce his established authority in 1946 when he saw the reemergence of the old party system of the Third Republic, whose baneful effects he so detested; on the other hand, the reemergence of the old party system might have been an indication that de Gaulle lacked some measure of authority, as the French wanted to return to some extent to the prewar political past. Obviously, de Gaulle's predictions came true: the Fourth Republic was not a clear break or rupture with the Third, even though there were some political innovations, new parties, and new party alignments; but overall, the Fourth Republic was simply a modified version of the Third (little different in scope or outcome), with governments coming and going with great rapidity. Using Kojève's framework, we might speculate that de Gaulle—who had to share his Mastership with all those who participated in the Resistance inside of France—was too far ahead of the French people during his brief time as Leader: whereas de Gaulle want to create a strong executive and to restrain the legislative branch, the French wanted no such thing (although their rejection and then half-hearted endorsement of the Fourth Republic in two referendums indicated that they were ambivalent or unsure at best). Of course, it should be emphasized that many people were wary or even fearful of de Gaulle coming to power as an executive president, believing that he would become an elected monarch, a Bonaparte, or even worse. A Leader cannot be too far ahead of his times. It was only when the Algerian crisis occurred in 1958, and when France was on the brink of a coup d'état and/or civil war, that people were willing to listen to de Gaulle's proposals for a new and genuine break with the past, and which they overwhelmingly endorsed. There is no doubt that more could be said and conjectured about the nature of de Gaulle's authority in 1946 and 1958, but *Notion* gives us ample material for reflection and avenues for further investigation.

The second appendix concerns Marshal Pétain's national revolution, whose motto was *Travail, Famille, Patrie* (work/labor, family, country/fatherland).[56] After briefly describing the character of revolution (from idea to realization), Kojève offers a few (somewhat elliptical) suggestions on how political institutions might be modified or new ones created to conform with his understanding of authority in the present context. It must be emphasized that Kojève's remarks have to do with a *national* revolution (whether Pétain's or Kojève's own), and thus how France might reconstitute itself as a nation in 1942 and beyond. Kojève never seemed to have revisited the suggestions he made here, although he is clearly interested in some sort of a national revolution in 1942: after all, there is no guarantee at this point that Germany will lose the war or that France will help to win it and to become fully independent. James Nichols helpfully suggests that Kojève's remarks show that he "takes the element of contingency in history very seriously indeed; he is altogether open to whatever political situation might come along and prepared to make amazingly flexible suggestions to deal with present realities. . . . In the circumstances of 1942, he remains open to the possibility that, for a time, the national political project may yet be what is required."[57] And Nichols is probably correct: in Kojève's next "contingent" writing (if we may so use the term) during the interwar period, "L'Empire Latin," he completely abandons the idea of national projects. At the end of the war, the world is now a world of superpowers; and if France wants to survive and to have influence, it and its allies must create their own empire to counter those of the Soviets and the Americans. The age of the nation-state is over.

Despite the above remarks, it must not be forgotten that Kojève never loses sight of the universal and homogeneous state as his polestar, even in these "contingent" writings. Thus, in the final paragraph of "L'Empire Latin" (dealing with the religious implications of his ideas), Kojève reminds us that the unification of all catholic churches would require the unification of the human race; that the unification of the human race must first proceed through and then transcend an era of superpowers and empires (even the proposed Latin Empire); and that it is only by working through this stage that we will achieve that "final state of unity which will permit the permanent elimination of political, economic, and social conflicts." In other words, in both *Notion* and "L'Empire Latin," the ideal state of the future continues to peak through, however dimly or sometimes furtively. In conclusion, we might maintain that at the core of all of Kojève's writings during the interwar period—both figuratively and literally—is the *Esquisse*, and thus the universal and homogeneous state, where the latter is most fully articulated, explained, and justified, and which provides the horizon of historical realization in the near or distant future. But however true this may be, it must also be remembered and emphasized that *Notion* provides a fundamental grounding and clarification of Kojève's later writings, making it one of his most foundational texts. As was mentioned at the beginning of the essay, and which Kojève affirms throughout, without an understanding of authority, we cannot understand the state—and this implies the universal and homogeneous state as well.

NOTES

1. See Dominique Auffret, *Alexandre Kojève: La philosophie, l'État, la fin de l'Histoire* (Paris: Bernard Grasset, 1990), 267–72. Apparently, because of his knowledge of German as well as of fine art, Kojève convinced his would-be executioner(s) that he and his Greek companion were "men of culture," and they were both released and allowed to go free.

2. Alexandre Kojève, *La notion de l'autorité* (Paris: Gallimard, 2004), English translation *The Notion of Authority: A Brief Presentation*, trans. Hager Weslati, ed. and intro. François Terré (London: Verso, 2014); *Esquisse d'une phénoménologie du droit* (Paris: Gallimard, 1981), English translation *Outline of a Phenomenology of Right*, trans., ed., and intro. Bryan-Paul Frost and Robert Howse (Lanham, MD: Rowman & Littlefield, 2000); and "L'Empire Latin: Esquisse d'une doctrine de la politique française (27 août 1945)," *La Règle du Jeu* 1, no. 1 (May 1990): 89–123, English translation "Outline of a Doctrine of French Policy (August 27, 1945)," trans. Erik de Vries, *Policy Review* 126 (August/September 2004): 3–40. All citations will be to the English translations of *Notion* (= *NA*) and the *Esquisse* (= *EPD*), with the first page reference to the English translation and the next to the French original (e.g., *NA* 1–2/49–50). In general, I have followed the English translations but have checked them against the French originals for accuracy and emphasis, and have sometimes altered them accordingly. I have also retained all of Kojève's stylistic usages, including his frequent employment of italics and capital letters.

3. This is according to Marco Filoni, in a personal email exchange with the author. These studies, however, never fully materialized, although extended discussions about the family and the state appear in the *Esquisse* (*EPD* 398–427/483–519 and *EPD* 117–69/122–87, respectively); in respect to work, in particular, and Hegel's master-slave dialectic, in general, they occur throughout Kojève's writings. On these issues and others, see more generally Marco Filoni, *Le philosophe du dimanche: La vie et la pensée d'Alexandre Kojève*, trans. Gérald Larché (from the Italian) (Paris: Gallimard, 2010), who is one of the scholars today most familiar with Kojève's published and unpublished manuscripts in the Fonds Kojève at the Bibliothèque nationale de France. Kojève references *Notion* in the *Esquisse* (*EPD* 160n38/175, 176/194, 352n36/423n1, 411n109/499n1) as well as a "Note on *Work*" (*EPD* 177n5/196), and in *Notion* he mentions a "brief article on the Family" (*NA* 71n2/152n), a "brief article on Work" (*NA* 106n1/202n), twice mentions a "brief article on the State" (*NA* 48n8/117n, 60n1/137n), and twice a "brief article on Right" (*NA* 9n1/59n, 73n3/155n). All of these "brief articles" may have ultimately been incorporated into the *Esquisse*.

4. A notable exception is James H. Nichols, Jr., *Alexandre Kojève: Wisdom at the End of History* (Lanham, MD: Rowman & Littlefield, 2007). Interestingly, Nichols allots a bit more space to *Notion* (50–63) than he does to the *Esquisse* (63–74). The remaining pages of his third chapter discuss "The Latin Empire" (75–79).

5. See *NA* 56–58/131–34.

6. See Emmanuel Patard, "Appendix A: A Critical Edition of Alexandre Kojève, 'Tyrannie et sagesse'" and "Appendix B: 'Tyranny and Wisdom,'" in *Philosophy, History, and Tyranny: Reexamining the Debate between Leo Strauss and Alexandre*

Kojève, eds. Timothy W. Burns and Bryan-Paul Frost (Albany: SUNY, 2016), 287–89 and 291–357. References to *On Tyranny* (= *OT*) will be to the third edition, Leo Strauss, *On Tyranny*, eds. Victor Gourevitch and Michael S. Roth, revised, corrected, and expanded edition (Chicago: The University of Chicago Press, 2013); references to Kojève's expanded edition (= *OTK*) will be to the edition by Patard in Burns and Frost. Kojève's discussion of authority begins at *OT* 143ff., and then more expansively at *OTK* 304ff.

7. *NA* 1–5/49–55.
8. *NA* 7–9/56–59.
9. *NA* 9–13/59–65.
10. *NA* 14ff./67ff.
11. *NA* 29–31/89–92.
12. *NA* 2/50–51, 17/70.
13. Alexandre Kojève, "Autonomie et dépendance de la Conscience-de-soi: Maîtrise et Servitude," *Mesures* 5 (no.1, January 14, 1939): 108ff. This article provided the opening chapter to both the French and English editions of the *Introduction to the Reading of Hegel*.
14. *NA* 15n/68.
15. *NA* 18/72.
16. Nichols, *Alexandre Kojève*, 50, states that "Kojève's identification of Hegel's incompleteness on this matter of authority is, in my judgment, his most serious critique of Hegel's system within the political/moral realm of human history. Kojève, of course, proposes to remedy this defect through his own comprehensive analysis."
17. Alexandre Kojève, "Hegel, Marx et le christianisme," *Critique* 1, no. 3–4 (août–Septembre 1946): 353n1. What follows the aforementioned quote in the note is also quite revealing and again demonstrates how influential *Notion* was for his understanding of politics as a whole.

One could, however, allow that the State is born from the mutual recognition of the victors of a *collective* fight for recognition. If several men fight together against common adversaries whom they end up by enslaving, they can mutually recognize each other as Masters without having fought among themselves. "Fellow citizen" would therefore be at the beginning identical to "brother-in-arms." But there is also the phenomenon of the political "leader" [*chef*] that Hegel does not analyze in his writings: the superiority (= authority) of one of the Masters can be recognized by the others without their becoming his slaves as a result of this.

It would seem that *Notion* was constantly making its appearances in Kojève's writings and grounding his thought before its eventual publication.

18. *EPD* 215–19/246–50.
19. *EPD* 219–27/250–60.
20. *EPD* 227–31/261–66; cf. 117–21/122–26, 131n11/140n1, 313–21/374–83, 400–402/486–87, 428/520.
21. E.g., *EPD* 154–61/168–77, 184/204–5, 229n15/264n1, 411/498–99, 425/516–17.
22. *NA* 18–21/73–76.
23. *NA* 21–24/77–81.

24. *NA* 19–22/74–78.

25. *NA* 24–28/81–88.

26. *NA* 31–32/92–94.

27. *NA* 33/94–95.

28. *NA* 34/96.

29. *NA* 34ff./96ff.

30. *NA* 43–48/110–17; cf. 88–89/175–76.

31. *NA* 36ff./99ff.

32. The case of the rule of the minority is a bit more complicated in that the minority is physically (or quantitatively) weaker than the majority, and therefore it must base its claim to rule on some qualitative superiority. Thus, Kojève insists that unless the authority of the minority is based upon one of the four ideal types (or combinations thereof), that authority will not be valid. But this does not mean that they (the minority) will be unable to rule over others (the majority). Kojève is clearly aware that the minority can exercise superior force over the majority (the Middle Ages or feudalism, for example, to say nothing of twentieth-century regimes)—and this is precisely why that minority must attempt to base its authority on one of the four recognized types to be authentic.

33. *NA* 38–39/102–4.

34. *NA* 39ff./104ff.

35. *NA* 41/107.

36. *NA* 40/105.

37. *OT* 145; *OTK* 308.

38. *NA* 48ff./117ff.

39. *NA* 49/118–19.

40. In order to solidify his claims even further, Kojève suggests that his metaphysical or temporal analysis is consistent with Aristotle's understanding of causation. The Past or Father is a material cause (the cause to its effect), the Present or Master an efficient cause (an action carried out in its immediacy), the Future or Leader the final cause (a project to be realized), and Eternity or Judge is a formal cause (the contemplative and disinterested decisions concerning justice) (*NA* 55–56/129–30).

41. *NA* 59/135, 91–94/179–85.

42. Cf. *EPD* 85–89/83–89, 166–69/184–87.

43. *NA* 62–63/140–42.

44. *NA* 64/142.

45. *NA* 64–65/143–44.

46. *NA* 69–70/150–51, 72–73/154–55.

47. *NA* 80/164.

48. Cf. *NA* 89/176–77.

49. *NA* 70–72/151–53.

50. *NA* 72–74/154–57.

51. *NA* 74–77/157–61.

52. *NA* 83–85/169–71.

53. *NA* 82/167; cf. 60–61/137–38, 76–77/160, 87/174–75.

54. The paragraph following the one quoted above adds yet another layer of perplexity and intrigue to what type(s) of authority(ies) might exist in the "ideal" end state.

Historical evolution goes from the unity of political "power" to the separation of "powers." Now, what we have just said "justifies" this state of things: in order for each "pure" type to reach the plenitude of its development, it has to be separated from the others. But this does not mean that Authorities must remain "divided," even *after* they have realized all their implicit possibilities. It seems, on the contrary, that they will have to reunite again. Political evolution would therefore start from the non-differentiated unity (the unity of the embryonic form), go through a period of division and development of the separated elements, finally leading to the totality—that is to say, to differentiated unity (the unity of the adult organism) (*NA* 83/168).

55. *NA* 95–101/186–94.
56. *NA* 101–7/195–204.
57. Nichols, *Alexandre Kojève*, 63.

BIBLIOGRAPHY

Auffret, Dominique. *Alexandre Kojève: La philosophie, l'État, la fin de l'Histoire.* Paris: Bernard Grasset, 1990.
Filoni, Marco. *Le philosophe du dimanche: La vie et la pensée d'Alexandre Kojève,* trans. Gérald Larché (from the Italian). Paris: Gallimard, 2010.
Kojève, Alexandre. "Autonomie et dépendance de la Conscience-de-soi: Maîtrise et Servitude," *Mesures* 5, no.1 (January 14, 1939): 108ff. Included as the opening chapter to *Introduction à la lecture de Hegel*, ed. Raymond Queneau, 2nd ed. Paris: Gallimard, 1968. English translation *Introduction to the Reading of Hegel*, trans. James H. Nichols, Jr. Ithaca, NY: Cornell University Press, 1980.
———. "L'Empire Latin: Esquisse d'une doctrine de la politique française (27 août 1945)." *La Règle du Jeu* 1, no. 1 (May 1990): 89–123. English translation "Outline of a Doctrine of French Policy (August 27, 1945)," trans. Erik de Vries, *Policy Review* 126 (August/September 2004): 3–40.
———. *Esquisse d'une phénoménologie du droit.* Paris: Gallimard, 1981. English translation *Outline of a Phenomenology of Right*, trans., ed., and intro. Bryan-Paul Frost and Robert Howse. Lanham, MD: Rowman & Littlefield, 2000.
———. "Hegel, Marx et le christianisme." *Critique* 1, no. 3–4 (août-Septembre 1946): 339–66. English translation "Hegel, Marx, and Christianity," trans. Hilail Gildin, *Interpretation* 1, no. 1 (Summer 1970): 21–42.
———. *La notion de l'autorité.* Paris: Gallimard, 2004. English translation *The Notion of Authority: A Brief Presentation*, trans. Hager Weslati, ed. and intro. François Terré. London: Verso, 2014.
Nichols, James H., Jr. *Alexandre Kojève: Wisdom at the End of History.* Lanham, MD: Rowman & Littlefield, 2007.

Patard, Emmanuel. "Appendix A: A Critical Edition of Alexandre Kojève, 'Tyrannie et sagesse'" and "Appendix B: 'Tyranny and Wisdom,'" in *Philosophy, History, and Tyranny: Reexamining the Debate between Leo Strauss and Alexandre Kojève*, eds. Timothy W. Burns and Bryan-Paul Frost. Albany, NY: SUNY, 2016, 287–89 and 291–357.

Chapter Ten

The Specular Philosopher

Alexandre Kojève and Jacques Lacan

Trevor Wilson

Among Alexandre Kojève's many collected papers, donated in 2001 by his partner Nina Ivanov to the Bibliothèque nationale de France, lies a copy of the first issue of *La Psychanalyse*, a review founded in 1956 by Jacques Lacan and other members of the newly formed Société française de psychanalyse. Edited by Lacan himself, this first issue of the review includes a discussion on language and linguistics, a translation of Heidegger, and a discussion of negation or *Verneinung* in Hegel.[1] The review had clearly entered Kojève's possession as a gift from the psychoanalyst to the philosopher, as evidenced by the inscription written on its cover: "for Kojève, who was my master (truly the only)."[2]

Although Kojève and Lacan shared a protracted friendship, developed across some of the most formative decades of their careers, these private moments of acknowledgment are nearly the sole testament to the extent of their collaboration. For Kojève, Lacan is never mentioned in any of the relatively few works published in his lifetime, and only a posthumous, passing discussion of psychoanalysis might suggest that Kojève had ever even thought about Lacan's discipline.[3] Lacan would publicly acknowledge Kojève's influence often, yet in his characteristically oblique style, as passing mentions of his previous training in Hegel at the foot of the master.

Yet despite this relative dearth of testimony, the camaraderie between the two was both deeply personal and integral to their respective intellectual development, such that it would indeed be difficult to examine the legacy of one without the other. While the two were of similar ages (Lacan was born in 1901, Kojève a year after in 1902), it would notably be Kojève who took on the status of intellectual mentor to Lacan: it is no surprise that Lacan's gift, an opening issue of a psychanalytical review, would contain numerous references to philosophy, as Kojève had effectively decades earlier provided Lacan the philosophical toolkit with which he would transform the practice of psychanalysis in France into his image. Indeed, Kojève's influence on Lacan invokes a broader disciplinary question: where does philosophy end and psychoanalysis begin? And while we might reflect on the role played by philosophy in the development of psychoanalysis, one might equally ask, as Pierre Macherey has done, how Lacanian psychoanalysis has fundamentally altered our understanding of philosophy through its adoption and transformation of its underlying principles.[4]

The formation of this camaraderie between Kojève and Lacan can be traced directly to Kojève's seminars on Hegel's *Phenomenology of Spirit*, held at the École pratique des hautes études from 1933 to 1939. From 1934 onward, Lacan, who had just several years earlier received his medical accreditation and begun clinical work as a psychiatrist, regularly attended the seminars. Toward the end of his first year of participation in the seminars, and the second year of the seminars overall, Lacan began to write directly to Kojève.[5] In his first letter (five in total are preserved in the archive), Lacan invites the philosopher to have dinner with his wife at their home. After this first dinner, Lacan once more invites Kojève to his home, this time for an undescribed but regular series of meetings of some kind—the invitation, and the meetings, have prompted speculation as to whether these informal gatherings were perhaps early prototypes for Lacan's own later seminars.[6] While it is unclear if Kojève ever did attend these later meetings, the possible proximity between Kojève's and Lacan's respective seminars nevertheless sheds light on a secondary, if unmistakable, influence of Kojève on Lacan: namely, one of form.

Through his reading of the *Phenomenology* and Hegel, the study of whom had long become outdated and only recently returned to prominence in the interwar period, Kojève had taught an entire generation the benefit of a return to text. Several decades later, in 1951, Lacan began his own seminars, first at his home and then at Sainte-Anne Hospital. These, too, took on the form of a return, this time to Freud and the method of the case study. Both Kojève and Lacan, in the spirit of what Paul Ricœur famously described as a "hermeneutic school of suspicion," argued in their returns that a close reading of a foundational text might reorient and reveal the underlying assumptions of a discipline, be it philosophy or the nature of the analytic encounter.[7] It is therefore impossible to ignore the structural parallels of these interventions, in either their style or ethos. That this method of intervention was shared between two figures was obvious to their peers: as Raymond Queneau rather succinctly described Lacan's work in his memoirs, "he does commentaries, according to Kojève's method, on Freud's texts."[8]

The preserved correspondence between Kojève and Lacan all took place in the year 1935. Incidentally, in that same year Lacan had intervened briefly in Kojève's seminars on the subject of madness in Hegel, although the intervention was excluded from the version of the seminars that was ultimately edited and published by Queneau.[9] In one of his letters written to Kojève, Lacan alludes to a text he had been working on that year devoted to the family "from a psychological point of view," hoping that Kojève might help him elucidate certain themes in his own work. While we lack the documentation to reconstruct their discussion of the topic, another curious manuscript, also found among Kojève's papers, suggests Kojève was thoroughly engaged with Lacan's work on the subject. The manuscript, dated to 1936 and entitled "Hegel and Freud: An Attempt at an Interpretive Confrontation," mysteriously disappeared after Kojève's death, and there remains only an outline detailing some of the themes that Kojève had sought to explore in the work: among others, the genesis of self-consciousness, desire, the origin of madness, and the essence of the family.[10] These very absences in the record are revealing, given the proximity of the topics to Lacan's work: according to biographer Dominque Auffret, Lacan had arrived at Kojève's home several days after the philosopher's death, in order to consult several papers.[11] Had Lacan, now well into his seminars, needed some final documents from these early years of their collaboration, approaching some fusion of philosophy and psychoanalysis? Rather than succumb to speculation, a return to the dual trajectories of their thought in the 1930s, seen in both Kojève's seminars and Lacan's early writings, ought to shed some light on the extent of their partnership, as well as the pivotal role played by Kojève in shaping the direction of Lacan's work.

EARLY LACAN IN THE SHADOW OF
HEGELIANISM: THE COMPLEX

The draft text mentioned by Lacan in his letter to Kojève was an article entitled "Family Complexes in the Formation of the Individual." Lacan had recently been commissioned by Henri Walloon to write the article as the entry for "Family" in the *Encyclopédie française*.[12] Spearheaded by the French Ministry of National Education and overseen by Lucien Febvre, the *Encyclopédie française* was conceived as a compendium on the current state of affairs in modern culture. Febvre had asked Wallon to compile a list of psychoanalytical texts, grouped under the framework of a "psychic paleontology," for the eighth volume of the collection devoted to mental life.[13] Wallon thus invited contributions from various figures within French psychology to participate, both more established names as well as relatively newer ones like Lacan.

In a testament to both his unorthodox approach and writing style, Lacan originally was asked to write two separate articles, yet once he had submitted the first article in September 1936, its confusing format and difficult composition provoked a near scandal in the editorial offices of the *Encyclopédie* and ended the possibility of any second contribution to the collection. In particular, neither Febvre nor Rose Celli, an author in her own right who was working as an editor for the encyclopedia, could make out Lacan's obscure passages on the Oedipal complex. The overwhelming opinion on the article was that it was poorly written by its author, thus requiring numerous rounds of edits before it saw publication—the drama piqued when an original, unedited version of the text eventually found its way into the hands of Anatole de Monzie, the French Minister of National Education and director of the *Encyclopédie française* project. Upon reading Lacan's work, Monzie allegedly shouted in irritation, "Let me translate this into normal language!"[14]

As Élisabeth Roudinesco notes, however, the controversy over this early text's publication illustrates to what extent, already in 1936–1937, Lacan was on the one hand justly recognized as one of the most brilliant figures of his time and, on the other hand, "how already his style was causing problems: his obscurity, illegibility, his reluctance to deliver a text within an allotted time, his slowness with regard to publication, etc." Roudinesco furthermore attributes the emergence of this notorious style to his foray out of psychology and into the world of philosophy, given his frequentation of Kojève's seminars at this time: "it all seems as though access to philosophy, still poorly mastered, led Lacan toward illegibility."[15] Perhaps somewhat paradoxically, the very style that distinguished Lacan's approach to psychoanalysis becomes the earliest and most frequent object of criticism. Philosophy, and in particular Kojève, is to blame.

Although the text remains relatively marginal within his corpus, "Family Complexes" is therefore a curious testament to Lacan's nascent career, both in style and theme, and it lays bare the early influence Kojève's seminars had on his thought process. Even though the article is not published by the *Encyclopédie* until 1938, Lacan reuses the material in a speech planned for the Fourteenth International Congress of Psychoanalysis, held in 1936 at Marienbad. Taken together with "Family Complexes," the speech is thought to be Lacan's first formal presentation of his theory of the mirror stage in early childhood development.[16] Lacan was not the first to outline a "mirror-stage" in a child's construction of self and reality—he was in fact greatly influenced by Wallon, who in 1931 had already published research on the role played by self-identification in the mirror for the development of subjectivity in the child.[17] On the other hand, Lacan's intervention is also intimately linked to that of Melanie Klein, who was then at the heart of a split within the psychoanalytical community over the analysis of young children. Klein had advocated for an examination of the ego formation in the child, in opposition to Anna Freud and those of the "ego psychology" school who sought to defend the child, and the integrity of its ego as an instrument of adaptation to reality.[18] While he does not formally acknowledge this influence or the debates in "Family Complexes," Lacan implicitly followed in Klein's wake, examining object relations in infancy, mostly between mother and infant but also between siblings, that help to construct and buffer the subject in its early development. The difference between Klein and Lacan, however, emerges in source material: whereas Klein's references largely remain case studies, Lacan takes clear inspiration from Kojève's Hegelian seminars, who had just prior lectured on the transition from consciousness to self-certainty in the *Phenomenology of Spirit*, as well as the mediation of subjectivity in the Master/Slave[19] dialectic.

Although, as its title suggests, "Family Complexes in the Formation of the Individual" describes how the infant comes to develop an individual personality within the confines of a family structure, Lacan addresses this topic through a distinction made between two key psychoanalytic concepts: complex and instinct. He differentiates the two from the perspective of the biological versus cultural formations within an individual's development, with "instinct" understood as biological and "complex" understood as cultural.[20] The family is a site of contestation between these two opposed influences: although one might initially define the family as a social group formed by biological or reproductive functions, Lacan argues that it would be incorrect to define the human family based solely on the act of procreation. To do so would therefore make the human family indistinguishable from an animal one. Instead, Lacan claims that the human family is defined by larger cultural relations that are imposed upon, and even subvert, these biological ones: "it is in the original order of reality in which social relations are constituted that one must understand the human family [. . .] its conditioning upon cultural factors at the expense of natural ones."[21]

In Lacan's argument, biological instincts are negated by cultural complexes, yet it is perhaps more accurate to say that, in the early stages of an individual's differentiation within a family, the two are dialectically mediated. The emergence of the complex is contingent upon the negation of biological instincts: "in this process one must recognize the character that distinguishes the human race, namely the subversion of every instinctual fixation, from which emerge the fundamental, infinitely variable forms of culture."[22] Despite the fact that a complex is predicated upon the negation of a biological instinct, Lacan stresses that the two must be seen as linked:

> In opposing the complex to the instinct, we do not deny a biological foundation
> in the complex, and in defining the complex through certain ideational relations,
> we link it however to its material base. This base is the function that it maintains
> in the social group: and we see this biological foundation in the vital dependence
> of the individual in respect to the group. Whereas the instinct has an organic
> *support* and is none other than the regulation of said support in a vital function,
> the complex only has the chance for an organic *relation*, when it replaces a vital
> lack through the regulation of a social function.[23]

In order to illustrate his point, Lacan offers several examples of complexes
that help to structure early individuation and that are formed at the expense
of biological functions. The first is that of weaning: Lacan stresses that
rather than driven purely by physiological factors, such as the duration of
lactation and availability of breastmilk, the decision to wean an infant off of
breastfeeding is entirely culturally regulated. This *negation* of the biological
instinct to breastfeed, moreover, produces in the infant a series of psychological complexes that stay with the individual long after the weaning period:
"traumatizing or not, weaning leaves in the human psyche a permanent trace
of the biological relationship that it interrupts."[24] The resistance of the infant
to weaning, Lacan argues, precedes the positive formation of a (nonbiological, psychological) complex in which the infant will seek to reestablish the
prototype or *imago* of a nurturing relationship [*l'imago de la relation nour-
ricière*] throughout his or her life.[25] Thus the negation of an instinct remains
preserved in the formation of a complex surrounding maternal sentiment that
plays a pivotal role in the infant's early individuation within the family.

This negation of biology or physiology, and the dialectical mediation between biological and cultural desires, greatly recalls Kojève's own
anthropomorphic definition of desire in his seminars—to quote Mikkel
Borch-Jacobsen, Lacan conforms rigorously to a fundamentally dualist ontology found within Kojève's philosophy.[26] Early in his seminars, Kojève had
explicitly sought to correct what he viewed as the major monistic flaw in
the *Phenomenology of Spirit*: the equation of humanity to nature. According
to Kojève, Hegel sought to develop a phenomenology of man, "man as he
appears [. . .] to himself in and by his existence," yet Hegel incorrectly
claimed that humanity was the same thing as nature, and therefore that his
phenomenological approach was applicable to nature writ large: "it is not universal, despite what Hegel thought. It is an ontology of Man ('Spirit') and not
of Nature."[27] The transformations that Hegel describes in the *Phenomenology*
are therefore uniquely human, Kojève argues, and recount the emergence of
humanity as a self-aware, historical agent.

Hegel's alleged error is made clear in Kojève's own interpretation of desire
in the *Phenomenology*. According to Kojève, human desire differs from

nature due to its formation around a lack—rather than desiring things like an animal, such as food, water, shelter, humans desire the recognition of another human. In the pursuit of this recognition, humans are ready to risk life and death as this recognition takes shape in prestige, dignity, and honor. Thus, Kojève claimed that in fact humanity, and human individuality, *begins* at the moment man is willing to deny his own natural being:

> To be man is to not be held back by any determinate existence. Man has the possibility of denying Nature, and his own nature, whatever that may be. He can deny his empirical, animal nature, he can *want* his death, risk his death. This is his negative being (a negator: Negativität): realizing the possibility of denying, and, through denying, transcending his given reality, being something more and other than simply a living being.[28]

Thus, for Kojève humanity, as separate from the natural world, nevertheless dialectically emerges by negating its biological function, and in so doing transforming the natural world into its own image.

This correction by Kojève of Hegel has lent credence to claims (and critiques) that Kojève anthropologized *The Phenomenology of Spirit*, and Lacan in "Family Complexes" appears to conform to this anthropocentric dualism. In describing the relationship between complexes and instincts, Lacan similarly identified, in the need to negate biological instincts in the earliest development of an infant's subjectivity, the formation of a human personality upon this negation. He draws furthermore an explicit link between the development of complexes, early individuation, and the same ferocity of the death drive that Kojève had seen in his anthropogenic philosophy.[29] Lacan writes that "the inclination to death, which is particular of the human psyche, can be satisfactorily explained by the concept that we are developing here: namely the complex, the functional unity of this psyche, does not correspond to vital functions but rather to the congenital insufficiency of these functions."[30] Early interruptions in the biological functions of the infant may threaten risk of death (as in, the weaning infant losing contact with its sustenance), yet it is precisely these interruptions that initiate the infant's individuation, or that permit the early subject to differentiate itself from its family through the development of the complexes. The weaning complex therefore signals for Lacan an important, early stage in the development of the individual, prelinguistic or symbolic, in which the process of suppressing a biological instinct to breastfeed brings forth the infant subject: the infant is aware that it is what its mother's breast is not.

Lacan in the article acknowledges his debt to Hegel (and, by extension, Kojève) in developing this point: "Hegel claims that any individual that does not struggle to be recognized outside of its familial group will never attain

a personality before death." In fact, Kojève had explicitly alluded to something quite similar in his seminars from 1935–1936, in which he discussed
Hegel's description of the early, historical transformation of the family in the
ancient world:

> Passage from the biological (animal) family to the human Family [. . .] within
> the Family, real and human action moves from the individual to the individual,
> this being understood as a Whole. From this comes death worship, for death is
> an achieved *totality* (individualization through death): it is not a natural, animal
> individuality (the cadaver) that is honored, but an individuality that is, through
> death, beyond Desire and the here and now, a totality that transcends instinct
> and the natural.[31]

Here, in Hegel's view of antiquity, Kojève highlights the early individuation
that takes place within the limits of private life. Individuals are recognized
as such, yet this individuality is confined to the familial household, has not
yet achieved a level of broader social recognition, and is therefore not fully
self-aware. It is only when the individual is viewed as a citizen, and therefore
comes to seek out recognition from others through the formation of a state
and civil society, that the subject achieves true self-consciousness: "as long
as man is a non-citizen, a private, individual person, he is a shadow, that is,
a death. To die on the field of battle is the deed of a Citizen; to die in one's
own bed fulfills the individual as a member of the Family."[32]

In a similar vein, although the weaning complex, in which the infant separates from his or her mother and seeks to cultivate an imago of the maternal
to compensate for her absence, constitutes one of the earliest moments in the
path toward subjective individuation for Lacan, it is only the development of
later complexes, those that stress the role of external recognition, that establish in the infant a fully formed sense of self. Lacan discusses two complexes
in particular: the intrusion complex, in which the infant both competes and
identifies with a rival sibling, and the Oedipal complex, in which the infant
similarly develops a rivalry and identifies with its parents. His discussion of
the intrusion complex borrows greatly from Hegelian terminology, thereby
highlighting the influence of Kojève's reading of the Master/Slave dialectic
and mutual recognition on Lacan's own formation of early infantile identity.

THE SUBJECT AS ITS OTHER: KOJÈVE'S MIRROR, LACAN'S UNHAPPY CONSCIOUSNESS

Lacan describes the intrusion complex as "the experience that the primitive
subject goes through, most often when he sees one or several of his fellow

human beings take part with him in domestic relationships, or, to put it another way, when he realizes that he has siblings."[33] When faced with the possibility of siblings who hoard the attention of their parents, the infant must come to occupy one of two positions: the infant is either in possession of the parents' affection or is an usurper, seeking to unseat a rival sibling. As with his description of the weaning complex, Lacan stresses that this rivalry, initially understood as a biological one, quickly takes on the shape of a "mental identification" in the formation of a complex, serving to define the social relations of the infant subject within a familial structure long after infancy.

Kojève in 1933–1934 had already discussed in his seminar the fourth chapter of the *Phenomenology of Spirit*, in which two consciousnesses struggle to be recognized by one another.[34] To summarize briefly that well-known moment in Hegel's work and Kojève's interpretation, the human subject desires to be recognized as a free and autonomous subject by others. In order to be recognized as such, the subject *forces* another to submit into recognizing it, yet the subject cannot truly be free and autonomous if it relies on another subject to recognize it. Hegel had described this as the shock of the subject who realizes that it "has for its object one which, of its own self, posits its otherness or difference as a nothingness, and in so doing is independent. [. . .] A self-consciousness, in being an object, is just as much 'I' as 'object.'"[35] The dialectic of the master, who is recognized, and of the slave, who recognizes, sets forth various moments in the historical development of consciousness, all of which find consciousness as phenomenologically split, torn between its status as subject and its necessary role as object to another subject.

Observing the interactions between infant siblings, Lacan identified a similar interplay between the competing subjects. When the infant sees another infant in a desired position (such as with its mother), the infant comes to recognize it as "another" object, and furthermore as an object of jealousy. As a consequence, however, rather than view the sibling solely as a rival, Lacan claims that the infants begin to develop a relationship based on two "opposed and complimentary attitudes."[36] On the one hand, the infant desires what the other infant has; on the other hand, however, the infant comes to confuse the other infant's role with his or her own. In Kojèvian logic, the infant desires what the other infant desires. Thus, Lacan argues, the intrusion complex is formed in the infant at a moment of a confusion, in which a rivalry with a sibling creates an ambiguity between an object and its own self-identification.

Notably, this cross-identification between competing siblings illustrates the same confusion present in the infant when it sees its own reflection in the mirror. Just as the infant subject acknowledges a "mental unity" in a fellow creature, its rival sibling, from six months onward it begins to do similarly for its own mirror image, projecting a mental unity onto its previously fragmented body. Lacan stresses, however, that, for the subject both with its rival and its own mirror image, a doubling effect occurs here between ego and object: "the ego is constructed at the same time as the other in the drama of jealousy. There is for the subject a tendency which draws satisfaction from relating to his mirror-image, the ego is a dissonance introduced into this specular satisfaction."[37] The infant subject sees an inherent unity in the mirror and establishes it as its ideal ego, yet this process initially confuses the infant, simultaneously alienating it from its own body by misidentifying with the mirror image it sees: it is not the same thing as its reflection.

While "Family Complexes" was Lacan's first attempt to outline the mirror stage in infancy, he developed the concept further in the speech he had written for the Fourteenth International Congress of Psychoanalysis in 1936. Although he was unable to deliver the speech in person, and the printed speech itself was lost, thirteen years later he would present on the very same topic at the organization's sixteenth session in Zurich.[38] In this more developed account of the mirror stage, Lacan provides further detail on the discordance incurred by the infantile subject, split in two by its identification with its reflected image. Lacan argues that this mirror image presents to the infant a gestalt, a frozen image of the "ideal-I" that "symbolizes the mental permanence of the *I*, at the same time as it prefigures its alienating destination."[39] The mirror stage is alienating precisely because it illustrates to the infant its status as object: the mirror image of the infant takes an active role *constituting* the infant [*constituant*] rather than being constituted by it [*constitué*].

Thus, while the mirror stage establishes a relationship between the infant and its reality, the very moment of establishing the infant's place in the world simultaneously reveals a sense of external dependency and produces paranoia: the mirror stage is a moment of "spatial capture," of the unity of the infant's identity, yet it reveals the "organic insufficiency" of the infant's natural reality.[40] At the conclusion of Lacan's 1949 speech, he invokes the problem once more in explicitly Hegelian terms:

> It is this moment that decisively tips the whole of human knowledge into being mediated by the desire of the other, constitutes its objects in an abstract equivalence through competition from others, and turns the *I* into an apparatus for which every instinctual pressure constitutes a danger, even if it corresponds to a natural maturation process.[41]

One finds a premonition of the paranoia that emerges in the infant during the mirror stage already in Hegel's description of the unhappy consciousness. Hegel described there how a single consciousness comes to embody both dialectical positions, in and for itself, at once: "the duplication which formerly was divided between two individuals, the lord and the bondsman, is now lodged in one."[42] This unhappy consciousness is thus that moment in

Hegel's *Phenomenology* in which the subject has both aspects of its nature but has not yet achieved true unity of self: "the Unhappy Consciousness itself *is* the gazing of one self-consciousness into another, and itself *is* both, and the unity of both is also its essential nature. But it is not as yet explicitly aware that this is its essential nature, or that it is the unity of both."[43] Hegel had presented Unhappy Consciousness as ultimately a religious attitude, with the subject torn between its mortal self and a divine one and unable to achieve satisfaction in its unification of the two. For Kojève, the only way for the subject at this point to achieve satisfaction is to reject any notion of the transcendent, to reject religion entirely: "to free oneself from this *unhappiness*, to arrive at *Satisfaction*, that is, to the realized fullness of one's being, Man must therefore abandon the idea of the *beyond*. He must recognize that his true and unique reality is his action freely accomplished in the here, for here."[44]

Lacan suggests that it is the Oedipal complex, and the process by which the infant takes up the authority of the parent, that serves as the crucial moment for the infant to overcome its paranoia as a split subject: "[the Oedipal complex] gives to reality a life-like density, it is also the moment of sublimination which in man opens up dimensions of reality that extend beyond self-interest."[45] This unification is achieved by offering the infant an external ego ideal, in the form of one's same-sex parent: the infant, split between itself and its constitutive mirror image, is able to sublimate its feeling of otherness into its identification with its parent. After having initially viewed one's parent as a rival, standing in the way of their object of desire (the mother), the infant acclimates by coming to both identify with and fear that same parent. This triangulation, for Lacan, is essential for the development of the infant's super-ego, as the infant establishes a "narcissistic defense of the subject" all while accepting the image of the father in order to adapt to its external reality:

[The image of the father] appears to the ego both as a support for its defenses as well as an example of its triumph. That is why this object normally comes to replace the structure of the double in which the ego first identified itself, and through which it can still mistake itself with for an other. It brings security to the ego by reinforcing this structure, but at the same time it opposes itself to the ego, as an ideal which alternately exalts the ego and depresses it.[46]

Thus, Lacan understood the Oedipal complex as a means of overcoming the paranoiac doubling of the subject that the infant adopts in the mirror stage. Notably, however, an infant's acclimation to reality and the stability of its ego requires libidinal repression, as the child must accept its inability to attain its object of desire and the authority of the father, in order to enter fully into the bonds of society, a topic Lacan would take up in much further detail later in his career.

Thus, in the 1930s Kojève and Lacan, through a joint reading of Hegel, had together sought to trace the deformations of the nascent subject as it gradually acclimates to his or her social reality: what paths, what detours, what negotiations must it take? Curiously enough, although they had perhaps not explicitly addressed this communality, both figures were indeed invested in the very same presocial configuration of consciousness: for Kojève, with his over-emphasis on the Master/Slave dialectic, an entire psychic drama takes place prior to the discussion of the family and state in Hegel's *Phenomenology*. For Lacan, the specular realm of subjectivity, as the infant sees itself as object in the mirror, imbues the nascent subject with fantasies, identifications, and cathexes long before the child learns to speak and understand language. In later years, Lacan would noticeably move away from such an openly Hegelian approach to psychoanalysis. This was in part due to an evolving set of influences—in particular, Roudinesco identifies the influence of Claude Lévi-Strauss, Ferdinand de Saussure, and structuralism on the uniqueness of Lacan's seminars as they begin in the 1950s. Indeed, Lacan's linguistic turn can be seen in his further development of the symbolic order: the moment at the conclusion of the Oedipal complex in which the child accepts the authority of the father and enters into the realm of language, in which linguistic rules parallel paternal ones. In these earlier years of his career, Lacan had not yet begun to formalize his approach to the real, imaginary, and symbolic orders, the discussion of which would shape his own influential seminars held from the 1950s through the 1970s.

Paradoxically, however, one stands to benefit from Lacan's relatively meager conceptual vocabulary of the 1930s, in which the psychoanalyst must borrow his terminology from Kojève in order to develop his points. Prior to Lacan's development of his own systematic vocabulary to describe his concept of the internally contradicted subject and competing regimes of signification, he relied on Hegelian language that had been honed and passed down by Kojève in his seminars. These conceptual similarities would persist long after he had matured into his own lexicon. As Lacan declared in 1953, in his famous "Discours de Rome" speech that is thought to inaugurate his turn toward linguistic structuralism, "it is impossible for our technique to fail to realize the structuring moments of the Hegelian phenomenology: in the first place the dialectic of Master and Slave [. . .] and generally everything which permits us to understand how the constitution of the object is subordinated to the bringing to realization of the subject."[47]

Lastly, in reading Kojève *through* Lacan, one comes to realize and admire the sheer specularity of Kojève's own philosophical metaphors. Recognition, so crucial for Kojève's anthropological reading of Hegel, takes place across a landscape of seeing: seeing oneself, seeing another, and seeing another see oneself. The Kojèvian subject struggles to overcome its sense of duplication, and wisdom is achieved only after having escaped this hall of mirrors. It would take Lacan's adoption of desire and recognition in Kojève to highlight one unacknowledged yet essential aspect of the philosopher's seminars: seeing is a source of pleasure and pleasure is a source of anxiety.

NOTES

1. Élisabeth Roudinesco provides a summary of *La Psychanalyse* and the Société française de psychanalyse in *Histoire de la psychanalyse en France. Jacques Lacan. Esquisse d'une vie, histoire d'un système de pensée* (Paris: La Pochothèque, 2009), 953.

2. Received correspondence, Jacques Lacan, NAF28320, Box 22.1, Alexandre Kojève Fonds, Bibliothèque nationale de France, Paris, France.

3. Kojève briefly discusses psychology in *Essai d'une histoire raisonnée de la philosophie païenne. I: Les Présocratiques* (Paris: Gallimard, 1968), 43–45.

4. Pierre Macherey, "Lacan avec Kojève, philosophie et psychanalyse," *Lacan avec les philosophes* (Paris: Albin Michel, 1991): 320–321.

5. The letters are kept in Kojève's collected papers: Received correspondence, NAF28320, Box 22.1, Alexandre Kojève Fonds, Bibliothèque nationale de France, Paris, France. A translation into English was made by Juan Pablo Lucchelli and Todd McGowan, "The Early Lacan: Five Unpublished Letters from Jacques Lacan to Alexandre Kojève," *American Imago*, 73.3 (2016): 325–341.

6. An explanation for this speculation is provided in ibid., 327–331.

7. Paul Ricœur refers to hermeneutic methods that "clear the horizon for a more authentic word, for a new reign of Truth, not only by means of a 'destructive' critique, but by the invention of an art of *interpreting*." See Ricœur, *Freud and Philosophy. An Essay on Interpretation*, trans. Denis Savage (New Haven: Yale University Press, 1970), 33. Ricœur's own work on Freud and philosophy were not without controversy, eliciting a telling criticism from Lacan. See Roudinesco, 1093–1094.

8. Raymond Queneau, *Journal, 1914–1965* (Paris: Gallimard, 1996), 852.

9. I am grateful to Lucchelli and McGowan for identifying Lacan's contribution, recorded in the published yearbook of the École pratique des hautes études, 332–333.

10. Dominique Auffret includes the full outline in *Alexandre Kojève: La philosophie, l'État, la fin de l'Histoire* (Paris: Grasset & Fasquelle, 1990), 447.

11. Ibid., 13.

12. The article has been reprinted as Jacques Lacan, "Les complexes familiaux dans la formation de l'individu," *Autres écrits* (Paris: Seuil, 2001): 23–84.

13. Roudinesco, 1678.

14. Ibid., 1680.

15. Ibid., 1680.

16. The speech was never published and Lacan claims to have lost the text. See however note 39.

17. Henri Wallon, "Comment se développe chez l'enfant la notion de corps propre," *Journal de psychologie* (1931): 705–748. As with Lacan after him, Wallon is generally thought to have introduced philosophical concepts into his psychoanalytical practice.

18. According to Roudinesco, these differences between Kleinians and Anna Freudians had already reached a head at the Marienbad conference in 1936.

19. Most translations of the *Phenomenology of Spirit*, including the one cited here, translate this dialectical moment as Lord and Bondsman. When referring to Kojève's seminars, I use Master/Slave to reflect his own translation of the terms into French.

20. Lacan had earlier stressed the difference between instinct and complex, in particular in his "Beyond the Reality Principle" (1936), where he defined the complex as the pathway through which "the images that inform the broadest units of behavior are installed in the psyche, images with which the subject identifies one after the other in order to play, as the sole actor, the drama of their conflicts." See Lacan, "Au-delà du 'principe de réalité,'" *Écrits*, 90.

21. Lacan, "Les complexes familiaux dans la formation de l'individu," 27–28.

22. Ibid., 28.

23. Ibid., 34–35.

24. Ibid., 31.

25. Ibid., 31.

26. Mikkel Borch-Jacobsen, *Lacan. Le maître absolu* (Paris: Flammarion, 1995), 239.

27. Alexandre Kojève, *Introduction à la lecture de Hegel* (Paris: Gallimard, 1947), 47.

28. Ibid., 63.

29. Kojève in his seminars does not mention existing psychoanalytical vocabulary for the human compulsion to death, despite Freud's having already formally developed a theory of the death drive in *Beyond the Pleasure Principle* (1920). It perhaps took the intervention of Lacan, who more formally straddled the fields of philosophy and psychoanalysis, to synthesize the concept as it had been articulated across both disciplines.

30. Lacan, "Les complexes familiaux dans la formation de l'individu," 35.

31. Kojève, *Introduction à la lecture de Hegel*, 119.

32. Ibid., 120.

33. Lacan, "Les complexes familiaux dans la formation de l'individu," 36–37.

34. Kojève, *Introduction à la lecture de Hegel*, 62–68.

35. G. W. F. Hegel, *Phenomenology of Spirit*, trans. A. V. Miller (Oxford: Oxford University Press, 1977), 110.

36. Lacan, "Les complexes familiaux dans la formation de l'individu," 38.

37. Ibid., 43.

38. Although there is some argument over to what extent the text parallels his speech in 1936, Lacan's speech from Zurich was published as "Le stade du miroir comme formateur de la fonction du Je telle qu'elle nous est révélée dans l'expérience psychanalytique," in *Écrits* (Paris: Seuil, 1966), 93–100.

39. Ibid., 95.

40. Ibid., 96.
41. Ibid., 98.
42. Hegel, *Phenomenology of Spirit*, 126.
43. Ibid., 126.
44. Kojève, *Introduction à la lecture de Hegel*, 90.
45. Lacan, "Les complexes familiaux dans la formation de l'individu," 51.
46. Ibid., 55.
47. Lacan, "Fonction et champ de la parole et du langage en psychanalyse," *Écrits* (Paris: Seuil, 1966), 292.

BIBLIOGRAPHY

Auffret, Dominique. *Alexandre Kojève: La philosophie, l'État, la fin de l'Histoire*. Paris: Grasset & Fasquelle, 1990.

Borch-Jacobsen, Mikkel. *Lacan. Le maître absolu*. Paris: Flammarion, 1995.

Hegel, G. W. F. *Phenomenology of Spirit*. Translated by A. V. Miller. Oxford: Oxford University Press, 1977.

Kojève, Alexandre. *Essai d'une histoire raisonnée de la philosophie païenne. I: Les Présocratiques*. Paris: Gallimard, 1968.

———. *Introduction à la lecture de Hegel*. Paris: Gallimard, 1947.

Lacan, Jacques. "Au-delà du 'principe de réalité.'" *Écrits*. Paris: Seuil, 1966: 72–92.

———. "Fonction et champ de la parole et du langage en psychanalyse." *Écrits*. Paris: Seuil, 1966: 237–322.

———. "Les complexes familiaux dans la formation de l'individu." *Autres écrits*. Paris: Seuil, 2001: 23–84.

———. "Le stade du miroir comme formateur de la fonction du Je telle qu'elle nous est révélée dans l'expérience psychanalytique." *Écrits*. Paris: Seuil, 1966: 93–100.

———. Received correspondence. Alexandre Kojève Fonds, Bibliothèque nationale de France, Paris, France.

Lucchelli, Juan Pablo, and Todd McGowan. "The Early Lacan: Five Unpublished Letters from Jacques Lacan to Alexandre Kojève." *American Imago* 73, no. 3 (2016): 325–341.

Macherey, Pierre. "Lacan avec Kojève, philosophie et psychanalyse." *Lacan avec les philosophes*. Paris: Albin Michel, 1991.

Queneau, Raymond. *Journal, 1914–1965*. Paris: Gallimard, 1996.

Ricœur, Paul. *Freud and Philosophy. An Essay on Interpretation*. Translated by Denis Savage. New Haven: Yale University Press, 1970.

Roudinesco, Élisabeth. *Histoire de la psychanalyse en France. Jacques Lacan. Esquisse d'une vie, histoire d'un système de pensée*. Paris: La Pochothèque, 2009.

Wallon, Henri. "Comment se développe chez l'enfant la notion de corps propre." *Journal de psychologie* (1931): 705–748.

Chapter Eleven

Alexandre Kojève's Economic Undertakings

Luis J. Pedrazuela

INTRODUCTION: THE THEORETICAL BACKGROUND

The philosopher and French high civil servant specialized in trade policy, Alexandre Kojève, shared with his interviewer Gilles Lapouge in 1968, the year of his death, the following words:

> I love this work. Intellectuals think that a given successful outcome is true success. You write a book, it becomes a top seller and that is the end of the story. Here it is different, for true success is something that happens. I have already told you about the joy I experienced when my customs tariff was accepted. You play a game of a superior nature. You travel, you belong to an international elite that has replaced aristocracy [. . .]. To be divine, what does it mean? It can either be the stoic wisdom or a game? Who plays the game? Gods play it, they do not need to react, thus, they play. They are lazy gods. . . . I am lazy, and I like to play . . .[1]

Lapouge adds that, as a high bureaucrat, Kojève rejoiced in staying at luxury hotels and giving speeches in their conferences halls and that he adored talking about political economy. The interviewer notes further that Kojève saw the world of 1968 as heading rapidly toward the Universal and Homogeneous State.

It is not only that the *undertakings* to which the title of this chapter refer deny Kojève's self-proclaimed divine laziness, but also that some of the notions that appear in the above interview are well-rooted in Kojève's own thought. As the main purpose of this chapter is to give an account of the economic undertakings in which Alexandre Kojève was tirelessly involved for more than twenty-two years, and to try to elucidate their real scope, we deem it advisable to go through some of said notions beforehand. This may allow us to envision Kojève's acts in the service of the French Ministry of Economic Affairs not as a disparate collection of public activities, but rather as a coherent whole.

If we start by the notion of "elite," to which Kojève in the previous interview shows himself proud of belonging, this notion may be linked to the distinction that the Russo-French thinker makes in his 1942 *The Notion of Authority* between those who experience authority and those who exercise it.[2] The latter are those who should fathom the psychological mechanisms of the former to make them believe that the authority that they exercise over them keeps to the *normal pattern* and should, accordingly, not be resisted. While the authority of the members of the elite is something that arises spontaneously sparing them any pedagogy whatsoever on how to acquire it, the perception of authority of those who are subject to it—to wit, those who make up the people that ought to *be politically educated*- needs to be shaped through pedagogy, or propaganda. Under the term *to make believe* Kojève's pedagogical conception of the exercise of power also appears in his 1964 essay, *The Emperor Julian and His Art of Writing*. The emperor Julian governs the people of Rome. The set of beliefs popular among the latter is something he can make use of to foster his own political agenda, namely: the eternal maintenance of the Roman State. Such beliefs make up the myths upon which Rome rests as a political community. By putting them in the service of his own concept of the Roman State, what the emperor does is to resort to theology, that is, to sanction essentially false stories cloaked in a credible form with a view to educating in a certain direction the specific individuals that form the Roman society. This is a perfectly legitimate thing to do as long the emperor's educational scope affects only the individuals in their specificity, it ceases to be so the moment the emperor switches his perspective to one that brings to the foreground the Society as a whole or, what amounts to the same, man in general. Such a change of perspective is relevant because through it the emperor moves from the practical to the theoretical realm, which is the one that deals with the State as such. If, in the practical sphere, irony permits to conceal one's own real political intent from the people for the sake of their education, inside the theoretical realm—the domain of *Nus*—myth-making and irony are excluded, and nothing but seriousness prevails.

Kojève's distinction between a practical domain pertaining to the pedagogical instruction of the individual taken as a specific part of society and a theoretical realm linked to a general theory of the State can be traced back to his 1943 *Outline of a Phenomenology of Right*. In this book Kojève puts forward a far-reaching definition of what a *group* or a *collective* is.[3] This definition might even run through some of the official notes that he wrote for the French Ministry of Economic Affairs as well as through the idea of economic *integration* that comes up in them. According to it, a member of a group can either be taken in his particular or in his universal aspect. If taken in the former aspect the individual is conceived in his specificity, in what constitutes his *here and now* and makes him different from the rest. By contrast, if taken in his universal aspect, the same individual is considered from a *general* perspective that makes abstraction of those differences. By ignoring that which makes him different and only focusing on that which he shares with the others, such a perspective conceives the actions of the individual member of a group as indistinguishable from those which anyone else would undertake in his place. Such a member stands, in consequence, for what Kojève names the *member whoever* of the collective or group in question. Moreover, the distinction between the specific individual member and the *member whoever* of a given society, group or collective is not a mere external one. On the contrary, the self-consciousness of the individual appears split-up between these two poles.

The will of a society, group, or collective is not formed by adding up the will of each of its specific individual members, but rather by the will of the *member whoever* as the bearer of a *general* quality that in the will of the specific member is completely absent. The *member whoever* is, thus, able to represent the group, whenever this is taken as a whole and understood from a *general* or theoretical perspective. Kojève's distinction between *actual and potential actions* comes to confirm the close relationship that the Russo-French thinker establishes between the general will of a group and theoretical knowledge. *Actual actions* are carried out by specific individuals who limit themselves to inserting in their worldly *here and now* the potency that is contained in *potential actions*. These, conversely, separate the conceptual essence from the empirical being by making abstraction of the *here and now* of the individuals taken in their specificity. Whereas *actual actions* are made up of bare acts that are immediately linked to the present circumstances of a given individual, *potential actions* relate to their will and intention and belong to the realm of speech in which "space is represented by the plurality of words and languages, and time, by the unity of their meaning."[4] *Integration* would be the process by means of which a State taken as a *whole of wholes* progressively extends its geographical base. Through such a process, universalities that so far appeared to be linked exclusively to a given State see themselves downgraded into mere particularities with respect to a would-be meta-State, very much as the specific individuals were stripped, at a former stage, of their singularities to the benefit of the general will of their own States. The phenomena of right and trade provide two efficient lanes for this process to run relentlessly towards its destination. By finally encompassing all of mankind, the would-be Meta-State results in something essentially different from what is usually understood under the term *State*. Comprising ever more categories of people, the *member whoever* of such a meta-state ends up coinciding with humanity itself. As this coincidence is tantamount to that which exists between the pair status/being and the pair contracts/will or action, the *human being* that constitutes such a humanity ends up functioning as the concept that forces into line all pre-existing differences. As already stated, the role that Kojève assigns to trade and right in this *harmonization* is not negligible. The agent of trade par excellence is the mediating slave or bourgeois, that is, he who works to exchange the product of his work instead of consuming it on the spot. Said product can be approached from a double perspective, namely, as the finished product, or, as the concept actualized by the slave's understanding and work. As a finished product, the product is indistinguishable from its fixed *here and now* as a thing. As a concept, by contrast, the product relates to the *concept-project* devised by the worker's mind according to his rational expectations. From a conceptual perspective, the product gives rise to an ever-changing set of universal needs that cannot be satisfied by consuming or assimilating the item produced. Only the exchange of the latter through its separation from the *here and now* of the worker's own body can lead to such a satisfaction. "The conceptual (logic) character of the product realizes and reveals itself objectively in and through exchange,"[5] states Kojève in this respect.

The concept of human work that underlies Kojève's idea of exchange is not mere labor, but first and foremost a social interaction based ultimately on a desire for recognition. As a spiritual reality, human work is defined by Kojève against the backdrop of other definitions of work that overlook its constitutive social aspect. For instance, cooperation among workers taken as mere producers, that is, as necessary coworkers grouped into a team to produce something is not, properly speaking, human work. Apart from also existing among animals, a mere cooperative account of work rests on an understanding of work in terms of the given thing or of the finished product but misses to capture its specific human dimension in terms of the *thing-to-be produced*. Yet, unlike raw materials or the product taken as a thing, the product taken as the *thing to be produced* implies the anticipation of the outcome of the work in the *concept-project* devised by the worker's mind. Additionally, in a sort of virtual exchange that takes place while the *concept-project* is being produced, the human coworker is due not the part that he himself produces, but that which is produced by another. This exchange, internal to the production process, is what Kojève calls *wage*.[6]

Now if, on the one hand, trade or exchange reveals the product's conceptual aspect and, on the other, *work-exchange* as such brings forth the universalization of the slave or bourgeois so that the mere formal or shell-like universality of the master can be replaced by a full one at the end of history, as Kojève asserts in his *Outline of a Phenomenology of Right*[7] and if, furthermore, *work-exchange* is something that liberates the slave or bourgeois from his earthbound animal existence and opens up to him the realm of the seas and the air,[8] then it is no less true that for Kojève such a liberation can only take place under certain conditions.

It can hardly develop, for instance, in a State or political society in which the notion of property depends ultimately on aristocratic warfare and in which trade or exchange can be curbed at will by the State. Fostering the existence of idle bondholders instead of stimulating the emergence of ever new needs thanks to the existence of a circuit between human work and universal needs based on exchange, the State in its Schmittian political form ought to be replaced by the global economic society hitherto stifled by it.

QUESTIONS

At this juncture, the question imposes itself: did Kojève enter the French Ministry of Economic Affairs in 1945 and keep to his existential commitment to trade policy after his retirement in 1967 and until his death with his boots on in 1968 to make the alleged emancipation of the slave happen?

Moreover, was Kojève's real intent from his post as a high civil servant, as he attributes to the philosopher in *Tyranny and Wisdom* "to influence the government"[9] and "determine or to co-determine its policy as such"[10] "with a view to introducing or to administering a philosophical pedagogy"[11] because "the philosopher cannot give up pedagogy? Indeed, the *success* of his philosophical pedagogy is the sole 'objective' criterion of the truth of the philosopher's doctrine?"[12]

THE PRACTICAL FOREFRONT

An introductory way to address these questions may be to evoke here the statement of one of Kojève's many work colleagues. François Valéry, son of the famous French poet Paul Valéry and, among other relevant positions, secretary at the conference on the Schuman Plan in 1950 and deputy permanent representative of France at the Organization for European Economic Cooperation (OEEC) in 1954, said in a French radio broadcast devoted to Kojève in 1986:

This means that Kojève placed himself ultimately at two levels. Still, his way of reasoning, for one cannot talk about Kojève without referring to Hegel, was structured in such a way that even the notes that he wrote about very concrete subjects, tariffs on exports or imports, for instance, gave the impression of relying on a powerful ammunition that did not appear in the foreground.[13]

As soon as in 1945, the WWII rubble still smoking, Kojève entered to work for the French Ministry of Economic Affairs thanks to the intermediation of Robert Marjolin—one of "his Hegelians," as he calls him in the introductory interview to this chapter. Marjolin was then director of the organism at which Kojève would develop his entire career as a French senior civil servant, namely, the DREE (Directorate of External Economic Relations). The overall task of this directorate was to promote France's external commercial policy and to foster the foreign trade of the country. By contrast, the distribution of the Marshall Plan's financial aid was not among its major concerns. Moreover, the DREE was far from being the sole organism with such commercial policy functions inside the complex French state machinery, and its plans had to be coordinated with four instances that reported to ministries other than that of economic affairs. Although jealousies between the different functional areas were not altogether absent, the truth is that during the twenty-three years that Kojève served in his post at the DREE, a smooth coordination among these entities was the rule rather than the exception. To a large extent this was due both to the meetings that their directors held on a weekly basis as well as to the close personal links that the latter were able to create.[14] Kojève grasped stunningly quickly how to position himself inside such an institutional network. By circulating within it the economic notes that he drafted he piqued the interest of the heads of its different organizational units. The close relationship that he had with three key figures of the time may have helped as well to the successful outcome of Kojève´s networking. Around ten years younger than him, such figures were in their thirties in 1945 and they belonged to the generation onto whose shoulders fell the *mission* of the reconstruction and modernization of France after the war. Regarding this generation, the French historian René Girault notes that it was greatly shocked by France's 1940 defeat against the Nazis and that both the reaction against such a defeat and the ideal of the rebirth of a postwar France were the motivation behind their actions.[15] One of these figures was the aforementioned Robert Marjolin. An ancient attendee of Kojève's lectures on Hegel in the 1930s, Marjolin left his head position at the DREE—which he had obtained thanks to Jean Monnet's recommendation—at the end of 1945 and went on to join the latter's efforts to set up France's modernization plan for three years. From 1948 to 1955, Marjolin would be the OEEC's first general secretary, and he would later participate in the negotiations of the Treaty of

Rome that resulted in the creation of the EEC in 1957. From 1958 until 1967, he was appointed to the vice-presidency of the European Commission for Economic and Financial Affairs.[16]

Oliver Wormser, who in 1945 entered to work at the Directorate of Economic and Financial Affairs (DAEF) under the Ministry of Foreign Affairs, was another personality closely attached to Kojève both at a professional and a personal level. He would end up becoming the DAEF's director in 1954 and stayed in this post until 1966. Wormser afterwards became French ambassador to Russia. After two years in Moscow and his refusal to become France's Minister of Economic and Financial Affairs, Wormser held the position of governor of the Bank of France from 1969 to 1975. Together with other French high civil servants—among them Kojève—Wormser's diplomatic and economic acumen served notably to thwart Britain's first application to join the EEC between 1961 and 1963.[17]

Bernard Clappier is the third personality worth mentioning. After working as inspector of finances at Vichy's industry department in 1943, from 1947 to 1951 he became the cabinet chief of Robert Schuman, French Minister of Foreign Affairs at the time. Clappier was also during a period vice president of the OEEC's exchange committee and simultaneously served, in his capacity as one of Jean Monnet's closest confidants, as a mediator between the plans of the latter and Schuman for postwar Europe. The 1950 Schuman Declaration and the following creation of the ECSC (European Coal and Steel Community) in 1951 owed their coming into being, to a large extent, to Clappier's mediating function. His refusal of Monnet's offer to become the head of the ECSC's financial board led him to accept the direction of the DREE, thereupon becoming Kojève's boss from 1951 until 1963. After serving twelve years as the head of the DREE, Clappier joined Oliver Wormser at the Bank of France as a sub-governor in 1965, replacing him in 1975 as governor.[18]

Marjolin being an old friend of Wormser and Wormser, in turn, linked to Clappier by more than just mere professional links, the clout of this triumvirate seems to have provided Kojève with a solid institutional basis, not only to display his acts in the international forums where the postwar world order was being devised, but also to get precious updates in relation to one of his major concerns: the removal of trade barriers and the universal expansion of trade.

If Kojève's inspiration for his economic undertakings as a high bureaucrat can be found in his own philosophical work and, more specifically, in the five explicit appeals to realize the Universal and Homogeneous State that can be found in it,[19] the scope of his official activities may well have been a total one, meaning by total one that encompasses humanity and the world as a whole.

The statement that Anne-Marie Moussa, a close friend, and work colleague of Kojève, made to one of his biographers may point in this direction. According to Moussa, Kojève's interests went beyond mere European issues and aimed rather at the entire world.[20] Relevant in this regard may be also the "counterattack" that Kojève led[21] against the Schuman Plan inside the French administration in 1951. If such a plan laid down the seeds of the future EEC, Kojève's *counterattack* against it proved his initial misgivings about the nature of Monnet and Schuman's *supranational* project. The Russo-French thinker was particularly distrustful of Monnet, whose initiatives he suggested closely monitoring since he thought he was moved by "a dubious interventionism."[22] Even if the ECSC that came out of the Schuman proposal was based on a *supranational* decision-making mechanism, Kojève sensed in it a threat for his own *supranational* project. A threat, in the first place, because in the Schuman Declaration the interests of France and Germany gained a dangerous prominence at the expense of those of the other countries.[23] If the latter joined the French-German economic pool, they risked being excluded from the broader economic integration that was underway since April 1948 under the umbrella of the sixteen-member OEEC. The OEEC was a US-sponsored organism that managed the distribution of the Marshall Plan's funds and whose decisions, contrary to those of the ECSC, needed the unanimous support of the national governments of its member countries. By focusing, moreover, on two specific products of such an economic relevance as coal and steel, the Schuman Plan risked fostering a return to bilateral relations as it would remove such products from the multilateral current of exchanges that was being set up in the world after WWII. In sum, the Schuman Declaration meant, for Kojève, a six-member and unbalanced Europe where the specificities of France and Germany would weigh too much, thereby putting at risk the economic integration so far achieved. Confronted with such an alternative, Kojève stood for the large Europe of sixteen that the OEEC represented in his eyes. Yet, even if his *counterattack* ultimately failed, Kojève's sense of *contingency* made no drama out of it. Far from it, he soon adapted his actions to the new circumstances. In line with this, Kojeve asserts in his *Kant* that for Hegelianism, actions undertaken for the sake of recognition do not necessarily lead to happiness and that satisfaction can be compatible with unhappiness.[24] Those who risk themselves for recognition—as opposed to Hegel's *beautiful souls*—must cope with a certain self-deprecation when facing failure, something that moral and religious individuals abhor. It should be noted also that Kojève's plan was defeated on only one flank, since his proposal for the elimination of trade barriers based on a common list of products was accepted about the same time.

If we now come back to Kojeve's networking, one is stunned by his ability to also make contacts on his own, without any institutional coverage. It is surprising in this sense how, by making use of his *Introduction to the Reading of Hegel* as a pretext to start up an epistolary exchange with a given figure, Kojève received letters as soon as in 1947 from, to name only two, Julian S. Huxley, coiner of the term "transhumanism" and at the time UNESCO's first general manager, and André Philip, none other than France's Minister of Economic and Financial Affairs back then. The former asked Kojève in his letter for a written contribution on the human rights problem for the UNESCO's commission on the subject, the latter acknowledged receipt, in his letter, of Kojève's *Introduction to the Reading of Hegel*.

Not less stunning is Kojève's ubiquitous position inside the French senior administration in 1948, hardly three years after his incorporation. If at the end of 1947 and beginning of 1948 he was in La Havana negotiating, in the wake of the GATT agreements, the creation of an International Trade Organization (ITO) which finally never came to fruition, during the same period his position inside the French "division of German issues" allowed him to closely follow the economic situation in Germany. Despite its functional dependency on the DREE, said division enjoyed a certain autonomy and was run from Baden-Baden by Jean Filippi, head of the "Directorate of German Economic Issues" who shortly afterward would become Kojève's boss at the DREE. Hubert Rousselier, a friend of Filippi since their times as senior officials at Vichy's Ministry of Finance, was the man leading the subdivision to which Kojève was assigned, among others, to handle the matters regarding the French occupation zone.[25]

THE MINISTERIAL NOTES

Besides this strategic positioning inside the senior French administration, Kojève based his economic undertakings, as pointed out earlier, on writing ministerial notes profusely and circulating them within the French State apparatus. Although he had not yet become a senior official, the template for some of these notes could well have been provided by his 1945 *Outline of a Doctrine of French Policy* or even by the program that in his 1942 *The Notion of Authority* he sketches to fill Pétain's "National Revolution" with a real content. This template would go along these lines: an idiosyncratic assessment of a present situation followed by the threat that such a situation poses to the maintenance of the *status quo* completed both by a call to action and an account of concrete measures accompanied by a list of the advantages that will come out from them. The purpose of the next pages is to convey an overview of some of these notes. This may allow us not only to capture the tension between present and future that may run through them, but also to witness the recurrent emergence of a refrain that already came up in Kojève's *Outline of a Doctrine of French Policy*, namely, the "English problem" as a nagging annoyance that Kojève's universal and homogeneous project seemingly faced from the beginning until the end.

September 1949: Hopes and Difficulties of the OEEC

Kojève wrote this note[26] at the end of August or beginning of September of 1949. As such it is a draft of an article that was later published in the September issue of the French weekly magazine, *France-Illustration-le Monde Illustré*. The note in question starts with Kojève's confirmation that the prevailing world's economic system is at the same time liberal and interventionist, its orientation being marked by the removal of the State's encroachment on the economic realm. For Kojève such a system is also Rooseveltian and authoritarian, to the extent that within it the States themselves are expected to take charge of their own economic dismantling by promoting the creation of mighty international organisms. However, not every State would be able to join an economic system defined in those terms. Before doing so, the economies of the concerned States should meet the liberal conditions that prevail within the international economic sphere. Otherwise, such States would lose their autonomy out of their own striving to participate in the latter. Such was the case, among others, of the European States after the war. Harry Truman's speech before the US Congress on March 12, 1947, was the "revolutionary" acknowledgment on the part of the United States that the creation of a worldwide economical realm beyond the state's control required a rise in the standard of living of the countries that aspired to take part in it. Said rise implied, in turn, the development of economies of scale. This was not feasible at a bilateral or interstate level, but only at a supranational one. The Marshall Plan and the creation in April 1948 of the OEEC as the organism in charge of distributing the financial funds among the different European states rested on Truman's speech assumptions and, thereby, addressed the European states not individually, but as a whole, that is, as making abstraction of their own individual interests. Yet, countering this collective integration and preventing it from being realized "over so short a period that it would seem utopian" stood the United Kingdom and its Commonwealth interests.

December 1949: Note on the Development of "Backward" Countries

Point IV of Harry Truman's speech of January 20, 1949, is key to this note. Kojève's references to it will become a constant in the 1950s both in his notes, and in his correspondence with Carl Schmitt. He seems to interpret it as giving "expression to a protean ideology of international development,"[27] hence the importance he attaches to it and, in its wake, to later US modernization programs. In this note on economic development, Kojève goes on to distinguish between autonomous *backward* countries and the colonial possessions of European mother countries. The development of the former should rest on Point IV funding policies, the UN playing thereby an essential intermediary function. The latter countries should, by contrast, avoid any UN-led intervention and, instead, pool their possessions inside the whole that they make up as OECE members. Regretfully, both the UN's role regarding the autonomous "backward" countries and that of the OECE concerning the European colonies would face opposition from Great Britain as this country would not give up its singular interests in certain "backward" countries for the sake of any whole.

May 1950: The Schuman Proposal and the OEEC

Barely one week after Schuman had addressed his proposal to the French cabinet, Kojève wrote on May 16, 1950, his note titled, "The Schuman Proposal and the O.E.E.,C." Its principal recipient was Jean Filippi, but Kojève copied it also to Olivier Wormser and Robert Marjolin. As stated earlier, Kojève expressed in this note his deep concerns about the plans that Monnet and Schuman had in mind for Europe. These concerns were so deep that Kojève took the trouble to write another note in the same vein three days later, in which he substitutes the terms "France" and the "ECSC's High Authority" for "OEEC's countries" and "European Investment Bank." The latter was, incidentally, an institution devised by Thierry de Clermont Tonnerre, former senior official of economy under Vichy and, at the time, deputy manager of the Interministerial Committee's General Secretariat (SGCI), the organism in charge of coordinating France's European political economy. Apart from reflecting such concerns, Kojeve's note of May 16 champions a method to eliminate trade barriers that is based on a consolidated common list of products of which steel and coal must also be part. According to Kojève, a trade liberalization procedure founded on said list would help both to achieve a multilateralization of trade and to discard any arbitrary measures that, under the pretext of liberalization, allow its proponents to shirk the long-term commitments necessary for Europe's economic integration to progress. If France, as the head of the OEEC's exchange committee, stood for it, said method would show furthermore the advantage of unmasking the countries less committed to the European integration by portraying them as sabotaging "the structural reforms that are indispensable to achieve a final integration of Europe." Setting out in the eyes of the international community the virtues of Kojève's common list method would ultimately lay bare, the "spurious interests" of the United Kingdom "and its Scandinavian satellites." In his note on the Schuman Plan, Kojève finally sees an opportunity to clear up the confusion that hitherto had prevailed in matters of European integration. If in his writing of 1949 he already underlined the incompatibility between the United Kingdom's two memberships, namely, that to the Commonwealth and that to the OEEC, in this note of 1950 Kojève puts forward the existence of two radically incompatible doctrines, to wit, the French doctrine and the "English" one. While the former openly asserts that the viability of the European countries relies on the achievement of a thorough economic integration, the "English doctrine" plays a double game with the sole purpose of fostering Great Britain's Commonwealth membership.

June 1961: The Agricultural Problem in the Western Modern World and the Mansholt Plan

In 1961, Kojève writes a note with the above-indicated title.[28] Due to its length, it is rather an essay than a ministerial note. Its importance is signaled by the fact that, in its introduction, Kojève relates its content to the Baumgartner–Pisani Plan and claims authorship over it notwithstanding the name of the two figures that the plan bears. He, thus, suggests to rename it the "Kojève Plan." Another aspect of this lengthy note worth mentioning is that Kojève addresses himself not to the usual group of French high civil servants, but to certain "initiates" that apparently ought to know who the real mind behind the plan is. If this were not enough, the peculiar nature of these pages that deal with agricultural issues comes also from Kojève having written at least two versions of them, one that he refers to as "Thomistic" and another one as "Marxist." Their relevance is further enhanced by the fact that the agricultural problem that they tackle would become one of the reasons behind General de Gaulle's final veto in January 1963 to the application for full membership of the European Economic Market that the United Kingdom initially submitted July 31, 1961.

Together with other French senior officials, Kojève played an important role in the negotiations between the British delegation and the continental representatives in Brussels during the roughly one year and a half that the former lasted. Contrary to the general welcome by the other EEC countries, the French attitude toward a British EEC membership was hostile from the very outset. Still, France was not in position to let this hostility surface openly. First, because this could lead to a dangerous confrontation with its other EEC partners and, second, because a harder stance on the issue required General de Gaulle to previously secure his political standing as the head of the Republic inside France. Hence, France's negotiating tactics would consist of enervating the British position by unduly protracting the negotiations. The unwieldy format of the United Kingdom's application, full of technicalities, made it easy for the French delegation to exploit the situation at will. At some stage of the discussions, a British negotiator wrote down the following verses:

Kojève
said to the General "I lift my glass
to the total destruction of western civilization."[29]

Among the words of these verses, there is one which perhaps captures the nature of Kojève's economic undertakings better than the others, namely, *total*. Like a "God that plays," Kojève would have also aimed, in his writings and actions as a senior official for the French Ministry of Economic Affairs, at achieving *total* solutions. In his note on the Mansholt Plan of 1961, for instance, Kojève plans a *total* solution to the predicament of the world's agriculture. Such a solution entails a radical overhaul of Great Britain's agricultural system—the ultimate source of the world's agricultural imbalances—on the one hand, and, on the other, the completion of the law of supply and demand of classical economics by doubling it with an analogous one stemming from a gift economy. In his 1963 note, "Attempt at a Solution to the English Problem for the Next Ten Years," Kojève insists, in turn, on the *total* perspective from which such a problem should be tackled by exposing, in somewhat different terms, a similar solution to the one of his note on the Mansholt or Kojève Plan, to wit: Great Britain's acceptance of the Baumgartner–Pisani Plan at a global level as a precondition for further measures meant to counter the consequences that such an acceptance would have for the United Kingdom. Finally, in November 1967, just over half a year before his death of a sudden heart attack at an economic meeting in Brussels, in a note titled "The G.A.T.T.'s Future Actions and the United Kingdom's Not Joining the E.E.C." Kojève—somehow anticipating that he is running out of time—urges the setting up of a plenary GATT session to tackle his newly devised *total* solution to the "English" problem, specifically, the creation of an enlarged Commonwealth that should include Japan.

Like an everything-but-lazy God, Kojève, thus, may have well played the role of a Kosma Prutkov[30] who, cloaking himself in the clothes of a French civil servant, sets out, unlike his literary model, to serve the serious task of creating a world state. Or alternatively, holding in his hand commercial policy tools instead of the painting brush of his uncle Kandinsky,[31] Kojève might as well have been keen on painting and repainting *total* solutions to the "English problem," as if this problem were the sole remaining blind spot in a perfect and self-transparent world canvas. Who knows? Be that as it may, Kojève's *total* solutions do seem to have been inspired by an attempt to bring into line human action, human desire, and human being in accordance with the watchword "to live well and in peace," which in his correspondence with Carl Schmitt, he willingly equates both with "nothing"[32] and with a pacifism turned so self-evident that no evidence would remain of the recognition once needed to reconcile the enemies.

NOTES

1. Alexandre Kojève, "Entretien avec Gilles Lapouge: Les philosophes ne m'intéressent pas, je cherche des sages," *La quinzaine littéraire* 53 (1968): 18–20.

2. Alexandre Kojève, *La notion de L'autorité* (Paris: Gallimard, 2004), 183–184.

3. Alexandre Kojève, *Esquisse, d'une phénoménologue du droit* (Paris: Gallimard, 1981), 436–438.

4. Ibid, 437, n. 2.

5. Ibid, 526.

6. Ibid, 528–529.

7. Ibid, 310–311.

8. Ibid, 527.

9. Leo Strauss, *On Tyranny: Corrected and Expanded Edition, Including the Strauss-Kojève Correspondence* (Chicago: University of Chicago Press, 2013), 163.

10. Ibid.

11. Ibid.

12. Ibid.

13. Statement of François Valèry at the radio broadcast hosted by Jean Daive, testimonio del programa, "Une vie, une œuvre, Alexandre Kojève, la fin de l'histoire," in France Culture, November 11, 1986. http://ttyemupt.unblog.fr/2012/09/07/alexandre-kojeve-par-jean-daive-transcription-radio/.

14. Laurence Badel, Stanislas Jeannesson, and N. Piers Ludlow, *Les administrations nationales et la construction européenne* (Bruxelles: P.I.E.–Peter Lang, 2005), 154, 183, 197.

15. Gérard Bossuat, *La France, l'aide américaine et la construction européenne 1944–1954*. Volume I. Nouvelle édition [en ligne]. Vincennes: Institut de la gestion publique et du développement économique, 1997 (généré le 09 novembre 2013), http:// books.openedition.org/igpde/2692, 14.

16. Badel, *Les administrations*, 164, 189.

17. Ibid, 142–144, 164.

18. This brief outline of Bernard Clappier's career history is based on Badel, *Les administrations*, 193; Bossuat, *l'Aide 1*, 10; Lorenza Sebesta, "El 'fin de la historia' de Alexandre Kojève y Europa, nuevos caminos para comprender las relaciones entre modernización e integración," *Puente@Europa, Universidad de Bolonia* 1 (2014). http://puenteeuropa.unibo.it/article/view/5460/5169, 62; Gérard Bossuat, *La France, l'aide américaine et la construction européenne 1944–1954. Volume II*. Vincennes: Institut de la gestion publique et du développement économique, 1997, 116–117, 122. http://books.openedition.org/igpde/2786.

19. These five explicit appeals to action can be found in (1) Alexandre Kojève, *Introduction à la lecture de Hegel* (Paris: Gallimard, 1968), 290–291; (2) Strauss, *On Tyranny,* 232; (3) Alexandre Kojève, "Hegel, Marx et le christianisme," *Critique,* 3, no 4 (1946): 339; (4) Alexandre Kojève, *Kant* (Paris: Gallimard, 1973), 77; and (5) Strauss, *On Tyranny,* 262.

20. Auffret, 409.

21. Bossuat, *L'aide II,* 120.

22. Ibid.

23. Alexandre Kojève's ministerial note, "Note pour M. Filippi. Objet: la proposition Schuman et l´O.E.C.E." May 16, 1950, Alexandre Kojève "Écrits à caractère administratif," Bibliothèque Nationale de France.

24. Kojève, *Kant,* 40, 44.

25. Badel, *Les administrations,* 185.

26. Alexandre Kojève's ministerial note, "L'O.E.C.E.," 01/09/1949–29/8/1949, Fonds NAF 28320 Alexandre Kojève "Écrits à caractère administratif," Bibliothèque Nationale de France.

27. Stephen Macekura, "The Point Four Program and U.S. International Development Policy," *Political Science Quarterly, Academy of Political Science* 128, no. 1 (Spring 2013): 127–160. https://onlinelibrary.wiley.com/doi/abs/10.1002/polq.12000.

28. Alexandre Kojève, ministerial note, "Le problème agricole dans le monde occidental moderne et le plan Mansholt," June 6, 1996, Fonds NAF 28320, Alexandre Kojève, "Écrits à caractère administratif," Bibliothèque Nationale de France.

29. N. Piers Ludlow, *Dealing with Britain: The Six and the First UK Application to the EEC* (Cambridge: Cambridge University Press, 1997), 200.

30. See the introduction to this volume.

31. See chapter 1.

32. Kojève, "Colonialism from a European Perspective," ed. y trans. Erik de Vries, *Interpretation,* 29, no, 1 (Fall 2001): 98. https://interpretationjournal.com/shop/alexandre-kojeve-colonialism-from-a-european-perspective-by-erik-de-vries-ed-and-translator.

BIBLIOGRAPHY

Auffret, Dominique. *Alexandre Kojève. La philosophie, l'état, la fin de l'histoire.* Paris: Grasset, 1990.

Bossuat, Gérard. *La France, l'aide américaine et la construction européenne 1944–1954.* Volume I. Nouvelle édition [en ligne]. Vincennes: Institut de la gestion publique et du développement économique, 1997 (généré le 09 novembre 2013), http://books.openedition.org/igpde/2692

———. *La France, l'aide américaine et la construction européenne 1944–1954. Volume II.* Vincennes: Institut de la gestion publique et du développement économique,1997. http://books.openedition. org/igpde/2786

Daive, Jean. *Une vie, une oeuvre, Alexandre Kojève, la fin de l'histoire.* Transcripción de la emisión radiofónica del 10 de noviembre de 1990 a cargo de Jean Daive http://ttyemupt.unblog.fr/2012/09/07/alexandre-kojeve-par-jean-daive-transcription-radio/

Kojève, Alexandre. "Entretien avec Gilles Lapouge: Les Philosophes ne m'intéressent pas, je cherche des sages." *La quinzaine littéraire* 53 (1968): 18–20.

———. *La notion de l'autorité*. Paris: Gallimard, 2004.

———. *Esquisse, d'une phénoménologue du droit*. Paris: Gallimard, 1981.

———. *Introduction à la lecture de Hegel*. Paris: Gallimard, 1968.

———. "Hegel, Marx et le christianisme." *Critique* 3, no. 4 (1946).

———. *Kant*. Paris: Gallimard, 1973

———. "Note pour M. Filippi. Objet: la proposition Schuman et l'O.E.C.E." Alexandre Kojève "Écrits à caractère administratif." Bibliothèque Nationale de France, May 16, 1950.

———. "L'O.E.C.E.," 01/09/1949–29/8/1949." Fonds NAF 28320 Alexandre Kojève "Écrits à caractère administratif." Bibliothèque Nationale de France.

———. "Le problème agricole dans le monde occidental moderne et le plan Mansholt." Fonds NAF 28320 Alexandre Kojève, "Écrits à caractère administratif." Bibliothèque Nationale de France, June 11, 1996.

———. "Colonialism from a European Perspective." Ed. y trans. Erik de Vries. *Interpretation* 29, no. 1 (Fall 2001): 9. https://interpretationjournal.com/shop/alexandre-Kojève-colonialism-from-a-european-perspective-by-erik-de-vries-ed- and-translator

Laurence Badel, Jaennesson Stanislas, and N. Piers Ludlow, eds. *Les administrations nationales et la construction Européenne*. Bruxelles: P.I.E., Peter Lang, 2005.

Ludlow, N. Piers. *Dealing with Britain: The Six and the First UK Application to the EEC*. Cambridge University Press, 1997.

Macekura, Stephen. "The Point Four Program and U.S. International Development Policy." *Political Science Quarterly. Academy of Political Science* 128, no. 1 (Spring 2013): 127–160. https://onlinelibrary.wiley.com/doi/abs/10.1002/ polq.12000.

Sebesta, Lorenza. "El 'fin de la historia' de Alexandre Kojève y Europa, nuevos caminos para comprender las relaciones entre modernización e integración." *Puente@ Europa. Universidad de Bolonia* 1 (2014). http://puenteeuropa.unibo. it/article/view/5460/516

Strauss, Leo. *On Tyranny: Corrected and Expanded Edition, Including the Strauss-Kojève Correspondence*. Chicago: University of Chicago Press, 2013.

Index

absolute knowledge: completion of history and, 148–50; vs. love of knowledge, 147; nonknowledge, philosophy as, 77; as a system of prejudices, 170–71

abstraction: concreteness and, 30–31; dialectical understanding of, 34–40; man of action and, 48n98, 168; modern science and, 146–47; risk of life as an, 125; of specific differences, 227

action: alignment of desire, being and, 237–38; cessation of, 111–15; freely accomplished, 219; historical wisdom and, 177–78; Kantian progressive, 71; man of, 10–11, 48n98, 151–52; philosopher in, 131–34; repercussion from, 185; revolutionary will and direct, 96; as the struggle proper to the slave-bourgeois, 62, 78–82, 164; tyrant or statesman's, 171–72; voluntarism, 20, 96, 98

animal: desire, 55, 214–15; earthbound existence, 229; as the natural extension of life, 66; vs. non-animal, 54, 56, 187. See also the bourgeoisie

anthropogenic: capacity of slavery, 81–86; desire for recognition, 156;

feature of technology, 87–88; fight/struggle for pure prestige, 107–8, 124, 189, 190; philosophy and the Freudian death drive, 215. See also death

anthropotheism: the idea of death and, 86–89; the modern project and, 83–86; non-humanist, 83, 87, 155–56; transhumanism, 233

appeals to action, 239n19

atheism: book (Kojève), 54, 63–65; consistency and radicality of, 83–90, 62–68

atheistic: humanism, 81–85; hypothesis, Society instead of God, 174; religion, 63

audience, 62; community of French writers, 159n38; the "Song of Departure" and Kojève's French, 150; warmongering mythologies, 123. See also propaganda

authority: as command without resistance, 125, 226; vs. constraint or force, 165–66, 187, 205n32; four types of, 196; genesis of, 192–94; vs. love, 171–74, 185–86; as obedience without manipulation, 165; subject to and holder of, 226; time and, 196; vs. right, 185, 200; universal and homogeneous, 166; as willing obedience, 165. *See also* "total"

Bataille, Georges, 33, 48n80, 123, 143, 145
the Beautiful, 35–41
the Bible, 3, 177
Bloom, Allan, 3, 99, 104, 115
Bonaparte, Napoleon: empire of, 142, 150, 155; Hegel's thought and deeds of, 17, 149; the "taking" (or conquest) and, 128. *See also* the statesman
bourgeois: agent of trade/exchange, 10–11, 113–14, 131–33, 227–29; capitalist order, 98; individualism, 151, 158n35; intellectual, 155; Judeo-Christian or, 164; mode of production, 10–11, 113; right, 114–15; status quo, 95. *See also* liberal
the bourgeoisie: aesthetics of, 17; hegemony of the present and, 5; repudiation of the past and, 198; as a revolutionary force, 154, 198. *See also* Truman's point IV
bourgeoisification, 98
Buddha: "Descartes and," 29–31
Buddhism, 65, 156; entries on (*Diary of a Philosopher*), 6
Buddhist: conception of death, 6; context and book on Kant (Kojève), 65–66; echoes in the notion of the "in-existent," 30; philosophy, 30; scriptures, 31; tradition, 64. *See also* emptiness

capitalism: "giving" vs. old capitalism, 131; ideology of, 98; liberal democracy and, 100–101. *See also* integration
Catholicism: Kojève's penchant for, 32, 155, 158n35, 202
Christian: death of God, 77–81; salvation undertones, 7, 57; theology, inversion of, 76

Christianity: dismantling of, 7; progress toward finitude and, 77
circular: dialectics, 14; logic of recognition, 173; system of knowledge, 143, 148–49, 176
colonialism, 132; colonial possessions, 235
communism: communist "experiment," 157n10; communist party, dogma, and revolution, 153–55; work/labor and, 109–10
community: "of the dead," 9, 96, 186; myths and political, 226; stable and peaceful, 188; supranational, 231–32. *See also* stable vs. unstable community
complex vs. instinct, 213–17, 222n20
concrete: vs. abstract or isolated particular, 168; advice, 166; art of Kandinsky, 34; concreteness as philosophical leitmotif, 35; *Gesamtkunstwerk*, 44; institutional arrangements, 112; totality, 42. *See also* posthistorical condition
conference in Düsseldorf, 129–34
conquest: of nature, 11, 96–103; for the sake of recognition, 166. *See also* the "Giving" and the "Taking"
constructivism: radical, as intellectual approach, 60–61; Russian art, 34
"contingency": contingent writings, 202
current affairs/current business: fulfilment of, 17; necessity and, 90; non-epicurean solution, 170; sense of, 18–19, 232; success and, 112; the tyrant's priority, 15, 162

death: of the author, 43; autonomy and its value in the face of, 124; awareness of, 72–73n22; of Christianity, 75; compulsion to, 222n29; expectation of, 66; fear of and its overcoming, 54–57; fight/ struggle to the, for pure prestige, 56, 107; on God's death and the slave's victory, 75–79; individualization and, 215–16; inversion of Christianity and 89–90; philosophy of, 83; real possibility of, 124; tyranny and fear of violent, 195

de Gaulle, 18, 157n10, 201, 236–37

Descartes, René: Cartesian dualism, 97; Cartesian system, 14, 146–47; intellectual intuition as inner understanding 170, 175. *See also* abstraction

desire: animal/natural vs. human/cultural, 54–55, 62, 79, 214; for another desire, 79; as anthropogenic mechanism, 90; for autonomy and respect, 187; dynamics of honor and, 124, 163–64, 215; vs. Hobbe's treatment of vanity, 107–8; liberation from, 73n25; modality of, 103–16; object of and the authority of the father, 219; of the other, mediation by the, 20; pedestrian, 98; for perfection, 172; for recognition, as the beginning of history, 156; sibling rivalry and, 217–18; to be desired, 124; universal and limitless, 166; vanity as the Hegelian-political virtue, 173; wordly glory, 167

Diary (Journal) of a Philosopher (Kojève), 1, 6, 7, 31; first version of, 45n11; on art, 31–32, 45n11

discourse (*Logos*)/ speech: *Concept, Time, and Discourse* (Kojève), 41, 143; non-contradictory, coherent, circular, 59, 123, 143, 148; Socratic public, 173–74; the tyrant as master of, 48n98; 168

DREE (Directorate of External Economic Relations), 21, 230, 233

dualism: end of History and liquidation of, 88; Hobbesian, 97; ring metaphor, 69–70

dystopian, 97, 100

Economic and Philosophic Manuscripts of 1844 (Marx), 106–9, 123

EEC (European Economic Community), 21, 231–32

elite, elitism, 101, 225–26; intellectual, 170; qua snobbery, 194

emancipation: individuality, abandonment of, 63–69; from nature and its paradoxes, 54–61; from religion and the fear of death, 68, 84; of the slave, 57, 151, 229; from work/labor, transcendence vs. non-transcendence of necessity, 109–11. *See also* suicide

empire: *L'Empire Latin*, 183, 202; Napoleonic, 142, 150; nonpolitical empire-like unity, 129; the One State and the "I" becoming "We," 68, 70; Russian, 1; self-consciousness and, 141–42, 150–56; socialist of private right, 110–18, 118n45; soviet, 100, 101; universal homogeneous, 110, 133

emptiness: and the inexistent, 28, 29; Japanization, snobbery, and, 48n80; Kandinsky and, 47n38; repetition, exhaustion and, 29; as triumph over nature, 57–58

end of History: "convergence theory" and, 99–101, 111–12, 131–34, 154; as a global assembly line, 133; as postmodern absence of novelty, 43. *See also* absolute knowledge; empire

the "English problem: the English doctrine vs. the French doctrine, 236; as a nagging annoyance, 234. *See also* Schmitt, Carl

exhaustion: of action and creative will, historical, 5, 11, 15; of current affairs and current business, 16, 162–63; of all logical possibilities, 148; of the possibilities of the artwork, 4, 39, 38; repetition, unoriginality and radical, 28, 44. *See also* absolute knowledge the family: the authority of the Father and, 191–92, 219; between biology and culture, as a first instance of individualization, 213–16; "Family Complexes in the Formation of the Individual" (Lacan), 211–16; patrimony, religion and, 9; personal intrigues within the, 164; the State vs., 126; "veneration of the dead," 9, 97, 215–16. *See also* love

fashion: Eugène Rubin (Evgenii Reiss), fashion photographer, 29; French community of writers and "fashionable" ideas, 159n38; Hegelian type of authority and, 196; lifestyle and dystopian vision, 100–101

Feuerbach, Ludwig, 59, 98

Fichte, Johann Gottlieb, 96, 141; dismissal of nature, 100

Ford, Henry, 131; Fordism, 112; Fordist, 132

freedom: limitless, 46n20, 58; from predication, 61–62; realm of necessity vs. realm of,105, 110, 156; risk of life, self-preservation and, 6, 54–55; unhappy consciousness and, 83–86. *See also* emancipation

Freud, Sigmund: case study method, 210; "Hegel and Freud," 211

Fukuyama, Francis, 100; Fukuyama's Hegel, 101

the general will: as a modern value, 9, 96; whole vs. the will of the parts, 194–95, 235

Gesamtkunstwerk (Total work of art): as a synthesis of theory and practice, 44

the given: the given thing and the finished product, 228; natural constraint or force vs. man's self-creating free will, 83–87; negation of the natural and social given, 87–88, 151; no a priori given limits of the posthistorical State, 42

the "Giving" and the "Taking," 130–34

Hamlet: Faust or, tragedy of, 175; *or Hekuba*, 124–29

Hegel, G. W. F: a Humanity bereft of individuality and, 61–63; nation, sovereign State and, 98–99, 155; unhappy consciousness and, 76–80, 94, 155, 219

Hegelianism, left-wing, 82; neo-Hegelianism, 142

Heidegger, Martin: *Being and Time,* 123; concept of *Dasein,* 97, 142; Heideggerian *resolve,* 98; Heideggerian saying, 99; Heidegger's thought, 156

historiosophical scheme, 154

Hitler: general will and *Volk,* 195; Napoleon and, 128, 198–99

Hobbes, Thomas, 97, 107, 123, 143, 157n4, 194

holism: holistic pretensions and the One State, 70; relationship part-whole, 68, 148, 194, 227–28

inexistent: aesthetics of the, 29–39; philosophy of the, 34–35. *See also* Buddhism; *Diary (Journal) of a Philosopher*

Ilyn, Ivan, 35; impasse (dead end) of Kojève's political thought, 188, 196; the Master's predicament, 64, 65, 80

initiates: to the "Kojève Plan," 236; to the science of dialectics, 167; vs. the "Uninitiated," 170

integration: of the different types of authority in the End state, 192–98; economic, 227–35; European, 235, 236; of levels of coherence and non-contradiction, 177; of the parts within the collective, 68, 227–28, 234

the "Intellectual": bourgeois, 155; engaged, 177; Hegel's own intellectual stance, 18, 106;

intellectual intuition, 161, 170; pseudo-religious or Christian atheist, 85, 130; the wise man, 163; tragedy of, 3, 129; true (*Réussite*), vs. intellectual success (*succés*) 225

Ivanov, Nina, 144, 209

Kandinsky, Wassily: abstraction, as an evolving notion, 33–34; the *concrete* paintings of, 28–33; the *empty* paintings of, 39; Kojève's essay on, 31, 44n4; ready-made forms, 32. *See also Gesamtkunstwerk*

Kant, Immanuel: book on (Kojève), 65–66, 73n25, 232, 72n4; as German philosopher, 149; Jacobinism, 102; Kant's system of right vs. Hegel's end state, 68–71; as modern philosopher, 104

Kitarō, Nishida, 72n22

Kirillov: a particular kind of, 8; a philosophical, 83

knowingly (*en connaissance de cause*), 28; vs. unknowingly, 101

Kojève's "counterattack," 21, 232

Kojève's networking, 230–32

Koyrè, Alexandre, 35, 47n49, 76, 123, 142

Lacan, Jacques: "at the foot of the master," 209; as Kojève's host, 210; as Kojève's pupil and *maître à penser*, 125, 150; philosophy, psychoanalysis, and, 210. *See also* Freud, Sigmund

Lapouge, Gilles, 225

law, right, and politics: "Commodity Exchange Theory of Law," 118n45; exclusive juridical group vs exclusive political group, 114, 127; the juridical reaches its definition, 122; juridical situation, 68; primacy of the juridical over the political, 68; primacy of the political over the juridical, 127; private socialist

internationalist right, 115; the third of right, 127, 113; time lag between politics and law, 127. *See also* empire

the "leader" type of authority: classical example, 191; concreteness as an ideal of political leadership, 48n98, 168; criticism of Hegel, 187–88; ideal disappearance of, 200; the leader with a universal project, 196; overcoming of the master's impasse 190; project to be realized, 205n40; revolutionary penchant, 198. *See also* the bourgeoisie; end of History

legitimacy vs. legality: as a Schmittian dichotomy, 127

liberal: attitude of the tyrant, 163; bourgeois individual rights, 98; humanism, 156; ideology, 101; liberals, 154; Lockean liberalism, 101; neoliberal, 128; understanding of wisdom, 151; world economic system, 234. *See also* capitalism

liberalization procedure, 236

the lord and the bondsman: paranoia and, 218–19; translation of, 124, 143, 157n4, 222n19

love: authority and, 185–86; family and, 17; *Hegel's Scientific Ways to Treat Natural Law*, 126; love and hatred/ private and public, 126; vs. recognition (admiration), 171–72; as substance vs. reason as subject, 96–97

Lukàcs, György, 97, 98, 113, 158n24

Lyotard, Jean François, 43

Machiavelli, Niccolo, 161, 171, 176, 199

madness: subjective certainty and, 178, 182

majority-minority: vs. Rousseau's general will, 194–95; as unauthentic authorities resting on quantity, 192–95, 205n32. *See also* authority

Marxism, Kojève's alleged, 103–16, 133, 158n35

"Master-slave" dialectic: in Marx's reading of Hegel, 104–8, 111; overemphasis on, 56, 76, 107, 155, 220; rebalancing of, 184

the member "whoever," 227, 228

ministerial notes, circulation of, 230–33

Mitrokhin list, 157n10

Monnet, Jean, 18–20, 230–35

Montesquieu, 197, 198

Moysset, Henri, 2, 125, 135n15

Nietzschean: anti-Christianism vs. Kojève's, 89; last man, 43, 154, 156; will to power, 98

Noah Harari, Yuval, 156

nonsense, 9, 15; futility, 75; "nothing," 238

OEEC (Organization for European Economic Cooperation), 229–37

ontology: dualist, 54, 155, 214; Heideggerian, 93. *See also* dualism

Orwellian, 97

Pashukanis, Evgeny, 118n45

pedagogy: disciples, success, truth and, 175, 229; practitioners of vs. subjects to, 226; propaganda or, 226; therapeutic education, 165; unlimited recognition as pedagogical task, 172. *See also* Tran-Duc-Thao

photography, 29–31; mechanical reproduction and, 32, 43

playfulness: "connoisseurs" or homo ludens; Kant vs. Hegel, as an ironic interplay, 71; Kojève's triple play, 2; the non-ironical domain of *Nus,* 226; play of a superior nature, 225; in the posthistorical empire, 28, 43, 154–56; seriousness, 13, 59–60, 123–34, 135n9. *See also* posthistorical condition

posthistorical condition: aesthetic connoisseurship, 43–44; BoBo snobbery, 199; in the final world, state, 42, 62, 97, 100–101. *See also* animal

postwar: changed conditions of the XX century, 99–100; French philosophy, 42; Europe and world order, 231–32; world of superpowers, 95, 99, 183

propaganda, 14, 104, 127, 226. *See also* pedagogy

revolutionary spirit: vs. reformist, 16; revolutionary overcoming of prejudices, 168; suicide or self-cancellation of the revolutionary idea and agent, 16, 153. *See also* absolute knowledge

Rousseau, Jean-Jacques: authority and general will, 9, 194–95; the Mauss-Kojève-Rousseau-Hegel link, 135n35

Schmitt, Carl: English *Seanahme,* 132–33; the friend-enemy distinction, 114, 126; a Katechonic view of history, 71; the overcoming of the political and, 13; "the real possibility" to kill, 122–24; Truman's point IV in the Schmitt-Kojève's correspondence), 243. *See also* Strauss, Leo

the Schuman declaration/ proposal, 231–36

self-preservation: and absence of freedom, 55; imperative to, 56, 62; instinct for, 63, 65; primacy of, 66; realm of life and, 97, 216; selfishness and pursuit of, 57–58. *See also* animal, desire

Smith, Adam, 109

Solovyov, Vladimir: aesthetics, "The Meaning of Art," 34, 37; contingency and necessity, 90; overcoming of the theandric conception, 82; unity of the divine and the human, 76, 79

Spinoza, Baruch: geometrical system, 147; life-world, 96–97

stable vs. unstable community: Hegel and Kant, unstable alternation, 71; Rousseau's "permanent and harmonic" general will, 194–95, 196; a stable political order, challenge of achieving, 184; unstable separation of powers, 197–99

the statesman: concrete totality (*Gesamtkuntswek*) and, 42–44; nonutopian stance of, 163; as a philosopher of the concrete, 48n98, 168; unlimited desire for recognition of, 166, 171–74

Stalin: death of, 99; "letter to," 144; Marxism and, 104, 153; Napoleon and, 71, 152; the proletariat, the general will and Lenin-Stalin, 195; Soviet Union under, 53. *See also* the "leader" type of authority

Strauss, Leo: the Athens-Jerusalem distinction, 75, 169; the debate with Kojève and the concept of posthistorical empire, 42; "Kojève's Hegel" vs. Strauss's Hegel, 100; mediation Schmitt-Kojève, 122, 124; reception among North American political theorists, 93, 99; slave-bondsman distinction, 157n4; Strauss's Paris period, 123

suicide: as atheism's most radical expression, 66, 83; the Buddhist subtext and, 72n4; collective, 61; emancipation and, 54–57, 64–69; as the realization of freedom, 64–66, 86–90. *See also* Kitarō, Nishida

Tolstoy, Aleksey Konstantinovich, 1–2

"total," 237; authority, 194; painting, 42

Tran-Duc-Thao, 15

Truman's point IV, 13, 130, 234–35

Vichy, France, 2, 125, 231–35

willing obedience, 3, 165

Zamyatin, Evgeni, 70

About the Contributors

José María Carabante is a professor of philosophy of law and political philosophy at the Faculty of Law at the Complutense University (Spain). He is the author of several monographs and articles on contemporary philosophy. His latest book is *Perfiles filosóficos* (Thomson Reuters).

Bryan-Paul Frost is the Elias "Bo" Ackal, Jr./BORSF Endowed Professor of Political Science at the University of Louisiana at Lafayette. He is the editor and co-translator (with Robert Howse) of Kojève's *Outline of a Phenomenology of Right* (Rowman & Littlefield, 2000) as well as contributor and co-editor (with Timothy Burns) of *Philosophy, History, and Tyranny: Reexamining the Debate between Leo Strauss and Alexandre Kojève* (SUNY, 2016). In addition to these, he has published on the political thought of Aristophanes, Aristotle, Raymond Aron, Cato the Younger, Cicero and Roman civic education, Rousseau, and Tocqueville and Emerson.

Isabel Jacobs is a PhD candidate in comparative literature at Queen Mary University of London. Her research explores Alexandre Kojève's aesthetics. In 2021, she was one of the organizers of a large international workshop on Kojève. She currently co-edits a special issue dedicated to Kojève and Russian philosophy. Her interests include global intellectual history, philosophy of science, and cinema. She holds an MA in Russian and East European literature and culture from University College London.

Jeff Love is a research professor of German and Russian at Clemson University. He is the author of *The Black Circle: A Life of Alexandre Kojève* (Columbia University Press, 2018), *Tolstoy: A Guide for the Perplexed* (Continuum, 2008), and *The Overcoming of History in War and Peace* (Brill, 2004). He has also published a translation of Alexandre Kojève's *Atheism* (Columbia University Press, 2018), an annotated translation (with Johannes Schmidt) of F.W. J. Schelling's *Philosophical Investigations into the*

Essence of Human Freedom (State University of New York Press, 2006), a co-edited volume, *Nietzsche and Dostoevsky: Philosophy, Morality, Tragedy* (Northwestern University Press, 2016), and an edited volume, *Heidegger in Russia and Eastern Europe* (Rowman & Littlefield International, 2017). His most recent work is a translation of António Lobo Antunes's novel *Until Stones Become Lighter Than Water* (Yale University Press, 2019).

Waller R. Newell is a professor of political science, philosophy, and humanities at Carleton University in Ottawa, Canada, where he helped found and teaches in the College of the Humanities, Canada's only four-year baccalaureate in the Great Books.

He was educated at Yale University, where he received a PhD in political science and at the University of Toronto, where he received a BA in arts and sciences and an MA in political economy. His latest book is *Tyranny and Revolution: Rousseau to Heidegger* from Cambridge University Press. www .wallernewell.com

Massimo Palma's main research field is twentieth-century German and French thought and literature. He wrote on Walter Benjamin, Eric Weil, and Alexandre Kojève, and recently published the books: *Group Photo with Master and Servant. Hegelian Mythologies in Koyré, Strauss, Kojève, Bataille, Weil, Queneau* (Rome, 2017) and *Your Eyes as Stones. Trauma and Memory in W. G. Sebald, Paul Celan, Charlotte Salomon* (Rome, 2020). He also edited and translated *Economy and Society* by Max Weber, Walter Benjamin's political writings, Georges Bataille's Hegelian essays, Georg Heym's *Umbra vitae*, and Fredric Jameson's *Benjamin Files*.

José Daniel Parra is a research professor in government and international relations at Universidad Externado de Colombia. He completed his PhD at the University of Toronto. He has published articles and book chapters on classical and modern philosophy, philosophical therapy, and the history of political thought and is the author of *Heidegger's Nietzsche: European Modernity and the Philosophy of the Future* (2019).

Luis J. Pedrazuela earned his PhD with a thesis on Alexandre Kojève at the University Carlos III of Madrid. He is currently a research fellow at the University of Leeds.

Alexei Rutkevich is a tenured professor at National Research University Higher School of Economics. He is a historian of philosophy, and his main works are on continental philosophy of the nineteenth and twentieth centuries.

Igor Shoikhedbrod is an assistant professor of political theory in the Department of Political Science at St. Francis Xavier University. He is also the author of *Revisiting Marx's Critique of Liberalism: Rethinking Justice, Legality, and Rights* (2019) with Palgrave Macmillan, as well as several academic articles focused on legal and political theory in *History of Political Thought, Contemporary Political Theory, Critical Horizons, The Canadian Journal of Law & Jurisprudence,* and *Critical Analysis of Law.*

Trevor Wilson is an assistant professor of Russian at Virginia Tech. He is a scholar of Russian and Soviet philosophy.

www.ingramcontent.com/pod-product-compliance
Lightning Source LLC
Chambersburg PA
CBHW022306280326
41932CB00010B/1002